Collaborative Customer
Relationship Management

Springer
Berlin
Heidelberg
New York
Hong Kong
London
Milan
Paris
Tokyo

Alexander H. Kracklauer
D. Quinn Mills · Dirk Seifert
Editors

Collaborative Customer Relationship Management

Taking CRM to the Next Level

With 99 Figures
and 7 Tables

 Springer

Prof. Dr. Alexander H. Kracklauer
Prof. D. Quinn Mills
Prof. Dr. Dirk Seifert
Harvard Business School
Soldiers Field
Boston, MA 02163
USA

akracklauer@hbs.edu and alexander.kracklauer@fh-neu-ulm.de
dmills@hbs.edu
seifert-d@gmx.de

ISBN 3-540-00227-8 Springer-Verlag Berlin Heidelberg New York

Cataloging-in-Publication Data applied for
A catalog record for this book is available from the Library of Congress.
Bibliographic information published by Die Deutsche Bibliothek
Die Deutsche Bibliothek lists this publication in the Deutsche Nationalbibliografie; detailed bibliographic data is available in the Internet at <http://dnb.ddb.de>.

Springer-Verlag Berlin Heidelberg New York
a member of BertelsmannSpringer Science+Business Media GmbH

http://www.springer.de

© Springer-Verlag Berlin · Heidelberg 2004
Printed in Germany

Hardcover-Design: Erich Kirchner, Heidelberg

SPIN 10904275   42/3130/DK-5 4 3 2 1 0 – Printed on acid-free paper

Preface of the Editors

Driven by rapidly changing business environments and more demanding consumers, many organizations are searching for new ways to achieve and retain a competitive advantage via customer intimacy and customer relationship management. In this context, new strategic frameworks and cooperative efforts with all participants along the value chain are needed to allow managers to synchronize their efforts with changes in shopping patterns of consumers. This book presents a new strategic framework that has already been tested successfully at global companies through a large empirical study. New management concepts like CPFR (Collaborative Forecasting and Replenishment), CRM (Customer Relationship Management), CM (Category Management) and Mass Customization are integrated in one holistic approach to jointly develop customer bonding and loyalty. Experts from companies like McKinsey, Procter & Gamble, Accenture, A.C. Nielsen as well as authors from renowned academic institutions like Harvard Business School and Technical University Munich offer valuable insights on how to redesign organizations to meet future requirements of consumers.

Structure of the Book

After the introduction of the concept of customer management in part 1 of the book, Mercer Management consultants Eric Almquist and David Bovet together with Carla J. Heaton from Marsh & McLennan explain in chapter 2 what companies have learned so far while implementing CRM and show key take-aways. Based on that, part 2 of the book explains how Collaborative Customer Management helps manufacturers and retailers to achieve joint success in the marketplace. Chapter 3 illustrates that Collaborative Customer Management is a further development of ECR on the demand side. Additionally, strategies and tools for Collaborative Customer Management are presented. A case study on Procter & Gamble clarifies the approach of Collaborative Customer Management. Chapter 4 explains the integration of Supply Chain Management and Customer Relationship Management. It shows how logistics and information technology add value to the consumer while simultaneously reducing cost. In addition it shows what possibilities exist to increase co-operation along the supply chain in order to better meet consumer demand. A case study by JDA's CTO, Scott Hines shows the way in which the integration of Customer Management and Supply Chain Management can lead to outstanding results. A study by Deloitte Consulting in chapter 5 reveals how customer satisfaction and profitability can be increased through customer management and supply chain management. The study, conducted in 28 countries, shows that companies in digital loyalty networks, which integrate CRM and SCM throughout the supply chain with modern IT are already realizing better earnings than comparable companies who have not.

The next part deals with the demand side of Collaborative Customer Relationship Management and looks more closely at CRM and Category Management. Chapter 6 and 7 show why cooperation in CRM makes sense and which results are realizable by using collaboration nets. The authors of the Technical University Munich show potentials and challenges of an individualization based approach and four models of an individualization based CCRM. AC Nielsen authors Matthias Groß and Jens Ohlig show in chapter 8, how market research institutes can help leverage the CM process and show the CM process in detail. Moreover, they demonstrate how Category Management can help to retain customers. Peter Barrenstein and Stefan Tweraser of McKinsey establish in chapter 9 why CM is particularly important now and offer guidelines for successful Category Management.

The next part of the book, part 4, looks into the relationship between CCRM and logistics. Collaborative Planning, Forecasting and Replenishment (CPFR), a new strategy for joint planning and supply management is introduced here via two contributions from industry experts. In chapter 10 Peter Hambuch of Procter & Gamble reveals how CPFR is employed by a large consumer goods manufacturer. In chapter 11, Georg Engler of Accenture discusses the progression from a pilot project to broad based use.

The fifth section of the book looks at future developments in CCRM. Chapter 12, written by A. H. Kracklauer, D. Q. Mills and D. Seifert together with P & G authors M. Leyk and S. Rübke deals with newest developments in the Category Management field and consequently talks about "New Ways of Category Management". M. Großweischede of the Competence Center for Multi-Channel-Management of the University of Essen introduces CCRM in the Internet and customer driven assortments for e-retailers in chapter 13.

The sixth and final section of the book draws conclusions from the preceding chapters and offers the essential 'take-aways'.

The book is to be viewed as a platform for the expression of the opinions of different important players in the field: manufacturers, retailers, consulting companies and IT-solutions providers. The opinions expressed by contributing authors do not necessarily reflect those of the editors. The articles distinguish themselves through different styles and approaches, offering the reader varying perspectives on Collaborative Customer Relationship Management.

Acknowledgements

The book would not have been possible without the help and the inspiration of many people and companies.

The editors would like to thank Accenture, JDA, and SAP AG, who sponsored our research.

Special thanks in particular to the contributing authors for sharing the knowledge and experience of their companies.

We would also like to thank the members of our research team. First of all we want to thank Anurag Mehndiratta, who gave us a lot of valuable insights based on his work at Siemens. Moreover, Alexander Adler, Mark Cicirelli, Kirstin Hornby, Julian Kurz, Carla Saraiva, Steffen Schneider and Michael Lark contributed in an outstanding way to this volume. Heartfelt thanks also to those whose personal involvement facilitated intensive debate on many ideas contained in this volume: Fred Baumann, Claudia Beckers, Steffen Bundesmann, Richard Downs, Dr. Stephan Friedrich, Prof. Dr. Hans Hinterhuber, Dr. Heiner Olbrich, Dr. Olaf Passenheim, Prof. Dr. U. Jens Pätzmann, Silke Slootz, Jim Uchneat, Jürgen Weltermann, Prof. Sean Willems and Prof. Dr. Michael Zerres.

And finally, our thanks to Prof. Michael Y. Yoshino and the Research Division of the Harvard Business School, who helped pave the way for the work presented here.

If you have questions, comments and criticisms regarding this book you may contact the editors via e-mail:

akracklauer@hbs.edu, dmills@hbs.edu, seifert-d@gmx.de

Boston, April 2003   Prof. Dr. Alexander Kracklauer
                                                    Prof. D. Quinn Mills
                                                    Prof. Dr. Dirk Seifert

Table of Contents

PART 1:

Customer Relationship Management: The Basics

In the early nineties, manufacturing and retailing managers in the US were confronted with a growing problem: stagnation. The only possible way to force competitors out and increase market share was through having aggressive pricing policies. But with stable costs and minimal gains in productivity, which were as common as stagnating sales, margins and profits suffered, and brand and store loyalty eroded. Manufacturers and retailers learned from companies like Wal-Mart and Procter & Gamble that cooperation is the cornerstone of value creation, and that collaboration in the supply chain could open up new opportunities for profitability.

CHAPTER 1

Customer Management as the Origin of Collaborative Customer Relationship Management

Alexander H. Kracklauer
BayTech IBS, UAS Neu-Ulm, Germany / Harvard Business School, MA, USA

D. Quinn Mills
Harvard Business School, MA, USA

Dirk Seifert
Harvard Business School, MA, USA

The marketing departments of retailers and manufacturers speak more often in their analyses about "hybrid" consumers – customers who do not demonstrate behavior consistent with simple categories. The smart shopper, one with a Jaguar in the parking lot of a discount hypermarket, is a reality, just as is the college student in a boutique wine shop. Because of this seemingly paradoxical customer behavior, it is becoming more and more difficult for retailers and manufacturers to identify and retain valuable customers.

Until now, both retailers and manufacturers have tried to grapple with this phenomenon individually. Many brand-name manufacturers have gone to great lengths recently to learn more about their customers. To that end, large investments have been made in consumer and market research. Consumer management is typically based on the few details a company has in its own database. Most retailers have only recently begun to systematically analyze the consumer's behavior at the point of sale and thereby to build a solid foundation for customer relationship management. Customer management concepts developed in-house in the past proved ineffective, as the quality of the data was insufficient.

Experience has shown that through a new management concept a few companies have been able to avoid the pitfalls of loosing value. The Collaborative Customer Relationship Management concept has been successfully implemented by leaders in the consumer goods sector. The consolidation and comparison of market and consumer data enables the exploitation of potential synergies. A broader database means significantly higher quality data. The identification and attraction of valuable and value-creating customers is simplified. The pilot projects executed show that, a joint and integrated approach to the identification, attraction, retention and development of new customers can be more successful than previous methods.

This book considers Collaborative Customer Relationship Management a comprehensive management concept and not, as is often the case in the recent and first mentions of the concept, strictly a technical solution to customer relations challenges.

1.1   The Customer Management Concept

CCRM is a new form of Customer Management. It's useful, therefore, to briefly describe the concept of Customer Management and its essential components. Customer Management consists of four elements, and can be illustrated as a phased model. All efforts are bound tightly with a deep understanding of the consumer, or customer insight. This detailed knowledge must be built systematically before it is made available. The diagram below shows the relevant components of Customer Management.

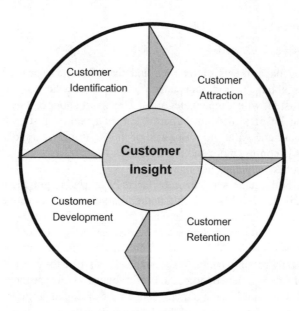

Figure 1.1:   The Concept of Customer Management

Identification

Systematic customer management begins with the definition of target groups and the collection of quantitative and qualitative data on these groups. A consumer segment is chosen which is most attractive to the firm. For example, consumer identification delivers information on the characteristics of profitable customers. It is important to know which products and services are of significance to the latter.

Customer identification also analyzes the customers that are being lost to the competition and how they can be won back. The tools of customer identification are customer segmentation, consumer market research and consumer target group analysis.

Attraction

All marketing and sales efforts are oriented towards attracting a target customer group. The core challenge here is to efficiently attract the relevant consumer segment. This involves realizing the correct form of communication and eliminating any sort of wasted effort. A firm must always consider its own marketing efforts in comparison to those of its competitors. The systematic construction of competitive advantages (price leadership or differentiation advantages) in the context of a company's market-driven activities facilitates better conditions for the attraction of customers. Hereby, former customers are targeted specifically with the intention of winning them back. Some tools of customer attraction are benchmarking, promotions, and free samples.

Retention

The long-term retention of profitable customers is one of the central concerns of customer management. The approaches to customer retention entail all relevant methods needed to achieve enduring customer loyalty (Figure 1.2). Customer satisfaction is the essential condition for retaining customers. Customer satisfaction is the result of a process of comparison between the customer's expectations (personal standard, image of the manufacturer, claims of the manufacturer, knowledge of alternatives) and his or her perceptions (actual experience, subjective impression of product performance, appropriateness of product for his needs). An enduring perception by the customer of additional value being provided by the manufacturer leads to sustained customer retention. In addition, a high quality shopping experience leads to a positive emotional association and lays the groundwork for the desired customer loyalty. The instruments of customer retention are one-to-one marketing, loyalty and bonus programs, personalization, and complaint management.

Development

The consistent expansion of transaction intensity, transaction value, and individual customer profitability is the goal of customer development. An increase in the wallet share is accomplished by leading the customer to other product or service offerings. This can be done, for example, by bundling together different products of a single manufacturer and selling them together at a discount. A valuable analysis concept in customer development is Customer Lifetime Value. It provides visibility to the transaction potential of the observed target group. Examples of tools for customer development are up- and cross selling and product and service bundling.

If a particular customer does not make any purchases over a certain time span, or does so only in reduced amounts, it is possible that he or she has been lost to the competition. It is important to identify this customer and to win him or her back. This is where customer development connects to identification and attraction.

Figure 1.2 shows the four elements of customer management and the select tactical tools for achieving the respective core tasks. Some measures like benchmarking, on-to-one marketing are useful in other phases of customer management.

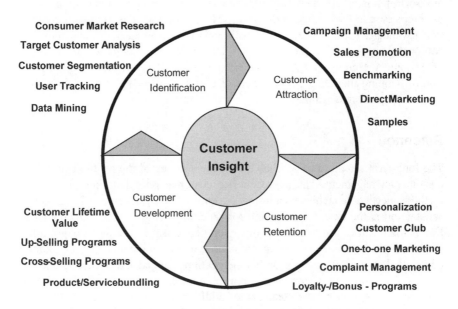

Figure 1.2:   Select Instruments of Customer Management

The consolidation of both manufacturers and retailers resources in Collaborative Customer Management leads to the realization of immense efficiency advantages: reduced marketing, IT, and logistics costs for individual partners, and a significant increase in the quality of customer relations. The book introduces the basic strategies of Collaborative Customer Management and explains through case studies and expert articles the new directions in customer relationships.

CHAPTER 2

What Have We Learned so Far? Making CRM Make Money – Technology Alone Won't Create Value

Eric Almquist
Mercer Management Consulting, Boston, USA

David Bovet
Mercer Management Consulting, Boston, USA

Carla J. Heaton
Marsh & McLennan, New York, USA

2.1   The CRM Arms Race

A confluence of market forces has steadily eroded the ability of companies to generate sustainable profits from ongoing customer relationships. In nearly all industries, the proliferation of new product and service offerings has provided customers with an overwhelming number of options from which to choose. The Internet, by giving customers an unparalleled ability to compare value propositions and aggregate their buying power, has further tipped the balance in the customer's favor. Digital technology has also extended this opportunity backwards along the supply chain, enabling powerful collaboration with companies' suppliers.

Companies have responded by spending aggressively to acquire new customers. U.S. companies are spending an estimated $110 billion on advertising through direct mail and telemarketing channels and $7.5 billion on Internet advertising in the year 2000. The returns on traditional marketing tactics, however, continue to dwindle. Credit card mailings, for example, have increased at a 12% annual growth rate over the past 10 years, but response rates have fallen at a similar pace to just 0.6%. Internet advertising, once touted as a low-cost direct marketing alternative, has not proven to be any more successful. The average banner ad click-through rate today is less than 0.5%, down from 2-3% in the mid-1990s.

Given the high cost of acquiring new customers, companies are also stepping up efforts to keep existing customers, especially the most profitable ones. Such efforts include reactive measures to sweeten the pot when customers threaten to leave, pricing adjustments to forestall attrition, and loyalty programs that reward continued usage. Customer retention initiatives are even more critical in a slowing economy, as reduced disposable income and greater price sensitivity make it more difficult and more costly for companies to maintain existing relationships or acquire new ones. Information on customer behaviour, when properly used, can raise the effectiveness of the entire supplier-to-customer value chain.

Faced with these challenges, many companies have readily embraced the promise of Customer Relationship Management (CRM). When Mercer Management Consulting recently interviewed chief financial officers and other senior executives from Fortune 1000 companies on their experience with CRM, many reported that they have turned to CRM because the competitive bar has risen. One business unit leader at a gas and electric utility said, "In recent years, we have stepped up our focus on CRM due to the expectation of greater competition."

There is serious money banking on the promise of CRM. The Gartner Group projects that spending on CRM applications and services, which totalled $23 billion in 2000, will grow at a compound annual growth rate of 27% and exceed $75 billion in 2005. Eager to capitalize on the opportunity, nearly 500 CRM vendors are marketing products and services that claim to help companies increase customer loyalty, target their most profitable customers and streamline customer data mining and sales processes.

2.2   Into the Money Pit

Despite the fanfare and large expenditures, CRM is not fulfilling its promise and dissatisfaction is mounting. Only 16% of companies that have implemented CRM software say it has exceeded their expectations, reports a March 2001 survey of

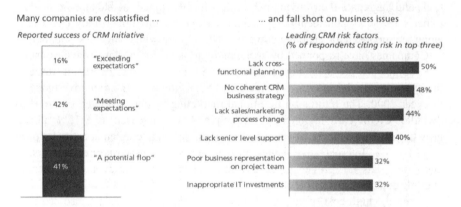

Source: Meta Group "Leadership Strategies in CRM" (Jan 2000); Data Warehousing Institute (Mar 2001)

Figure 2.1:   The Failed Promise

1,200 business executives and IT managers conducted by the Data Warehousing Institute. Forty-one percent consider the effort "a potential flop" (Figure 2.1). Other surveys cite dissatisfaction with CRM at even higher levels.

Why this disappointment? In our experience, the overriding reason is that many executives view CRM as a technological solution. They focus myopically on installing the latest computer system, and push business issues into the background. Bill Brender of Brender & Associates observes, "The CRM vendor community is not selling solutions that help the customer; they're selling technology in a box." Not surprisingly, we often see situations such as that described by one senior sales and marketing executive: "We turned a manual mess into an automated mess, and as a result we just made the same mistakes faster and more efficiently."

Viewing CRM as a technological "silver bullet" causes companies to ignore or rush past critical business issues that must be addressed first. They fail to develop a comprehensive strategy. They cut corners on the cross-functional planning needed to prepare the organization to deploy new CRM capabilities and underestimate the organizational change required to leverage the new technology. Finally, they neglect to build a business case for CRM, embarking on major investments without knowing how the new technology supports their business design or estimating the magnitude of the expected benefits.

Indeed, Gartner research shows that 85% of companies that buy CRM software pick the wrong tools because they fail to define their business objectives or execution path before they invest. Millions of dollars later, while the technology may have produced small operational improvements, it did not significantly boost profitability. As one CFO of a large agricultural products firm told us, "When an investment fails to meet expectations, it's not because the technology failed to perform as specified, but because we did not define the customer need up front and we chose the wrong technology."

2.3   Core Principles

How can companies avoid this frustrating and costly scenario and instead help CRM make money? What distinguishes the few firms using CRM effectively is a clear focus on growing customer value – on building customer relationships that enhance the long-term flow of profits to the company. These firms view technology as a tool to help build profitable relationships. Their primary focus is not "which technology?" but rather, "how do we derive economic benefit from managing our customer relationships better?" They hold CRM initiatives to the same financial standards as any major investment. There is a clear business case specifying what, when, how and how much. And there is a clear plan to make it happen. The effective use of CRM can be distilled into four principles (Figure 2.2).

CRM succeeds in delivering value when you ...

• Develop a customer value growth strategy to drive CRM initiatives

  – Begin with a customer-centric strategy that defines value growth objectives, the key business leverage points, and the appropriate role of technology. Never lead with technology.

• Capture and use the customer information that really matters

  – Focus on key customers, channels, and touchpoints and gather the information most relevant to value creation. Resist the "360˚ view" that results in too much data of too little consequence.

• Make value metrics the drumbeat for CRM activities

  – Develop metrics to prioritize and track CRM initiatives based on their ability to build customer value and boost productivity.

• Create a dynamic learning organization to accelerate value growth

  – Systematically build customer knowledge by using "test-and-learn" methods to continuously refine offers and go-to-market strategies.

Figure 2.2:   The Four Principles

2.4   Develop a Customer Value Growth Strategy to Drive CRM Initiatives

As a first step, companies should embrace the notion of managing for customer value growth and develop a clear strategy to acquire, develop, and retain profitable customers. Every move should be based on its potential to create value; initiatives should be prioritized by their contribution to overall financial performance. Decisions about customer selection, value proposition development, business process organization, supplier choice and management, and employee motivation should be made with an understanding of their impact on customers' current and potential value.

A customer value growth strategy must be forward-looking in order to anticipate emerging customer priorities. Charles Schwab, for example, has been able to sustain long-term success by consistently anticipating emerging customer priorities

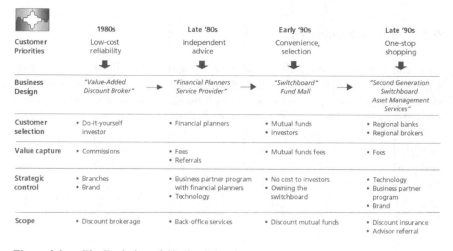

	1980s	Late '80s	Early '90s	Late '90s
Customer Priorities	Low-cost reliability	Independent advice	Convenience, selection	One-stop shopping
Business Design	"Value-Added Discount Broker"	"Financial Planners Service Provider"	"Switchboard" Fund Mall	"Second Generation Switchboard Asset Management Services"
Customer selection	• Do-it-yourself investor	• Financial planners	• Mutual funds • Investors	• Regional banks • Regional brokers
Value capture	• Commissions	• Fees • Referrals	• Mutual funds fees	• Fees
Strategic control	• Branches • Brand	• Business partner program with financial planners • Technology	• No cost to investors • Owning the switchboard	• Technology • Business partner program • Brand
Scope	• Discount brokerage	• Back-office services	• Discount mutual funds	• Discount insurance • Advisor referral

Figure 2.3:   The Evolution of Charles Schwab

(Figure 2.3). In the 1980s, when customers began to demand low-cost reliability, Schwab had already positioned itself as a value-added discount broker. By the late 1980s, when customers realized that they needed independent advice and guidance, Schwab was ready with a partnership with financial planners in place. In the late 1990s, Schwab debuted the "one-stop shop" model, once again a step ahead of its customers and the competition. Technology has played a key role in Schwab's customer-facing activities as well as its back-office operations, but always as a tool to help build the next business design rather than as the driving force.

Zara, an innovative fashion manufacturer and retailer in Spain, exemplifies a customer-driven strategy and a networked business design, supported by the right technology. Zara identified a need to serve young, hip, urban women with cutting-edge clothing at reasonable prices. The value proposition revolves around delivering fresh fashion to these consumers fast. Zara's "value net" business design (Figure 2.4) begins with frequent digital communication of buying trends from stores to designers. The company uses small lot sizes, automated cutting machinery, outsourced local assembly, and centralized distribution to deliver on the customer promise. Results are dramatic: Zara can take new clothes from sketch-to-store-shelf in an astonishingly fast 15 days, compared to industry norms of nine months. In Zara's case, the customer strategy drives a high-performing networked operation linking customers with the company and with its key suppliers. Technology holds its importance, (the company was an early adopter of PDA devices and used them to communicate the latest observed fashion trends), but clear customer thinking and smart operations have always come first for Zara.

Winning companies also go beyond cross selling and up selling to current customers. They manage customer value growth dynamically over the customer lifecycle (Figure 2.5). The lifecycle view of customer value creation opportunities,

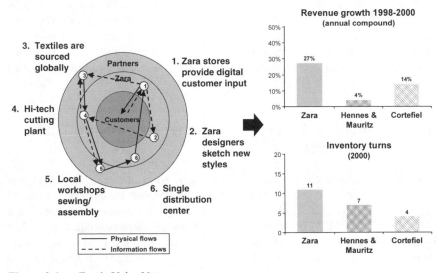

Figure 2.4:   Zara's Value Net

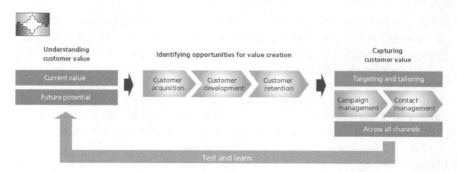

Figure 2.5:   Customer Value Management

from acquisition to development to retention, depends on a nuanced understanding of the customer's behavior, needs, and purchase occasions. What's dynamic about the strategy is the continuous series of actions taken to capture value throughout the lifecycle, including targeted promotional campaigns and multi-channel customer contact, with continuous test-and-learn loops informing future actions.

Mercer's work with a leading European credit card issuer illustrates the point. The company first determined the potential value of a new business design that would leverage customer information. Only then did it proceed to rapidly build and deploy new capabilities to acquire and develop profitable customers. In-market tests helped to target high-value customers, design attractive offers, and develop ways to service customers differentially based on their existing and potential value. At the same time, the company realigned its organizational capabilities to support the new strategy:

It created more flexible customer management processes, accelerated test-and-learn cycles, and established new governance mechanisms for value-based decision making. CRM technology investments played a role, to be sure. But the technology was just one of many considerations, not the gating factor for change. The rewards of this approach have been more than $30 million of incremental income in the first year of market tests, with capabilities now in place to drive continued value growth.

2.5   Capture and Use the Customer Information That Really Matters

Many CRM vendors claim that capturing every interaction with each customer across all channels is essential for building a customer-centric business. Attracted by what appears to be an elegant solution, many companies overemphasize a "360° view." In reality, however, this view is not all encompassing. It is limited by static, often outdated information about current customers gathered through current touch points, and fails to illuminate the value of prospective customers and changing market dynamics.

A more effective view is value-oriented, forward-looking and externally facing (Figure 2.6). Companies must gather data that will allow them to measure customer-level profitability, prioritize different initiatives and track their success. Such data illuminates not only the current behavior of today's customers, but also the future priorities of current and potential customers, the company's share of their wallets and the appeal of competitors' value propositions. Only by taking a truly comprehensive view, one that takes into account money left on the table for competitors, can companies create a differentiated approach that grows customer value.

Value-oriented	Forward-looking	Externally oriented

• Revenue potential
  – Cross-sell/up-sell
  – Information resale
  – Lifetime value
 	
• Cost to serve
  – Marketing and acquisition cost
  – Service intensity
  – Preferences
 	
• Media
  – Channels
  – Other service attributes
	• Use of experimental stimuli to
	  test buying sensitivities to factors
	  such as price, service, and brand
	
	• Problems with current products
	  and services
	
	• Unmet needs for products
	  and services
	
	• Attitude toward brand
		• Customer wallet share
		
		• Non-customers
		  – Needs, priorities, and problems
		    with competitor products and services
		  – Category, product, and provider usage
		  – Brand perceptions
		  – Lifestyle data
		  – Media/channel usage
		
		• Suppliers
		  – Product development
		  – Demand data
		  – Real-time order status
		  – Profitability

Figure 2.6:   Capture the Information that Matters

Collecting and analyzing the right data helps focus investment dollars on the improvements that really matter to customers and ultimately affect the bottom line. In the interviews conducted by Mercer, executives across several industries identified giving their customers "a seamless high-quality experience" amongst their top priorities. These executives saw many areas where their service fell short, but recognized that finite resources could not support the delivery of superior service across the board. What they lacked was a process for understanding how and where to allocate resources in order to best improve the customer's experience.

Once again, the answer lies in understanding the levers for customer value growth and having the relevant information on hand. By creatively combining customer research and behavioral, financial, and operating data, companies can identify the most important elements of the customer experience; for example, which service interactions and channels matter most to customers, and which improvements will cause the greatest lift to loyalty or value.

As companies increasingly rely on external hardware and service providers, the exchange of information becomes multi-layered. To ensure just-in-time delivery of inputs, for instance, it is critical for a company's suppliers to enjoy timely insights into end-customer demand. In the office furniture industry, Michigan-based Herman Miller was the first to pass dealer order information directly back to its key suppliers. The firm uses a combination of homegrown e-tools that span the full gamut of operations, from customer product selection to generation of bills-of-materials, continuous updates on supplier deliveries, and supplier payments. This digital information flow allows Herman Miller to effectively manage its unique value proposition, thus delivering office solutions to customers within two weeks of order placement and so reliably that dealers book the installation date when they take the order.

Mercer helped one global provider of financial products and services to target such spending on multi-channel customer service improvements. The company isolated the revenue impact of channel interactions and service improvements across different customer segments and determined, in each segment, the key drivers of behavioral loyalty. This led to focused investments in upgrades to Web and phone channels, which translated into a $50-$75 million increase in revenues (Figure 2.7).

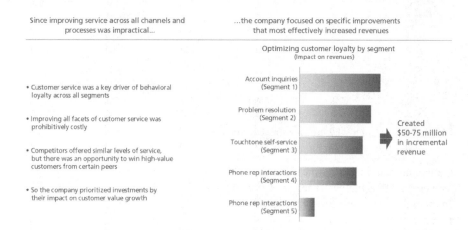

Figure 2.7:   A Mutual Fund Provider Focuses its Resources

2.6   Make Value Metrics the Drumbeat for CRM Activities

Most of the companies interviewed by Mercer had invested in CRM with two objectives in mind: to grow revenues by increasing customer satisfaction, and to cut costs by improving the sales process. Despite these good intentions, they have had difficulty measuring the incremental impact of CRM initiatives. As one marketing executive at a financial services provider said, "The specific financial impact is hard to determine because there are so many other variables which affect financial performance but cannot be isolated."

As a result, few firms measure the success of their initiatives. The metrics they do employ typically have little relevance to value creation. Many companies look at measures of customer loyalty, which CEOs recently surveyed by the Conference Board ranked as their greatest management challenge. Yet customer retention rates, often tracked as a proxy for customer loyalty, are a poor indicator of value creation. Buying habits and preferences vary from customer to customer, and so does profitability. A credit card company with 100% customer retention will be less profitable than a competitor that attrits debtors with high default risk from its

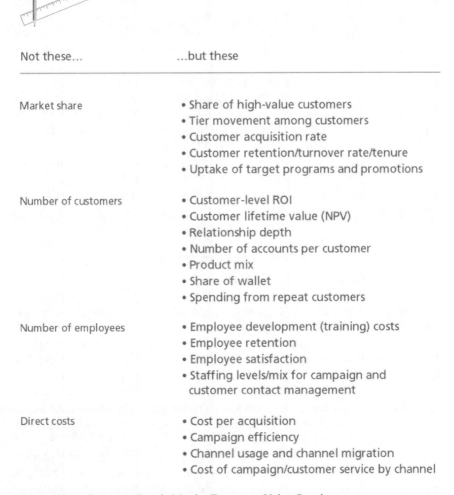

Not these...	...but these
Market share	• Share of high-value customers • Tier movement among customers • Customer acquisition rate • Customer retention/turnover rate/tenure • Uptake of target programs and promotions
Number of customers	• Customer-level ROI • Customer lifetime value (NPV) • Relationship depth • Number of accounts per customer • Product mix • Share of wallet • Spending from repeat customers
Number of employees	• Employee development (training) costs • Employee retention • Employee satisfaction • Staffing levels/mix for campaign and customer contact management
Direct costs	• Cost per acquisition • Campaign efficiency • Channel usage and channel migration • Cost of campaign/customer service by channel

Figure 2.8:   Customer-Centric Metrics Encourage Value Creation

portfolio of customers, but retains lower-risk, high-revolver cardholders. Capital One, for instance, has realized this opportunity. By using sophisticated modelling to identify high-value individuals and tailor a superior offer, Capital One has achieved one of the lowest charge-off rates, as well as one of the highest average account balances, in the credit card industry.

Accordingly, the goal should not be to increase customer loyalty across the board, but rather to acquire, retain, and develop the most valuable customers. The first step is to understand the costs to acquire and maintain customers and the value created by improvements in customer interactions. One can then create metrics such as customer lifetime value and customer-level ROI that will help to identify the most valuable customers. Rather than focusing solely on customer retention or market share, the more effective approach is to track the share of high-value customers and analyze trends such as movement between service tiers. By developing metrics aligned with their customer value growth objectives, companies can effectively analyze market trends and the effect of their initiatives on the bottom line (Figure 2.8). The same segmentation approach should also be applied to channel selection.

Using the right value metrics will help the organization to focus on the activities and investments that are growing customer value. Such metrics can align the efforts of internal and customer-facing departments, as well as external partners and suppliers who are increasingly essential to delivering on the customer promise. Ultimately, these metrics should sound a regular beat that reminds everyone what the goal is and provides clear indications of progress and future direction. At Capital One, senior executives meet weekly to review market test results and plan subsequent customer actions. There is little ambiguity about how value is created from customers.

2.7   Create a Dynamic Learning Organization to Accelerate Value Growth

Companies implementing CRM systems often stumble because they fail to realign the organization around their business objectives. If senior management fails to support the CRM initiative or to convert high-level strategy into specific operational requirements, employees will conduct business as usual. A typical pitfall is the failure of different departments to collaborate on CRM "test and learn" activities. In marketing experimentation, for example, everyone from suppliers to product developers, marketers, channel managers, call centers, and service staff might be involved. If collaboration is not aligned, the market experiments are likely to produce mediocre results or even fail.

At a minimum, all employees must work toward a common goal of customer value growth. This is no small challenge in corporations composed of multiple business units. As one senior financial executive at a landscape equipment manufacturer remarked, "Several divisions often have the same customers, but each one wants to have it their own way. Getting them all on the same page is like pulling teeth."

To define a common goal, senior management and the business unit leaders must agree on how they will measure and capture value. They can then specify what process redesign and capabilities are required. And they must communicate this plan internally and create an environment in which everyone is rewarded for advancing these goals. At Herman Miller, for example, the current performance of complete, on-time customer product shipments is prominently displayed at the entrance of the Zeeland, Michigan assembly plant. The operations vice president routinely hands out $100 bills to line workers who can answer a few key questions about the company's latest results for commonly understood operational goals tied to customer satisfaction.

Structural changes can get a company on track, but they are not sufficient. To become truly differentiated in the marketplace, a company must develop the culture and capabilities necessary for continuous improvement. It must become a learning organization that systematically gathers and acts on the customer information needed to refine its offers, processes, and business design. This transformation requires a commitment on several fronts:

- Continued senior management support and investment for testing and learning.

- A culture that encourages all employees to share and learn from new information.

- Training and compensation initiatives that empower and motivate employees to gather, analyze, share, and learn from information.

- The flexibility to modify or even reinvent strategies and processes.

Federal Express exemplifies such a customer-focused learning organization. FedEx tracks its progress daily via an automated system and disseminates value-based indicators such as customer ROI and yield per package on the company Intranet. Cross-functional teams analyze trends in service quality indicators to identify problems and target opportunities for improvement. All employees are eligible to receive bonuses linked to explicit metrics-based goals, and are required to take annual "customer care" training to reinforce the focus on customer value growth.

Like Federal Express, a learning organization does more than use pilot programs before committing to a full rollout. It thrives on adaptation through frequent, rapid-fire test campaigns. Accelerated test cycles allow the company to rapidly capture and leverage learnings from multiple customer initiatives (Figure 2.9). Various tools can help companies develop a test-and-learn culture, such as the Nexperiment™ methodology, an advanced experimental design technique for modifying and testing customer value drivers quickly and efficiently (see sidebar, "The coming age of marketing experimentation"). This same experimental approach can be applied to channels.

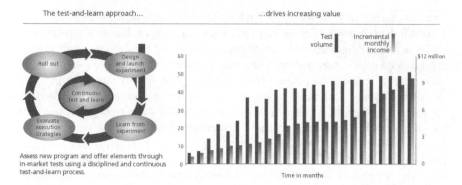

Figure 2.9:   A learning Organization

2.8   Getting Back on Track

To make CRM make money, think business first, technology second. Strategic considerations, which target long-term value growth, should firmly control one's management of customer relationships. Then a customer-focused learning culture inside the organization can be created and marketing decisions can be based on comprehensive and value-driven analysis. By harnessing one's energies to develop stronger, more profitable customer relationships, one can fully leverage existing CRM system investments (see sidebar, "Direct Marketing Services: creating a world-class 'customer development company'").

To determine whether your enterprise is focused on customer value growth, ask the following questions:

- Understanding customer value: What are our customers worth today?

- What could they be worth? What are their needs and priorities, how are they changing, and why?

- Identifying opportunities for value creation: Do we know what levers to pull to improve customer acquisition, development, and retention? Are we actively managing our customers to maximize value and profit?

- Capturing customer value: Do we offer our customers a unique and compelling value proposition? Are we targeting and tailoring those value propositions appropriately?

- Testing and learning: Are we measuring and monitoring the impact of satisfying customers on business results? Are we continually adapting and reinventing our processes based on the results observed? Are we using the power of experimental designs in marketing initiatives?

- Investing for value growth: How much have we spent or do we plan to spend on CRM initiatives? Can we link these expenditures to value creation? Have we prioritized initiatives based on their customer and bottom-line impact?

Answering these questions will reveal the nature of disconnect between the promise of CRM and actual results. Then you can redirect your organization's energy and resources to get CRM back on track to value creation.

The Internet has turned out to be a surprisingly tough place to do business. Customers are notoriously impatient, and if they hit a snag online or see something unappealing, they just click to another Web site.

The Internet does have a redeeming characteristic, however: It's a great place for conducting test-and-learn experiments to optimize marketing programs. In the physical world, it's often expensive to test different advertising campaigns, merchandising formats, or product prices. On the Web, however, companies can quickly and cheaply develop online experiments, analyze the results, and reconfigure the elements of their marketing programs to realize the full potential of the offer.

Take the case of Crayola.com, a portal launched by Binney & Smith that sells Crayola art supplies and features art activity ideas for parents and teachers. To succeed, Crayola must attract potential customers to its home page, draw these visitors to its e-commerce store, and then convert them into buyers. So like many other online retailers, Crayola sends e-mails to potential customers with their promotional offer and features banner ads on its website to attract them to its store.

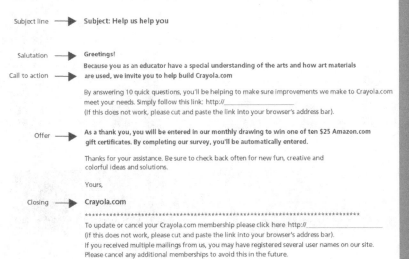

Figure 2.10:   One Version of Crayola's E-mail

Here the company runs into trouble. Its e-mail and banner ad are among the hundreds of marketing messages that bombard people each day. Only a tiny fraction elicit the desired response, and response rates to Internet messages are notoriously low. Crayola's initiatives were no exception.

If the company could determine what drove response rates, its marketing campaign would be far more efficient and effective. Its e-mail, for example, is a bundle of stimuli including the salutation, a call to action (to buy, view, or register), the various features of the offer, and the closure (Figure 2.10). Which stimuli were best?

Data mining techniques cannot solve this problem, because they analyze past behavior and thus are limited to whatever stimuli happened to be introduced into the market. Moreover, historical data do not equip marketers to sort out the separate effects of each stimulus or a particular combination of stimuli.

A more effective way forward is experimental design, with methodologies that have been developed over many decades in process manufacturing, psychology, medical clinical trials, and transportation planning. Experimental design, when properly applied, creates value in marketing because it allows a very large number of options to be understood by testing a small, scientifically chosen subset of those options.

Crayola approached its marketing challenge as a three-step "stimulus-response chain" and used Mercer's Nexperiment™ methodology to increase success at each step. A "brute force" evaluation of just three different salutations, four calls to action, five promotional offers, and six price points in an e-mail would have required a control cell and three hundred

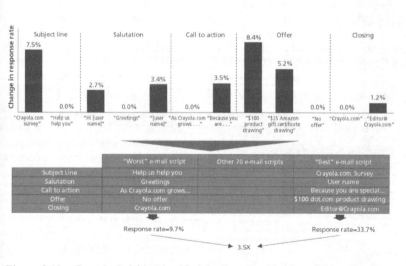

Figure 2.11: Crayola Quickly Identified the Best Combination of Stimuli

sixty test cells. But Nexperiment was able to quickly evaluate just a small subset of combinations.

The results? Within several weeks, Crayola had determined that its "best" e-mail script was nearly twice as effective as its "worst" in attracting educators and more than three times as effective among parents (Figure 2.11). For converting these visitors into buyers, the best combinations converted nearly four times as many shoppers into buyers and nearly doubled revenues per buyer. Increased yields over the entire stimulus-response chain helped make Crayola's online effort profitable.

To date, experimentation has been limited to a few areas such as direct mail in credit cards and e-mail and banner ads in online retailing. But the best marketers will take an integrated view of the customer and coordinate all interactions across loyalty programs, call centers, Web sites, and so on. As digital channels come to permeate all aspects of business, experimental design will combine online and offline elements. In a world of increased noise and clutter, experimentation will help companies get their offers, prices, and channel tactics more quickly refined so that they can raise the odds of success.

Direct Marketing Services, North America's largest direct marketer of insurance and related products, had been a highly profitable business. But at the end of the 1990s, DMS saw a rapid deceleration in revenue growth, its margins shrink, and its earnings stagnate. The company's new CEO, Bob Romasco, quickly recognized the need to chart a new business strategy.

Working with Mercer, DMS examined how it generated profit and how it might best respond to shifting customer priorities and competitive pressures. The process led to a new strategy, one that was captured by the transition from the company's old vision statement "We want to be a world-class direct marketing company" to the current "We want to be a world-class customer development company." This opened opportunities for DMS to become a multi-product, multi-channel enterprise and provided the critical business framework to organize its CRM initiatives.

With its new customer development strategy in place, DMS could gather the value-oriented, forward-looking, and externally oriented information that mattered. The firm proceeded to:

- Segment customers by attitudes, needs, demographics, and behavior

- Calculate the current and potential value of each customer to understand which were the most and least valuable

- Develop metrics to clarify objectives throughout the organization, set expectations, and evaluate the progress of its customer development initiatives

Case 1: The Coming …

Case 2: Direct Marketing Services

Because DMS understood the value drivers behind its business and had a set of metrics and objectives in place, it could get to work creating customer value. Brainstorming sessions identified new business designs, value propositions, and product portfolio changes that could better meet customer needs. Optimization models and experimental design techniques were employed to target and tailor offers to current and prospective customers.

These data-driven marketing methods allowed DMS to customize value propositions along multiple dimensions, including price, brand, products, and channel, based on customer behavior and needs.

In parallel with these targeting and tailoring efforts, DMS turned itself into a learning organization. It set up test-and-learn prototypes to refine a series of marketing activities, such as the scripts and pricing of offers made by its call centers. In each case, DMS created a system to extract and analyze the test results, synthesize the learnings, disseminate the knowledge and adjust the underlying business process.

As Romasco instinctively understood, creating a learning organization involved far more than a new set of tasks and skills. DMS indeed any winning CRM company needed an energetic organization that could take initiative, respond creatively to customer information and learn from market tests. Far from burying business initiative beneath a sea of numbers, it's critical, as Romasco said, that "the talent in the organization be proactive, not passive."

As a direct result of these customer value growth initiatives, DMS quickly increased cross-selling, up-selling, and retention rates. It deepened and broadened its customer relationships, created over $50 million in incremental customer value, and developed key strategic advantages over its competitors.

Figure 2.12: How Direct Marketing Services Used CRM

PART 2:

Collaborative Customer Relationship Management – How to Win in the Market with Joint Forces

The first part of the book is about the concept of *collaborative* customer relationship management (CCRM) and about the integration of supply and demand chains.

The authors Alexander Kracklauer, D. Quinn Mills and Dirk Seifert show how CCRM works and explain basics of CCRM (Chapter 3). Companies are primarily working together in logistics due to the fact that potential cost reductions are obtained there most easily. This limited perspective blinds retailers and manufacturers to the extensive possibilities in marketing and to the recognition of the customer as the deciding factor in their success or failure. In this article, the writers describe the goal, the strategy and the value of CCRM, and also intensively discuss the importance of joint customer retention management. The authors then show applications of CCRM. They look at the customer touch-points between retail and the consumer and identify a number of opportunities for manufacturers and retailers for adding value in the framework of CCRM. A. Kracklauer and N. Warmbrunn show in a case study a real life example of how CCRM works in retailer supplier relationships and what results can be achieved.

Chapter 4, written by Alexander Kracklauer, D. Quinn Mills and Dirk Seifert together with Michael Barz, describes the integration of Supply Chain Management and Customer Relationship Management. The authors show that CCRM can be supported by two basic tools: a) *logistical support activities* in order to meet the needs of the customer and b) *structural as well as technological support* in order to align business activities and harmonize information sharing. They explain logistic-driven activities like joint supply chain management and CPFR (collaborative planning, forecasting and replenishment). Last but not least, they give a short description of how information technology and multifunctional teams can, as a structural setup, help to reach the goals of CCRM. Again, a case study of JDA CTO Scott Hines shows a real life example, how the integration of supply and demand chains can ramp up business results.

Chapter 5, written by Jim Duffy, Peter Koudal and Stephen Pratt (Deloitte Consulting) show the tremendous impact that integrating supply and demand chains has on consumer businesses. Their global study shows that those businesses who can link customer management and supply chain operations are much more likely to boost performance in sales, market share and other key measures.

Collaborative Customer Relationship Management (CCRM)

Alexander H. Kracklauer

BayTech IBS, UAS Neu-Ulm, Germany / Harvard Business School, MA, USA

D. Quinn Mills

Harvard Business School, MA, USA

Dirk Seifert

Harvard Business School, MA, USA

Since the early nineties, the concept of Efficient Consumer Response (ECR) via vertical collaboration has raised the potential level of collaboration among manufacturers and retailers to new heights. ECR consists of two areas of cooperation: logistics and marketing. ECR implementation in the consumer goods market to date has been primarily in logistics because potential cost reductions are more easily obtainable there.

In the future, however, it is of critical importance that advances be made in cooperative marketing. Historically, Category Management has been seen as *the* instrument for such cooperation. The partnership between manufacturers and retailers was generally limited to an exchange of "cash cow-sleeper" lists. Categories were analyzed with respect to revenues and unit sales but a penetrating examination and its assimilation into retail strategy was rarely done.

This limited perspective blinded retailers to the extensive possibilities in marketing and to the recognition of the customer as the deciding factor in success or failure. While in cooperative logistics, innovative processes like CPFR were being intensively discussed, only a few improvements, like Day-to-Day Category Management were to be seen in cooperative marketing. Current developments in Customer Relationship Management show, however, that real potential exists in being able to use modern information technology (IT), and that a focus on the customer means more than mere Category Management (CM). Collaborative Customer Relationship Management is a concept that develops further on the demand side of ECR, integrating CM and going beyond it.

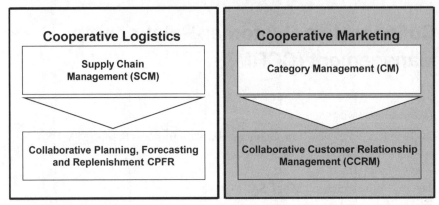

Figure 3.1:   Integration of Collaborative Customer Relationship Management in the ECR Concept

3.1   Collaborative Customer Relationship Management

Efficient Customer Relationship Management consists of four different phases. First, it is about the identification of profitable and unprofitable customer groups through customer value analysis. Second, it involves winning a target customer who has been identified through the analysis. Third, it involves developing ties with the target customer. Fourth, a relationship is developed with profitable target consumers and efforts made to expand consumer spending. In the established consumer goods market, *customer retention* is regarded as the core of customer relationship management. In a saturated market with low returns on sales, focus on retention and bonding seems to be *the* method for increasing earnings. Customer retention, ultimately, needs to be understood as a product of customer satisfaction – the consumer is enthusiastic, recommends products or services, buys the brand again and may even make larger purchases.

Since manufacturers and retailers operate under similar circumstances in the marketplace, are subject to the same developments in consumer behavior, and react in part with identical measures, it is appropriate to consider the components of Collaborative Customer Relationship Management in the framework of the relationship between manufacturing and retailing.

3.1.1   What Is Collaborative Customer Relationship Management in the Consumer Goods Market?

Traditional customer relationship management was characterized by retailers' and manufacturers' individual initiatives. In the future, it may no longer be possible for a company to conduct its customer management alone. Against a backdrop of increasingly changeable consumer behaviour, it is becoming ever more difficult to accommodate changing customer needs in the marketing and product mix. The customer, often criticized as a bargain hunter, is consistent in his or her search for the best value. But the best value need not be the lowest priced offer. Numerous studies prove that consumers are prepared to pay premium prices if the product or service satisfies their needs in a particularly convincing way.

Retailers must try to meet customer desires and at the same time attempt to offer the customer something extra. Through attractive shopping environments or brand names, retailers and manufacturers seek to differentiate themselves from the competition in order to keep customers long-term. In such a situation, synergies can be realized. The satisfaction of consumer needs can proceed more efficiently and economically if retailers and manufacturers work together. Joint direct mailings, e-mail campaigns, and other marketing measures are valuable from the standpoint of cost savings and knowledge exchange. The customer can be seen from the retailers and manufacturers perspective to create a more comprehensive picture. The customer is not only a consumer; he or she is also a shopper. Managers speak of the two moments of truth in which customer management must prove itself: While a product is being purchased and during its use. On this subject, there is much knowledge already available on both the retailer's and the manufacturer's side. The value of Collaborative Customer Relationship Management lies in the joint use of these resources.

3.1.2   Collaborative Customer Retention Management

The identification, attraction, acquisition and development of profitable target customers for bilateral sales and profit development is to be understood under the term Collaborative Customer Relationship Management, and the outstanding role of customer relationships in the consumer goods market must also be acknowledged. In times of evaporating returns, companies must persevere in winning the fight over Customer Lifetime Value. While it is true that attracting customers is a prerequisite for keeping them, it is also a very expensive undertaking. The costs, according to estimates are about five to eight times as high as corresponding investment in existing customers to support their loyalty.

Therefore, the topic of customer relationships, more than any other, should be addressed as the most promising instrument in the consumer goods market. s a rule, limited means require a concentration on existing customers. Collaborative Customer Retention Management addresses this topic and can be defined as the joint and directed use of methods for lasting relationships. The common goal is to achieve store and/or brand loyalty with select customers and customer groups.

The roots of Collaborative Customer Relationship Management and Customer Retention Management lie in the concept of vertical marketing. It is about harmonious dovetailing of marketing ideas along the value chain of the market system, which allows for a better exploitation of consumer demand and simultaneously

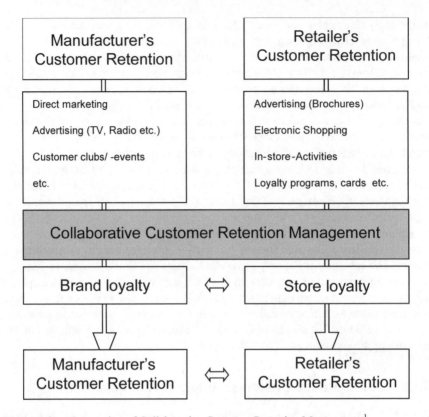

Figure 3.2:   Integration of Collaborative Customer Retention Management[1]

more economical distribution. Consequently, vertical marketing indicates coordinated control and regulation of corporate activities directed at the market.

Based on this conception of vertical marketing, three basic strategies can be derived, within which the long-term policies of the manufacturer should move forward the retailer. Hereafter, these three essential strategies will be illustrated in the combination of retailers and manufacturers.[2]

3.1.2.1 Selection Strategy

The selection strategy entails decisions on the type of firm in retail or the desired degree of distribution (including number of distributors).

---

[1] According to Goerdt 1999, p.17

[2] Irrgang 1993, p.63ff.

3.1.2.2   Stimulation Strategy

The stimulation, or push strategy, is characterized by an intensive retail oriented treatment of the market. The push strategy is responsible for 'forcing' goods into the market and trade channels.[3] The tools of the push strategy include rebate and conditions policies, personal sales talks, services rendered (return of unsold or damaged goods) and retail advertising. The typical objectives are acceptance of assortments or optimal support through sales agents. In the next step of adding value, retailers try, with the help of their marketing tools, to pass the goods on to the consumer. Currently, customer retention management measures, like bonus and rebate systems, are being initiated but without the participation of manufacturers.

The pull strategy, on the other hand, entails intensive communication and information exchange by the manufacturer for his or her brands vis-à-vis consumers with the goal of creating a "demand suction" with the retailer. Through the increased demand intensity of the customer in the retail outlet, the sales agent (retailer) should be moved to carry the product and benefit from consistent demand to support it. Examples of the use of the pull strategy include product sampling, television and radio advertising and consumer oriented print ads.

3.1.2.3   Cooperation Strategy

The cooperation strategy entails long-term vertical cooperation concepts with the goal of grounding a value-adding partnership. This form of collaboration indicates a comprehensive partnership of at least two independent companies, which control the products, services and information flow with a view to maximizing value creation potentials.

Horizontal cooperation (also known as Affiliate Relationship Management (ARM) in e-business) attempts to bring companies at the same level in the supply chain to a broader market. It involves using alternative distribution channels, or simply adding value directly to the customer. In contrast, vertical cooperation (a.k.a. Supplier Relationship Management (SRM)) aims to build partnerships with companies along the value chain. Supply chain partnerships between suppliers and retailers recognize partnerships with those who precede them in the value chain, liberate considerable potential for efficiency, if structures and processes in the participating companies are coordinated for that purpose. Strategic competitive advantages can be achieved through collaboration in logistics, marketing and operations.

When the collaboration between retailing and manufacturing in the past was determined primarily through the coordination of Category Management, one sees today increasingly close cooperation in customer retention management. This strategic shift opens the possibility of exploiting the most varied of synergy potentials in addressing the customer, a topic explored in detail below.

---

[3] Nieschlag, Dichtl, & Hörschgen 1997, p.535

3.2   Goals of Collaborative Customer Retention Management

The goal of Collaborative Customer Relationship Management is to offer manufacturers, retailers, and consumers additional value and thereby to create a win-win-win situation. The following figure 3.3 clarifies this with examples of increased utility for the three groups just mentioned.

Consumer	Retailer	Manufacturer
Tailored customer service	Efficient collaboration with the manufacturer	Efficient collaboration with the retailer
Multi - Channel advertising (TV, Radio, POS, Web etc.)	Differentiation from Competition	Use of the Synergy effect
Discriminating and personalized service and products	Discriminating Shoppers Customer insight	Status of preferred supplier with retailer
Customer oriented product mix	Distinction of customer oriented product mix	Better customer insight
Higher customer satisfaction	**Higher sales growth Store loyalty**	**Higher sales growth Brand loyalty**

Figure 3.3:   Creating a Win-Win-Win Situation

The consumer profits from Collaborative Customer Retention Management above all through an optimized cost benefit ratio. Collaborative activities like supply chain management and vendor managed inventory increase product availability. Category Management brings about consumer-oriented assortments and provides customers an improved shopping experience.

Manufacturers and retailers can profit from Collaborative Customer Retention Management primarily through growth of profits. On the one hand, this is made possible by cost reductions in the process chain and by streamlining logistic processes. On the other hand, increased sales result from consumer oriented product mixes and new marketing concepts, which draw new customers and at the same time enlarge the purchases of regular customers. The prerequisite for this is a structural change on both sides. With these measures, retailers and manufacturers create better store and brand loyalty respectively and thereby customers who guarantee a competitive advantage. Lastly, the stabilization of customer relations contributes to a higher realization of Customer Lifetime Value. After this discourse on cooperation in customer retention, we will return to a comprehensive concept of Collaborative Customer Relationship Management.

3.3 Applications of Collaborative Customer Relationship Management

Where can retailers and manufacturers sensibly cooperate on strategy? When one looks at the points of contact between retail and the consumer, a number of opportunities for manufacturers and retailers for adding value in the framework of Collaborative Customer Relationship Management can be found. As an example, the customer informs himself on the Internet about new products, buys it in a local outlet, receives points on his customer card and communicates his opinion and experiences on the telephone to customer service representatives.

3.3.1 Sales and Marketing

The opportunity for creating value in the sale of products grows with collaboration between partners, while consumer data can be contributed primarily through the manufacturer. Qualitative and quantitative market research by the manufacturers

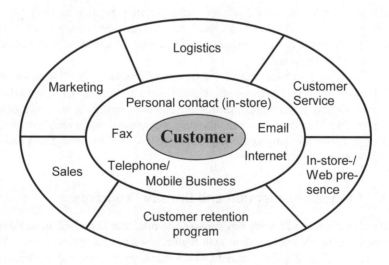

Figure 3.4: Application of Collaborative Customer Relationship Management

can be an essential instrument for adjusting the product mix to suit customer demand. Together with the opportunities for analysis by the retailer (scanner data or receipt analysis, etc.), many chances arise for collaboration. For example, the market research of a manufacturer of paper products could reveal that women use mainly sanitary napkins after a pregnancy. Retailers can confirm through receipt analysis to what extent mothers with babies purchase sanitary napkins concurrently with diapers. Through an appropriate planning and optimization of product mix in the area of sanitary napkins/diapers at the retail outlet, the bundled purchase can be facilitated.

In close connection with sales are points of contact with marketing. This area is one with successful models of manufacturer-retailer partnerships already in existence. Cooperatively prepared promotions and jointly run direct mailings are examples of the possibilities, which can result from a collaborative marketing program.

3.3.2 Logistics

The concrete goal in logistics is the elimination of inefficiencies that occur through uncoordinated processes in the supply chain, as for example when products and information lie idle, or unnecessary buffer stock exists. The objective is to economize the entire supply chain through a transformation of the system from an accumulation model to a customer-focused flow principle. This starting point, as well as that of marketing contain further potential for value-adding collaboration and will be expounded upon below.

3.3.3 In-store/Virtual Presence

In both the in-store and virtual presence of the retailer the manufacturer can likewise be of assistance. In American retail outlets it is commonplace that retailers prepare shelf presentations in certain product groups, which are then implemented after approval by the retailer.

On the retailer's website, manufacturers can offer additional information about their products and product categories respectively. On the other hand, manufacturers can advise about product availability of respective brands in the stores of their retail partners. Manufacturers can also use information garnered through their websites to undertake geographic segmentations and thereby send direct mailings to the retailer's core customer area.

3.3.4 Customer Retention and Loyalty Programs

Customer retention and loyalty programs (customer cards and clubs among others) are further venues for cooperation with high efficiency potential. As a rule, these programs are initiated and organized by manufacturers, retailers, or in a horizontal cooperation. The customer is offered rebates, or special services, and in exchange data is collected and analyzed. Bonus cards or customer clubs are used to distinguish one's self from the competition. This makes collaboration in this area more attractive, because special offers and bonuses for particular or especially loyal customers can be made available. Thereby, opportunities for manufacturers and retailers arise to identify market segments profitable to both, and to link retail outlet and brand name together.

3.3.5 Customer Service

In the area of customer service, collaboration between manufacturers and retailers cannot be avoided. In customer service, elements can be combined which bring with them a structural change in the relationship with the customer. Examples of this are call centers, and repair and delivery services. Because much product information is only available to the customer from the manufacturer, it is the latter that can provide many of the details about products sold in stores. Additionally, manufacturers can also deliver information beyond what is specifically product-related.

In the face of continually declining consumer loyalty, the starting points just described for manufacturers and retailers offer possibilities for creating value and retaining customers. The data obtained from different points of contact with the consumer can be jointly analyzed and used for a jointly directed approach to the customer.

3.4 Collaborative Customer Relationship Management Strategy

In practice, as illustrated above, there are many facets to the opportunities for creating value in the context of comprehensive customer management. If they are conceived in terms of a long-term collaboration, they can be referred to as strategic networks, strategic alliances, or strategic coalitions; thereby differentiating themselves from conventional forms of collaboration, which as a rule, are usually short-term in their orientation, and on the scale of the whole corporation, are relatively insignificant.

The adjective 'strategic' emphasizes in another way the 'new' quality of corporate collaboration. Internal resources are seldom sufficient to meet the challenges of the developing marketplace. Cooperation appears sensible insofar as it improves responsiveness to continually changing markets, technologies, and consumer needs. Above all, it appears that the consumer, in the face of a broader palette of goods and services (through e-business, etc.), is growing more sophisticated and correspondingly coming to demand more value. The consolidation of resources for the satisfaction of consumer desires appears thereby to be a logical move.

The new techniques of Collaborative Customer Relationship Management are composed of strategic and operational elements. They entail a consistent orientation to customer needs as well as the elimination or reduction of all activities that do not add value with the objective of generating enduring competitive advantages.

In the strategic section, a joint assessment of the current situation is first completed. An important part of this is the strategic analysis, in which a systematic search for occasions and necessities of strategic decisions, as well as a precise diagnosis of the roots of suspected strategic problems takes place. The primary purpose of the strategic analysis is the investigation and preparation of strategic decision-relevant information. Familiar instruments of strategic analysis are for example, gap and portfolio analysis, life-cycle analysis and the SWOT model (strengths, weaknesses, opportunities and threats). For instance, it can be determined that a company's marketing efforts are a weakness, which hinders its success. Here one could find a way to incorporate the expertise of a partner whose strength lies in this area.

The complexity of cooperating in value creation requires a structured approach in order to guarantee the success of a partnership. The following matrix shows a corresponding structure for levels of cooperation in customer management.

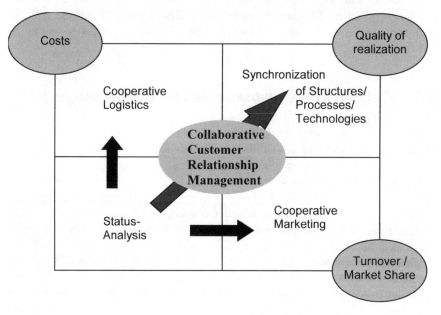

Figure 3.5:   Strategic Matrix of Collaborative Customer Relationship Management[4]

---

[4] According to Zeiner & Ring 1999, p.253

After the strategic analysis comes the fixing of objectives (costs, market share, sales and the quality of the realization respectively), and decisions about cooperative logistics, cooperative marketing, and synchronization of structures, processes, and technologies. An example is given below.

The cooperative logistics and synchronization of processes and technologies between the partners is akin to Porter's model of the value chain as supporting activities for the central instrument of customer management: cooperative marketing.[5] The importance of the combination of the areas becomes apparent because in the cooperative promotion planning as an element of marketing, the logistics must also be considered. If in planning a promotion for diapers, with an aggressive pricing policy at a large hypermarket chain 250 or more full trucks must be anticipated, effective logistics plays a large role in the success of the promotion.[6] The growing network between manufacturers and retailers, joint business planning, and the connection between logistic processes, enabling technologies, and marketing prohibit a purely functional approach.

The following section describes the realization of strategic objectives through appropriate instruments in the framework of Collaborative Customer Relationship Management.

3.5   Instruments of Collaborative Customer Relationship Management

The following instruments form the operative part of customer management and enable the realization of strategic objectives. The instruments presented here are those that currently have the most significance. In the area of marketing, they divide themselves into structural, technological, and logistics measures.

For the joint processing of customers, three different instruments of marketing will be explored in depth: Co-Marketing, Category Management, and Joint Market Research. Developments in Customer Retention, like Customer clubs, Complaint Management, In-store theater, Website and e-Mail programs, etc. will be illustrated briefly.

---

[5] According to Porter the primary activities within the value chain are indivisible with the manufacture, marketing and sales of a product. The secondary activities, corporate infrastructure, human resources, development of technology and procurement, support the primary activities. Porter 1999, p.66.

[6] Compare with the articles on CPFR in this volume.

Figure 3.6:   Marketing-Oriented Instruments of Collaborative Customer Relationship Management (Demand Chain Collaboration)

3.5.1   Co-Marketing

Co-Marketing is based on non-hierarchical collaboration between manufacturers and retailers in marketing and promotions. The main purpose is to develop loyalty to and the image of brands and product lines. This is accomplished through joint implementation of consumer oriented marketing concepts. Through the analysis of consumer studies in the context of market research, and benchmarking, large potential can be revealed whereupon specialized sales promotions can be based.

For manufacturers this represents a new chance to influence the management of their brands at the point of sale. For retailers this means new opportunities to distinguish themselves from the competition through outlets and affiliated brands.

The co-marketing concept also requires of participants a change in both thought and action. Performance and returns must be in balance, so that each side can bring its strengths to bear in order to jointly satisfy the demands of the consumer. The marketing and sales department must grow closer with this concept, each identifying with the strategy, and feeling equally responsible for the success of the brand. Only in this way can promotions be tailored for each retailer, which consider the philosophy of the product line, and the marketing principles of the retail organization.

Case Study 1: Co-Marketing between Compaq and RadioShack

The following shows the tremendous benefits, Co-Marketing can provide all partners. A co-marketing agreement between Compaq and Radio Shack established Compaq Presario Internet PCs as the only PC brand sold in up to 7,100 RadioShack stores and dealers nationwide. The companies co-market a line of RadioShack-exclusive Compaq PCs that are specially designed for Internet and educational use and are sold within a unique "Store within a Store" setting called the Compaq Creative Learning Center. In addition to offering the Compaq Creative Learning Series of Internet PCs, the companies also enable customers to purchase other Compaq consumer products and to custom-configure Compaq PCs to meet their requirements. Compaq and RadioShack decided to prolong their alliance that had originally started in 1998 to 2001 due to three primary factors: 1) a working and strategic relationship that has exceeded both companies' expectations; 2) better than anticipated sales of Compaq Internet PCs at RadioShack; and 3) a shared strategic focus on providing consumers with a new level of easy Internet access and use.

"There is no question that the RadioShack/Compaq partnership has been extremely beneficial for both companies and for our customers," said Mike Larson, senior vice president and group general manager, Consumer Products Group, Compaq Computer Corporation. "This agreement will allow us to continue to offer a one-stop Compaq shopping and service destination in virtually every U.S. neighborhood through America's most trusted consumer electronics chain. In our shared commitment to providing a complete and fulfilling in-store experience, we now want to expand that vision to provide the best Internet products and services possible for our customers." Besides financial success, the alliance between Compaq and RadioShack reflects a shared commitment to making the Internet part of everyone's day-to-day activities. Both companies have announced strategic partnerships with Microsoft's MSN Internet service. Compaq, a front-runner in technological advancements, provides consumers with all the tools needed to experience today's e-Lifestyle. The consumer experiences this benefit through hardware and software specifically designed for simple Internet usage, including one-button access to the Web. "Compaq's management team shares our vision of making the Internet easy and accessible for the American consumer," commented David Edmondson, chief operating officer for Tandy/RadioShack. "Our strategic alliance with Compaq helps us further accelerate the adoption of new and emerging technologies, which in turn supports our strategy of becoming America's Home Connectivity Store. The Compaq Creative Learning Center will continue to play a key role in helping us "connect places" via the Internet and other digital media. By integrating Compaq's technical proficiency and quality Internet PCs with the expertise and superior service of RadioShack, consumers benefit from a seamless buying solution. RadioShack's trained salespeople and proficient home-installation team take consumers from the initial steps of acquiring a computer to actually zipping onto the Web and signing up for Internet service, facilitating the immediate integration of the Internet into their daily activities – from online shopping, travel planning and immediate news retrieval to next-generation applications in home entertainment, home security and Internet access.[7]

Jointly developed projects, like the ones just described, are an expression of the potential that lies in the area of promotions in collaborative business relationships. This is not only true for the offline collaboration. Online relationships (as affiliate or supplier relationship management) can help to boost revenues even further.

3.5.2   Category Management

In the late eighties, a high profile player in the consumer goods economy began Category Management as a further development of product management, in which an orientation to the consumer was often neglected. Category Management (CM) is an approach to systematic assortment optimization in retail. The entire range of products is divided into categories. An important metric for differentiation is the perception of the customer. Products that the customer believes belong together are assembled in a group. The categories are managed as strategic business units, in order to increase usefulness to customers and thereby to improve earnings.

In total, CM entails three tactical elements: Efficient Store Assortment (ESA) that enables the retailer, usually in cooperation with the manufacturer, to distinguish himself or herself from the competition through a customer oriented product mix and an optimized in-store presentation. There are already retailers which take ESA to the level of using area' for several different purposes in the course of one day. In the morning, a customer would find sandwiches, hot coffee, and newspapers. In the evening, the same corner would be stocked with beer and barbecue supplies. Thinking in categories means asking: "What does the customer need

---

[7] http://www8.techmall.com

before work?" or "What does he need for a barbecue?" In the opinion of some authors, CM goes beyond that to include service offerings, as for example with a summer fest.[8] Further, it is about speaking to target groups with appropriate product groups; e.g. single serving frozen foods for singles.

The second tactical element, Efficient Promotion (EP) aims for customer attraction and lasting customer retention. The growing number of promotions at the POS however has reduced their effectiveness while low prices attract primarily the unprofitable bargain hunters. Special offers punish loyal customers who purchase the product in question on a regular basis at the normal price. Therefore, Efficient Promotion tools should be used to reward customer loyalty.

Case Study 2: Kmart and Wal-Mart

Kmart is a very good example of how important efficient promotion planning is in order to survive in the market. Kmart tried to win in the market with ad circulars, which seek to attract customers through the promotion of sale prices on everything from treadmills to toothbrushes to towels. Not only are the circulars very expensive to create, print and distribute, but by requiring stores to stockpile the promoted items every week to meet demand, they wreak havoc on inventory systems. The circulars accounted for 10.6% of Kmart's operating expenses, compared with 0.4% at Wal-Mart. Wal-Mart instead took based on heavy market research another approach: it simply created the image of having low prices everyday. A cartful of items according to Wal-Mart would cost less than anywhere else. Based on careful collaborative category management efforts, Wal-Mart eliminated most of the costly newspaper advertising. This resulted in much lower selling, general and administrative expenses than competition, helping Wal-Mart to keep selling prices below other consumer- and hypermarkets. [9]

And finally, Efficient Product Introduction (EPI) serves to systematically multiply real product innovation and support its successful introduction. Ninety percent of all products introduced in the last two years have disappeared from the market.[10] The main reason is that so many are copycat products, which do not offer consumers additional value.

To summarize, the objectives of Category Management are shown in the following figure.

---

[8] E.g. Lingenfelder 2000, p.2

[9] Figures taken from The Wall Street Journal, 01/18 2002, p. B1: Expensive Ad Circulars Help Precipitate Kmart President's Departure

[10] Nielsen/Young, 1999

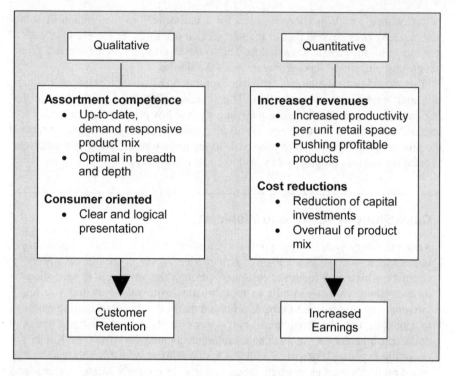

Figure 3.7:   Goals of Category Management[11]

The condition necessary for successful realization of CM is open, continuing collaborations between manufacturer and retailer. If there is an absence of readiness for bilateral and continuous information exchange or the necessary trust, CM will not be possible.

CM aims to design the product mix more responsively to consumer desires than ever before. Thereby, the goal of exploiting the potential of the market through optimal assortments is also achieved. The advantage of this was shown by a study from Coca Cola Retailing Research Group Europe. As early as 1993, the Group concluded that sales could be increased by 15 to 20 % through collaborative design of the product mix.[12]

Implementation of CM in the framework of Collaborative Customer Relationship Management will be discussed at the end of this section.

---

[11] According to Goerdt 1999

[12] Coca Cola Retailing Research Group Europe 1993

3.5.3   Joint Market Research

The effective management of a category as a strategic business unit is unthinkable without detailed knowledge of the customer and the particulars of the marketplace. The knowledge that retailers have about consumers however, is paltry. It is often the case that retailers have no detailed understanding of the trends and desires of consumers in important product categories.[13]

The task of market research is to provide a differentiated analysis of customer structure and consumer behavior with the objective of obtaining clear market segmentation. This enables a targeting of the identified customer group with the appropriate goods and services. At the beginning of a detailed analysis, many investigations therefore look to the demographics of the retail outlets of the retail organization under consideration.[14] The distribution of buying power, or the age and domestic structure of particular customer groups are essential indices. Beyond that, analysis of individual purchases allows a differentiated view of consumer behavior. Market research firms like AC Nielsen are usually sources for relevant market and consumer data. Consumer studies and retail outlet analysis based on this information is possible.

Joint Market Research is of special importance here. Through the consolidation of knowledge on the consumer the opportunity arises to complete the consumer puzzle as illustrated in the following diagram.

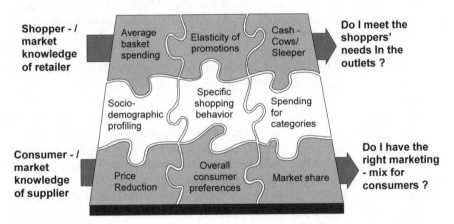

Figure 3.8:   Cooperation in Market and Consumer Research[15]

---

[13] Mei-Pochter, Schächer & Loos 1999, p.42

[14] Cantrell 1998, p.85

[15] Mei-Pochter, Schächer & Loos 1999, p.42

Within the consumer puzzle pieces like demographic profiles, specific shopping behavior, and average basket spending have received relatively more attention. Manufacturers and retailers have devoted less attention to cooperative market research, but it offers an approach to the problem of obtaining specific knowledge about the consumer *and* the shopper *and* their behavior. Consolidated resources and competences facilitate an outstanding synergy effect. The following case study on cooperative market research clarifies the use in the field.

Case Study 3: Cooperative Market Research between Retailers and Procter & Gamble

One of the leading international manufacturers of consumer goods and ECR pioneers, Procter & Gamble brings its own market research to its collaboration with retail. Cooperative market development is performed on the basis of a so-called 'shopper study'. These are data, which view the consumer not only as a user of products, but also as a buyer in the most varied distribution channels. In an annual review, the position of each chain is analyzed in different categories and a comprehensive picture can be drawn.

The first component of the shopper study is the Nielsen household panel. Supplemented by demographic data, scanner evaluations and market studies, statements on loyalty of the customers in the retailers' outlets and the coverage of excess demand by the competition can be made. This facilitates the identification of the competition in a product group. It is often the case that a competitor is not of the same type of business, but possibly a discounter who is the main competitor of a convenience store in a particular product group.

The second component of cooperative market research analyzes the image of distribution channels and reports on the propensity of consumers to buy in different categories. Basis of the analysis are huge, country specific customer surveys, provided by leading market research consultancies. Thereby P&G becomes concrete data on the attitudes and values of shoppers. The central questions here are, "Which expectations do consumers have of a distribution channel?", "How well does that channel meet certain criteria?" (generally and with regard to specific categories), or "How is the performance of a certain selling concept seen in comparison to the competition?" The market research of P&G is not limited to the level of situation analysis, rather beyond that it offers concrete measures for cooperative market development. The retail partner profits from a better understanding of his actual competition. At the same time, he increases his knowledge of his actual and potential customers.[16]

---

[16] Biester 1999, p.40

3.5.4   Other Customer Retention Programs

Customer Retention Programs are a further opportunity to work collaboratively on sales, profit and security in relationships with customers. In the marketing mix, there are in each case different tools available for retaining the customer. Depending on the focus, increasing interaction or satisfaction or eliminating barriers to change, the result is a number of possibilities for cooperation. In product policy for example, joint product development, joint offers of additional service, and performance guarantees as well as value-added services are possible. In pricing policy, loyalty cards, setting 'the right price' based on customer questionnaires, as well as rebates and bonus systems are useful instruments. Manufacturers can help retailers by investigating consumer behavior relative to price difference, coupons, or other devices or incentives for cardholders. In the framework of communications policy, direct mailings, event programs, joint online marketing and service numbers can be used to retain customers. Customer clubs, magazines, and complaint management are further means of communications that can be used jointly. In the context of distribution policies, the Internet, prizes, product sampling, direct delivery and subscriptions can be filled with life.

Many of the tools mentioned here can be combined. For example, direct mailings can be sent from a manufacturer into the core area of a retailer advising of special deals available of the manufacturer-retailer team. In addition to the special offer, one can mention about a contest being hosted by the retailer. The contest can serve to increase the awareness of a product introduction, sales of a particular manufacturer's goods and to position the retailer as an innovative merchant. In the direct mailing, a coupon can be sent along for a test sample or something similar to motivate the customer to shop at a particular retail outlet. Both manufacturer and retailer can ease the financial burden of marketing through joint advertising efforts.

The customer club, as a particular form of customer retention will be described here as an integrated concept. Different customer retention measures can be combined in order to offer the consumer additional value and to improve the image of the respective company. Here too, manufacturers and retailers can also work together on cooperative market research. At the end of this section, a case will be used to show how this works. The goal is not only to increase revenues, market share and long-term profit, but also to expand customer insight through optimized consumer databases. Club magazines, cards, special offers, and special events are common means for making customer clubs attractive to select target groups. Important in any event is the establishment of enduring communications with the customer and to formulate genuinely unique enticements.

A further important tool of customer retention is complaint management. For customers who express their dissatisfaction with products and services, there is an appreciable difference between expectation and actual experience. With insufficient complaint management, a trend towards negative word of mouth advertising and inactivity can develop, or in the best case: complaints. This is the best case because the reason for the dissatisfaction can be investigated and the customer won back. Even here, the expertise of predecessors in the supply chain can be of use. If for example the manufacturer of electric toothbrushes has identified the unavailability of replacement brushes as a reason for dissatisfaction, he can work together with the retailer on a response in distribution policy.

The manufacturers of technically sophisticated products can be linked to the retailers through service numbers. If customers have problems, the manufacturer can be contacted via the retailer. In consideration of the purchasing power of the retailer and his or her desire for customer satisfaction, it could be expected that manufacturers would address non-functioning customer hotlines.

In addition to the opportunities just described, cooperation in the virtual medium offers new starting points. Mobile marketing and opt-in e-mail's potent campaigns are representative of many possibilities the collaboration between online-shops and supplier will be shown in detail in a later chapter in that volume. Beyond that, the design of not only in-store displays, but of complete departments is an emerging trend. With target group specific 'solutions centers', the needs and desires of customers can be satisfied in a special way through for example an especially broad and deep assortment coupled with services and special offers. Here manufacturers can consult and support. At the end of the section, a successful example will be presented. The approach to the customer via the Internet can also be jointly designed in many ways, beginning with overviews of which retailers have a particular product in stock and on to e-mail marketing.

3.6   Measuring Performance in Collaborative Customer Relationship Management

The concept of performance measurement and evaluation should, per agreement among partners give a realistic reflection of the project. The results of this evaluation can be used as guideposts for the enterprising retailer. This can be done with the help of a scorecard. This is a list of criteria, which illustrates the framework for performance evaluations. The scorecard is an instrument of performance evaluation and the determination of the status quo in the context of Collaborative Customer Relationship Management. Ideally, the members of multifunctional teams keep a score involved in the project. The scorecard helps determine how much progress has been made towards established goals. Additionally, it identifies potential and supports management in the formulation of new priorities and strategies. The scorecard is thereby an important analytic technique combined with elements of forecasting and control.

A good application of continuous measurement is a balanced scorecard. The essential idea of this approach is that economic success can be traced to factors, which stand behind financial goals and ultimately determine success. The balanced scorecard creates a new framework for the integration of strategic measures. Different indices, which comprise the consumer's perspective, internal business processes, as well as learning and growth area derived from an explicit and consistent translation of corporate strategy into concrete goals and measures. The following figure clarifies this relationship.

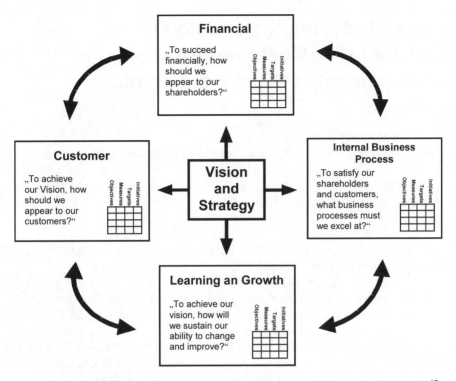

Figure 3.9:   The Balanced Scorecard as a Supporting Element of Strategy Implementation[17]

The balanced scorecard does more than improve the transparency of indices of business performance. Especially companies whose business divisions enjoy high autonomy, e.g. retailers with independent distribution channels, use the balanced scorecard as a management system with primarily strategic and above all imple-mentations tasks. It is also therefore well suited to deliver valuable information to the value chain partners. With the consumer-oriented perspective of the balanced scorecard, the identification of performance factors which add value for the cus-tomer stand in the foreground. In the contribution by Mills et al. entitled *"New Ways in Category Management"* found in this volume, an example of the joint scorecard in CM is given.

In the US, some retailers allow their suppliers to view their scorecard results via the Internet. Manufacturers are then in the position of reconciling objectives at the product and product group levels.

---

[17] Robert S. Kaplan & David P. Norton, Using the Balanced Scorecard as a Strategic Man-agement System", Harvard Business Review (January-February 1996): 76.

Case Study: Implementation of Collaborative Customer Relationship Management at Procter & Gamble

Alexander H. Kracklauer
BayTech IBS, UAS Neu-Ulm, Germany / Harvard Business School, MA, USA

Niko Warmbrunn
Procter & Gamble, Schwalbach, Germany

An example of Collaborative Customer Relationship Management can be found in the collaboration between P&G and a North American trade partner.

Collaborative Customer Relationship Management holds that, as with planning concepts generally, the strategic framework comes first, and then the tactical measures. Before any decisions are taken, a strategic analysis is done. With projects such as the one to be described here, it is indispensable to gather information and experiences on the retailer in question, the competition, and the consumer. Hereby, the scanner data from retail partners, especially in conjunction with customer cards and other shopper and consumer data, is referenced. These deliver data on what, how much, and from whom something was bought. These evaluations are supplemented with shopper analyses by P&G. That means manufacturing partners can support the retailer by providing him or her with information on the consumer and the competition. Since a manufacturer is only usually concerned with a few categories, and retailers often with hundreds, the manufacturer is better situated to deliver detailed data than the retailer. The following discussion illustrates part of the work done in collaboration between the manufacturer, retailer and P&G.

Consumer Structure and Consumer Behavior: The Search for the 'Right' Customer

Joint Market Research demands that appropriate data are available and exchanged. This analysis is then refined in the individual companies by multifunctional teams, formed prior to the partnership. Excerpts from the initial P&G survey show the following results.

Shoppers can be divided into two different groups: loyal customers and occasional shoppers. Based on this definition in this illustration, the shoppers distinguish themselves through the number of shopping trips and through the average

Table 3.1:   Consumer Structure of the Retailer

	Loyal Buyers	**Occasional Buyers**
Number of total shoppers	14%	86%
Shopping trips per year	53	12
Expenditure per Trip in $	27.74	15.96
Expenditure per Year per customer at retailer	1,474.50	196.06
Total expenditure in $	20,643	16,861
Distribution	56%	44%

expenditure per trip. On a yearly basis, it is clear that a loyal customer is eight times 'more valuable' than the occasional shopper.

Examination of the data revealed that 14% of the regular customers are responsible for 56% of sales. The majority of occasional shoppers, 86% represent only 44% of total revenues. Further benchmarking data shows that this supermarket chain has a large share of unprofitable occasional shoppers relative to its competition, where usually no more than 70% of all shoppers are only occasional and loyal shoppers are in the range of 30%.

Other keys to the consumer behavior, as well as motivation and attitude of the customer, come through gap analysis based on consumer interviews. This places the anticipated demands of the consumer in the light of the actual situation and describes how consumers perceive the supermarket. This analysis showed that, in the eyes of the customer, the retailer is too expensive and that the product range is too narrow.

The dissatisfaction of the customer is also clearly evidenced by the small penetration[18] of the supermarket of 1.8%. A competitor comparable in terms of number of stores and location achieved 2.1%. Additionally, a downward trend was apparent in the retailers market share.

The objective of the strategy had to be to recover lost market share. The multi-functional teams agreed that the first step would be to establish the grounds for the low and declining market share of the retailer.

---

[18] Percentage of buying households from all American households

Low Market Share as an Indicator of Insufficient Customer Management

An analysis of market share can reveal not only the successes and failures of the product groups under consideration, but also the root causes of those results. Correspondingly, an analytic break down of the market share must be done. P&G defines its market share as follows:

$$\text{Market share} = \text{Penetration} \times \text{Loyalty} \times \text{Intensity Index}$$

Market share is therefore a multiple of:

- Percentage of buying households (penetration). Example: of 100 million national households, 3 million have made one purchase at the retailer. That equates to a penetration of 3%.

- Percentage of demand of a customer in a product group that a retailer covers (loyalty). Example: For the product group 'salty snacks' the retailer's customer spends $100 on average and 40 of those dollars in his store. That equates to a loyalty of 40%.

- Average expenditure of a customer in a product group in comparison to average national expenditure (intensity index). Example: If the national average expenditure for 'salty snacks' is $125, the hypothetical customer has an intensity index of 80. ($100/ $125 (average customer) x 100). The retailer has shopper with a 'small purse'.

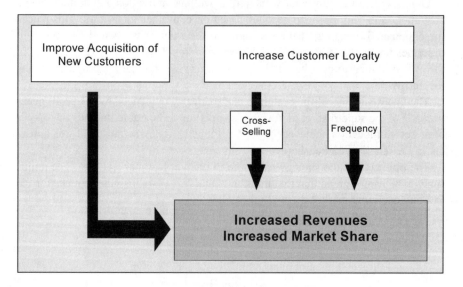

Figure 3.10:   Options for Increased Revenues – Market Share

After the market share is defined as such, the following options for the retailer and P&G present themselves:

1. Increase penetration through the acquisition of new customers.

2. Increase loyalty and the intensity index by improving the profitability of existing customers, transforming occasional shoppers to loyal customers, thereby retaining free-spending households.

Since loyalty is determined by frequency and purchase amount, two possibilities for increasing loyalty are available: Cross-Selling and Frequency.[19] Cross selling for our purposes is considered the equivalent of bundled purchases. Frequency refers to an increase in the number of shopping trips.

Based on the available data on occasional shoppers, both options should be pursued. Thereby, the assumption is made that all 2,567,000 occasional shoppers have the same shopping habits. This means that they make on average 12 shopping

Table 3.2:   Shopping Scenarios

Option   **A**

More purchases: Increase number of shopping trips per year by one among half of the occasional shoppers.

Shopping trip/year		Expenditure in $		Number of Shoppers		Sales in $
13	×	15,96	×	1.283.500	=	266.300.580
12	×	15,96	×	1.283.500	=	245.815.920
				Increase		20.484.660

Option   **B**

Cross-Selling: Increase average purchase by $5 among half of the occasional shoppers.

Shopping trip/year		Expenditure in $		Number of Shoppers		Sales in $
12	×	20,96	×	1.283.500	=	322.825.920
12	×	15,96	×	1.283.500	=	245.815.920
				Increase		**77.010.000**

---

[19] Beyond these possibilities are two more: up-selling through volume discounts or premium price strategies. These options should not be explored here in greater detail.

trips per year, totaling $491,631,840. We assume that we could impact a) shopping trips (+1 shopping trip/customer) or b) basket spending (purchase increase + 5$/customer/trip) among half of the occasional shoppers.

The illustration lets one speculate that sales can be more efficiently increased by higher average purchases than by increasing the number of shopping trips per annum. It seems simpler to sell more to a consumer who is already in the store than to attract new customers. Further analysis showed that the average purchase lay below the average for the retailer's specific type of business. Attracting new customers would also entail higher acquisition costs. Nonetheless, the idea of attracting new customers should not be forgotten. In view of shrinking penetration, investment on this front seems unavoidable.How can both goals be achieved?

Joint Market Research: Which Target Groups Are Relevant?

After a theoretical analysis of the options, the next step to a solution was to ask: "Which target groups are relevant and valuable for the retailer?" Both sides agreed to first identify the right customer in order to achieve penetration expansion (new customer acquisition), increased loyalty (higher frequency and cross-selling) and intensity indices through target group marketing. Retailer and P&G asked themselves, "Which lifecycle group offers the most potential to the supermarket?" They divided the customer base into singles, families with children and families without children.

After a deep analysis of consumer and shopper data from both the retailer and P&G, it became clear that, 'families with children' were underdeveloped relative to the competition and consequently held potential. The following diagram, a component of the analysis, clarifies the approach.

The index shows the penetration of the retailer's supermarkets and that of his competition in comparison. For example, the competitor reaches 19% more households with children than the retailer and 38% more than the national average for supermarkets. Despite the fact that during the national comparison families with children were over-represented in the region and thereby of diminished value, disadvantages relative to the competition are apparent. The competition has better penetrated the market and reached all strata of customers more effectively. In comparison to the national average, the retailer's supermarkets have fewer unprofitable single-households in their customer structure and reach more profitable large households. Nonetheless, the penetration of the competition in all target groups is clearly higher and here lies the opportunity for the retailer.

A further analysis considered the purchasing power of the target group. Here too there is great potential. Of the households in the target market, 35% have children. These account for 43% of sales for everyday purchases. Thereby, families with children are by far the most relevant and highest volume target group. Again though, the competition has proven itself better at exploiting this potential than the retailer being considered here.

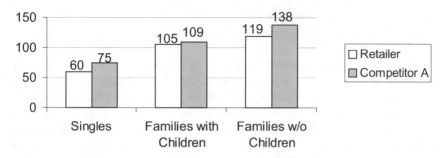

Figure 3.11: Household Penetration of the Retailer and that of Competitor "A"

Additional analyses showed that, in particular families with children ages 0 to 6 present a problem. A simultaneous investigation made clear that in *the* category for this group-baby-care, this retailer had a below-average market share. In a fair share analysis, the dimensions of the potential became clear. The fair share in this project was defined as the retailer's market share in terms of the value of everyday goods. The course of the two preceding years showed that in the category of baby-care, the retailer was 1.2% below the average possible market share for everyday purchases.

This target group was very interesting: the group 'young families with children' made more shopping trips than the 'average customer' per year, spent more per trip, and generated thereby more revenue per year than other families. Likewise, the fact that young families with children change supermarkets less often makes this target group interesting. Based on the potential of this profitable target group, the objective became one of optimizing the category baby care, in order to come up to the fair share and thereby to increase total market share.

Category Management and Co-Marketing for Retaining the Target Group

For retailers, this means expanding product and service leadership in order to stand out from the competition. In Category Management, this means an emphasis on presentation, (target group-oriented assortment, no out-of-stocks, etc.) and innovation (first to present new products). The goal must be to offer the target group a superior product with outstanding service and to communicate this through television, radio, and direct mailing. Thereby, the supermarket should develop a pull-strategy in order to draw in new customers.

On the other hand, the potential of existing customers cannot be neglected. Every possibility to increase the average expenditure through bundled or premium purchases should be used. This can be done by, among other things, showing competitors prices on shelves, as well as through other instruments of CM like best placement for premium products, or co-location of products commonly used at the same time. The task must be to offer and to enhance one-stop shopping for every need.

This should be accomplished through Collaborative Customer Relationship Management. To retain the target group long-term, P&G and the retailer analyzed receipts and customer card data, as well as focus group discussions to ascertain the most important consumer desires of the target group. Thereby, it came to light that in particular with diapers[20], the choice of supermarket is determinant and thereby must be raised to the level of a key line. The idea of creating a Baby Care Center (Baby Club) in the supermarket was borne in mind with the ambition of generating more volume, increasing average expenditure, and strengthening the loyalty of families.

In this project, the term 'Baby Care Center' came to mean a spatially distinct place for all baby articles. The center should be built on five successive elements.

1. Placement and Marketing

   To this element belong selection and weighting of categories within the baby care center. Core categories should be diapers, baby towels, baby care, and infant nutrition, while these categories determine the choice of supermarket for parents. Next to the articles, which regularly appear on the shopping list, high-margin impulse items like baby clothes and toys are placed. Seasonal assortments further increase the attractiveness of the Baby Care Center.

2. Efficient Spatial Arrangement

   The design of supermarkets must consider the target group consumer's expectation of easy shopping. This means that the arrangement of all products for babies is found in one place with clearly arranged shelves and signage. Additionally, the 'logical' consumer behavior of parents should be observed. Core categories should be the easiest to find, and have the most space devoted to them.

3. Pleasant Shopping Environment

   The customer's expectations of easy, pleasant, and high quality shopping should be supported by wide aisles, cash registers with short lines and no sweets, and parking lots for parents with children, changing rooms for babies, lounges and refreshment centers, as well as a broad and deep assortment. Additionally, the choice of colors, music, lighting and a play corner for children make shopping into an experience.

---

[20] Diapers have the highest penetration in this target group among baby products and serve therefore as a destination category.

4. Target Group Information

In order to really offer the consumer more value, the transfer of information can represent a decisive competitive advantage. Of the target group households with their first-borns, 40% of them desire advice on baby care and product information. This information can be passed along at the POS through schooled personnel, extensive descriptions on the shelves and books or brochures, and in customer magazines or videos.

5. Co-Marketing

Through additional marketing, manufacturers and retailers attempt to commend the attractiveness of their supermarkets and brands. Examples of this are events, direct mailing (with coupons), or Baby Club customer cards.

Where families were attracted through special offers in the past, e.g. through sale prices, the Baby Care Center should retain the customer long-term with a broader and deeper assortment that covers newborns through school children. This product mix offers the target group genuine additional value. Beyond that, loyal customers are rewarded with a cash bonus, e.g. a 10% rebate when total purchases exceed a certain threshold. This strengthens customer loyalty. The granting of the rebate was decidedly under the usual 20 to 25%, which the retailer offered in conventional campaigns. At the same time, an additional marketing program for the Baby Club was initiated via television, radio and Internet advertising. Both sides brought their expertise to the table in acquiring and retaining customers.

An example of marketing cooperation was the use of a link to the "Pampers Parenting Institute" by P&G in the retailer's online marketing campaign for the Baby Club. From this website, one could find tips and advice on baby care and health.

Beyond that, the retailer hoped that through targeted design and assortment presentation a positive light would be reflected onto other categories, weaknesses in individual areas like negative price image would be partially compensated and an overall good impression given. Features like rationalization of the purchasing process, clarity of the product arrangement, pleasant surroundings, or well-planned product mix can actually become important criteria or image building and thereby to making the retailer a destination store.[21]

An important aspect of the Baby Care Center was in-store presentation. The assortment, which has been directed at Baby Club customers, gives the consumer new ideas and an overview of possible purchases, which can also lead to additional sales (the shelf as "shopping list"). The customer saves time, and one-stop shopping is possible. At the same time, attractive in-store presentations make shopping into an experience for young mothers. The design of the presentation should stimulate demand and lead to an impulse purchase. Here the resources of P&G and the retailer worked hand-in-hand: P&G designed the shelves in close cooperation with the retailer and accompanied the implementation.

---

[21] Möhlenbruch 1994, p.203

Next to shelf optimization, it is also important that no gaps in inventory appear because the reaction to gaps from consumers has a negative impact for retailer and manufacturer alike. According to market research by the manufacturer of Pampers, in 22% of the cases, a change to a different brand occurs in the same store. This is a problem for P&G, not however for the retailer. In 32% of the cases, the purchase is delayed. This is a problem for both, while the risk of a change to another market and another brand is present. In 46% of the cases, a competitor purchased the Pampers. This is the biggest problem for the retailer, because not only the Pampers are not sold, but other articles tied to their purchase meet with similar fate as well. Through analysis of stock turnover, preparation of the shelves and warehouses, and a de-listing of slow turning skus that block valuable shelf space, this problem was solved. Especially those responsible for logistics and the Category Manager of the multifunctional teams from retailer and manufacturer worked on the proper solution.

Results

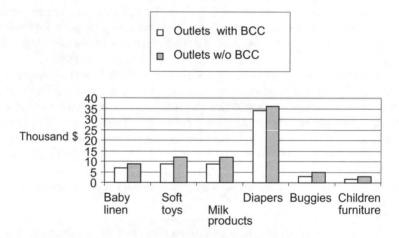

Figure 3.12:   Revenue Comparison of Supermarkets with Baby Care Centers to Regular Supermarkets

As the following data show, the combination of increased penetration and customer loyalty made the Baby Club a successful project for Collaborative Customer Relationship Management.

Only three months after the introduction of the Baby Center, the first results were convincing for all concerned. All products in the assortment showed dramatic growth relative to the previous year. In particular, the high-margin non-food segments like baby linen, soft toys, buggies and children furniture were able to nearly double the sales. This shows, how a new placement in the proper context can awaken buying impulses.

Other objectives were achieved. Five months after introduction of the Baby Care Centers, increased revenues brought the retailer close to the 12% fair share in the baby care category. The retailer achieved an increased market share in baby care of 1.1% in comparison to the previous year, and a hike in revenue of 13%.

On the assumption, which is supported by receipt analysis, that for every dollar spent on baby care, the total purchase is raised by three dollars, there is an additional increase in revenues associated with everyday purchases. In fact, there was also a corresponding increase in market share in terms of overall value correlated to baby care. The growth of the channel could be traced to the Baby Care Center above all. The customers were also satisfied with the retailer: polls showed a distinct improvement in the judgment of value and overall image of the retailer.

Through the increased attractiveness of the supermarket, P&G profited too. In the first six months after the introduction of the Center, sales of P&G products rose 16%, and through this disproportionate growth, their share of baby care products sold through the retailer. This can all be traced to the increased efficiency of the assortment, (no out-of-stocks) as well as the fulfilment of the customer's wish for bulk sizes. The strongest P&G product, Pampers, rose to first time category leader with the retailer in front of the strongest national brand, Huggies.

It proved a win-win-win situation. The retailer received, in addition to market share, a better appraisal of the value-for-money it offers customers, and consequently a higher overall rating too. P&G won too: through consumer dictated product mix, improved product availability, and joint marketing, sales and market share were increased. And finally, the retail and brand customers won a better selection of goods, improved availability, and other incentives led to substantial more satisfaction with the supermarket and the brand.

References

Biester, S. (1999): Gemeinsamer Blick zum Kunden, in: Lebensmittelzeitung 19th Nov. 1999, P.40

Cantrell, P. (1998): Who is your customer? – Category Management, in: Aftermarket Business, Nr.8, 1998, p.85

Goerdt, T. (1999): Die Marken- und Einkaufstättentreue der Konsumenten als Bestimmungsfaktoren des vertikalen Beziehungsmarketings, Erlangen 1999

Irrgang, W. (1993): Vertikales Marketing im Wandel- Aktuelle Strategien und Operationalisierungen zwischen Hersteller und Handel, München 1993

Kaplan, R. and Norton, D.P. (1997): Balanced Scorecard: Strategien erfolgreich umsetzen, Stuttgart 1997

Kracklauer, A. and Seifert, D. (2001): Gemeinsam näher am Kunden; Markenartikel 3/2001, p.50-59

Kurt Salmon Associates (1993): Efficient Consumer Response – Enhancing Consumer Value in the Grocery Industry, Washington 1993.

Lingenfelder, M. (2000): Abschied vom Produkt- Ist Category Management mehr als eine vergängliche Mode, in: Marburger Uni Journal 7/ 2000, p.2-6

Mei-Pochtler, A., Schwächer, M. and Loos, C.(1999): Kundenmarketing – Kooperatives Kundenmarketing ist oft noch ein Fremdwort, in: Lebensmittelzeitung 26.th Feb. 1999, p.42-43

Möhlenbruch, D. (1994): Sortimentspolitik im Einzelhandel, Wiesbaden (1994)

Nielsen (1992): Category Management-Position your Organisation to Win, Chicago 1992

Nielsen/Young Consulting (1999): Nur jedes zehnte Produkt bleibt am Markt, in: Horizont 29/1999, p. 10

Nieschlag, R., Dichtl, E. and Hörschgen, H.(1997): Marketing, Berlin 1997

Porter, M. E. (1999): Wettbewerbsvorteile – Spitzenleistungen erreichen und behaupten, 5. Aufl. Frankfurt a. Main/New York 1999

Seifert, D. (2001): Efficient Consumer Response – Supply Chain Management, Category Management und Collaborative Planning, Forecasting and Replenishment als neue Strategieansätze, 2. Aufl., München 2001.

The Coca-Cola Retailing Research Group Europe (1993): Kundenloyalität im Lebensmitteleinzelhandel: Projektergebnisse auf der Basis von Fallstudien, März 1993

Zeiner, R. and Ring, T. (1999): Efficient Consumer Response – Der Weg ist das Ziel, in: Heydt, A. (Edit.): Handbuch Efficient Consumer Response – Konzepte Erfahrungen, Herausforderungen, München, 1999, p. 237-254.

CHAPTER 4

The Integration of Supply Chain Management and Customer Relationship Management

Alexander H. Kracklauer
BayTech IBS, UAS Neu-Ulm, Germany / Harvard Business School, MA, USA

D. Quinn Mills
Harvard Business School, MA, USA

Dirk Seifert
Harvard Business School, MA, USA

Michael Barz
Business Consultant, Wiesbaden, Germany

It's not only the focus on CRM that allows companies to outperform their competition. Companies so far rarely integrate supply chain management and customer relationship management. By integrating these business processes companies are able to break through and achieve a number of improvements in their financial and performance metrics that would have been unachievable using only stand alone CRM & SCM techniques. JDA Chief Technology Officer Scott Hines coined the term ISCRM; Integrated Supply Chain and Customer Relationship Management. Later in this part of this book, a local US case study of JDA and a global study conducted by Deloitte Consulting show how the integration of demand-generating and supply-chain operations through information technologies help companies to create an outstanding value proposition. Superior performance in sales, market share, customer service etc. can be achieved by creating digital loyalty networks. To build this network, companies must develop not only a customer strategy, but also a partner and supply chain strategy to support customer loyalty. There is great potential in the development of ECR via focusing on the consumer to meet his or her needs. There is also significant potential in the integration of the supply and demand sides with the help of respective IT capabilities and well-developed digital platforms.

As mentioned in the last chapter, logistic functions have to serve customer relationship management processes. Data coming from the consumer have to be translated into the logistic value chain in order to get the right products at the right time

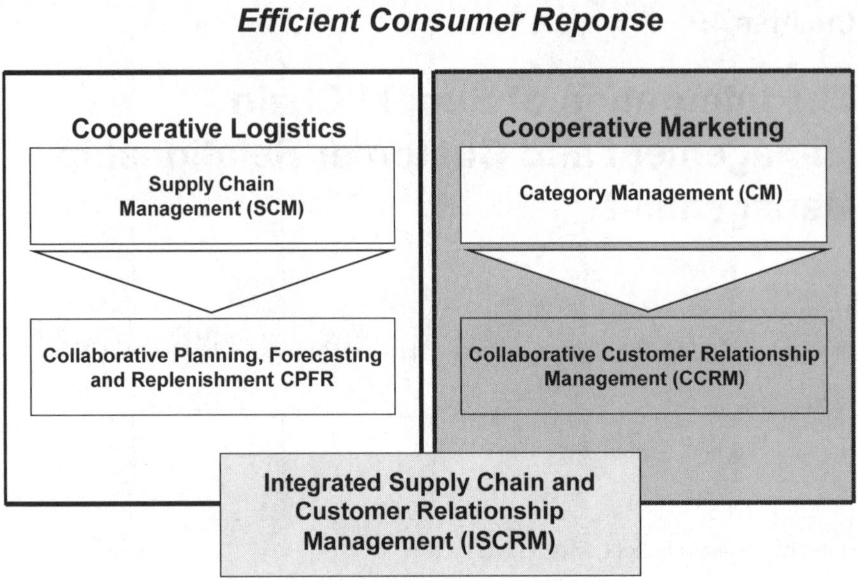

Efficient Consumer Reponse

Figure 4.1:   Integrated Supply Chain and Customer Relationship Management

to the right place and in the right quality. This must be achieved by structural arrangements to get the data interchange through the value chain e.g. through interdisciplinary teams which work at the interfaces between different companies.

A very important role to integrate SCM and CRM plays the IT infrastructure – vertically and horizontally integrated IT networks require a coordination of corporate strategies of the participants in the value chain. The following chapter deals with these challenges and shows ways to achieve integration.

4.1   Logistics-Oriented Support for Collaborative Customer Relationship Management (Supply Chain Collaboration)

In order to be successful in marketing, retailers and manufacturers must have product presence and products that are up-to-date, and available. The realization of frictionless product and information flows are central to quick, flexible, and reliable coverage of demand at a reasonable price in order to respond to customer demands and market forces. Thereby, logistics as a complete concept for the planning of product and information flows of retailers and manufacturers, whose objective is higher product availability, responsiveness to demands and environment changes, and cost reduction for goods and information transfer, comes to the fore. Logistics are removed from the customer's perceptual field, but are essential to customer satisfaction and retention because he reacts to performance at the POS; e.g. out-of-stock situations and stale products. Of particular importance is the condition that savings on logistics be passed on to the customer. As an example, Wal-Mart, with its aggressive pricing has nonetheless good earnings due to its efficiency in logistics.

4.1.1 Supply Chain Management

In logistics, the optimization of the value chain can be subsumed under the term supply chain management (SCM). SCM describes the economic exploitation of unused resources along the entire value chain. SCM is a form of vertical alliance, which ideally incorporates everyone from the producer of raw materials all the way through to the customer. All participants in SCM think, plan, control and act not in terms of functions, but rather processes. The organization of the process chain changes from an anticipatory, plan oriented push-system to a reactive, demand driven pull-system that shows substantial affinity with the just-in-time concept.

This leads to a reengineering of the entire supply chain between manufacturer and retailer. Manufacturers want to exploit their full production capacity and re-tailers want to plan their inventories with maximum precision. This can lead to inefficiency in the cooperation. Manufacturers use several measures, like promo-tions or rebates, to achieve ever-larger shipments, ergo to sell more products. The articles that are not actually produced in response to demand are pushed into retail outlets or warehouses. Due to limited space, there exists high pressure to liquidate inventory. The consequences are continually sinking sale prices and declining margins, which ultimately affects both manufacturers and retailers equally. With SCM, this will be brought to an end when manufacturers and retailers work coop-eratively and make the customer the focus of their decision-making. A purchase is registered at the cashier and information on the consumer's purchase is collected and passed on to the manufacturer. The retailer foregoes making a purchase order, and instead transfers data to the manufacturer on inventory and sales based on consumer information. Manufacturers and retailers now use this information to alter product lines and assortments in response to shopping habits and consumer needs. As the customer ultimately determines the price, she becomes the starting point.

The consumer, with her needs and habits, is the focus of all considerations. The optimization of the process chain is supported through IT like Electronic Data Interchange (EDI) or Data Warehouse, while the orientation to efficiency demands the consistent reduction or elimination of all tasks in the value chain that do not add value for the customer [1].

---

[1] Seifert 2000, p.23

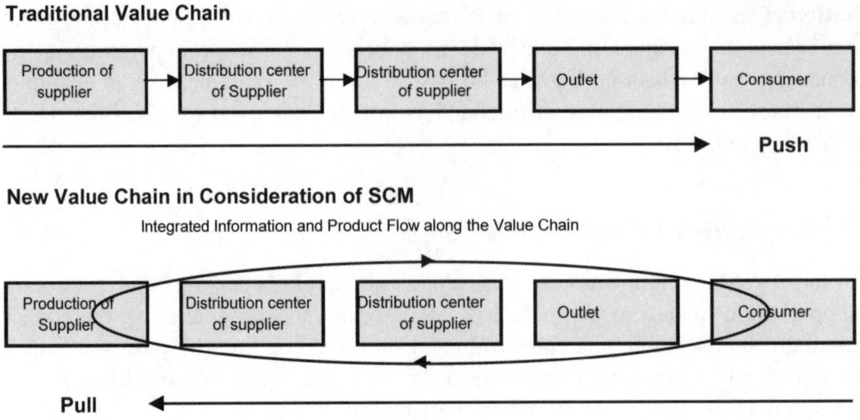

Traditional Value Chain

New Value Chain in Consideration of SCM

Integrated Information and Product Flow along the Value Chain

Figure 4.2: Reengineering the Value Chain[2]

Supply chain management presumes that manufacturers and retailers consider themselves as part of a unified logistics system, in which retail delivers information as quickly as possible via the Internet on inventories, promotions, and sales, and the manufacturer ensures a continuous, demand driven supply of product. This tactic is known as Continuous Replenishment (CRP). Other measures in SCM are Cross Docking (CD), Vendor Managed Inventories (VMI) and Internet based process optimization.[3] CD is a transfer of goods wherein the sequence or amount is changed en route without warehousing. With VMI, the supplier takes over complete responsibility for the retailers' inventory. The basis for suppliers' planning is sales data and current inventory, or a delivery plan from the receiver based on these data. They all lead to a reduction of inventory, and thereby lessen idle capital.

In the past, work among the participants in the value chain always led to conflicts in the trade channel. Every member of the process chain was intent on minimizing his own logistics costs. The optimization of logistics at one stage of the value chain often leads to additional costs for predecessors and followers in the chain. SCM offers a decidedly different approach to the comprehensive optimization of the value chain.

Through new technical mechanisms like the Internet, new concepts are developed in SCM. One of these is Collaborative Planning, Forecasting and Replenishment (CPFR). CPFR is a first attempt to achieve integration of supply chain and demand chain activities, as it combines different demand chain tools like demand planning and sales forecast with logistic activities like replenishment. As explained in detail later, by integrating these business processes all companies along the value chain are able to achieve a number of improvements in their financial and performance

---

[2] According to Kurt Salmon Associates 1993, p.1; Zentes 1996, p.4.

[3] e-Procurement, e-Ordering, e-Tracking and e-Payment

metrics that would have been unachievable using only stand alone CRM & SCM techniques. Increases in value can be achieved by driving out costs from the value chain as well as increasing turnover. Improved accuracy of demand will lead to more customer satisfaction and loyalty as well as to reduced inventory carrying costs.

4.1.2 Collaborative Planning, Forecasting and Replenishment

Closely related to Supply Chain Management tools is Collaborative Planning, Forecasting, and Replenishment. The CPFR concept grew out of the fact that, the original orientation to processes of SCM was enormously successful, but in some individual cases less so. The reasons for that were poor communication, unconnected systems and a shortage of collaboration. Furthermore, the typically insufficient planning quality of the sales data was based on the fact that manufacturers forecasted based on algorithms and historical data.

The risk of running out of stock is clearly a problem for most successful products. Understanding the level of out-of-stock is the first step in working against it. Also billions are held in inventory, showing enormous reduction potential, which can be exploited through distinguished sales planning. CPFR represents a further development of SCM. Manufacturers and retailers active in the framework of CPFR do joint sales planning using all available data. The inclusion of commonly managed data clearly distinguishes CPFR from SCM. The goal is to increase sales forecast accuracy. Based on this market forecast, production, delivery, warehousing and advertising are coordinated. Product demand is automatically controlled through IT. The results of CPFR are for example: less time spent by products in the value chain, higher product availability, and reduced warehousing costs. Additionally, information on changing consumer behavior is simultaneously to all participants in the supply chain. Thereby, they can react to sudden changes in demand and eliminate expensive inventory liquidations. This shows how the nature of the relationship between trade partners is changing from one of seller-buyer to collaborator-collaborator, from purchase orders to joint forecasting and planning.

4.2 Structural and Technological Support for Collaborative Customer Relationship Management

The control of complex and consumer oriented strategies demands evermore closely integrated processes and structures. This trend already exists in other fields such as construction and engineering. The structure of individual business divisions and in particular, the classic sales and purchasing structure, is changing. In the foreground is complete solutions for cooperation between manufacturers and retailers, which in part is a prerequisite for things like Category Management projects. In information technology as well, entirely new requirements and a different infrastructure are being recognized as a prerequisites for cooperation. Alone in the consumer goods economy, numerous projects focused on collaborative technology are being driven by the sales side. Topics like trade promotion management, cooperative planning tools like Syncra in CPFR, and developments in Advanced Planning and Scheduling, are being discussed not only by experts. More than anything, the Internet is opening new dimensions in the use of technology, through things like extranets or Web-EDI. These new forms of communication are amenable to broad use in Collaborative Customer Relationship Management. Electronic marketplaces like Transora will support Collaborative Customer Relationship Management as a communications platform and give thereby innovative users competitive advantages.

In other areas like Web Order Management (WOM) or portal technologies, opportunities for collaboration and bilateral knowledge transfer are arising. In data warehousing larger amounts of data can be collaboratively shared and mined. Before that topic is explored, a view of how collaborations are organized is presented.

4.2.1 Multi-Functional Teams

Category Management and Co-Marketing as well as all other instruments of Collaborative Customer Relationship Management have one thing in common: they require a team-oriented collaboration. In contrast to most sales and purchasing departments, these are multi-functional. The goal is to bring together the specialized knowledge of different functions and task groups. A team structure is appropriate for the intra- as well as inter-organizational collaboration.

Consumer goods manufacturers operate in a difficult environment. Retailers reduce the value of established brand names when they create their own labels. Furthermore, retailers are operating more globally. This increases the pressure on manufacturers' margins. For many consumer goods manufacturers, the question becomes one of how they will operate in such markets.

From key account management comes a new form of customer-supplier relationship. The purpose is essentially an integration of manufacturer and customer organizations. The accomplishment of this demands the formation of cooperative multifunctional teams for key account management, while the relationship between the respective partner organizations has a strategic significance.

Such multifunctional teams work to reduce costs along the entire value chain and to increase sales. Instead of the traditional, confrontational one-on-one relationship between sales and purchasing, a number of exchanges are introduced between them representing the marketing, finance, logistics, and IT departments from both parties. Among manufacturers, these teams are less concerned with particular brands or categories; rather they are oriented to specific key accounts. This customer driven definition implies that the respective key account manager is in the role of being a team leader or coordinator. On the retail side, teams are usually oriented to specific product groups or categories.[4]

The following figure diagrams the material just covered, and shows in a second step a solution for the new relationship between manufacturers and retailers.

---

[4] Hahne 1998, p.196

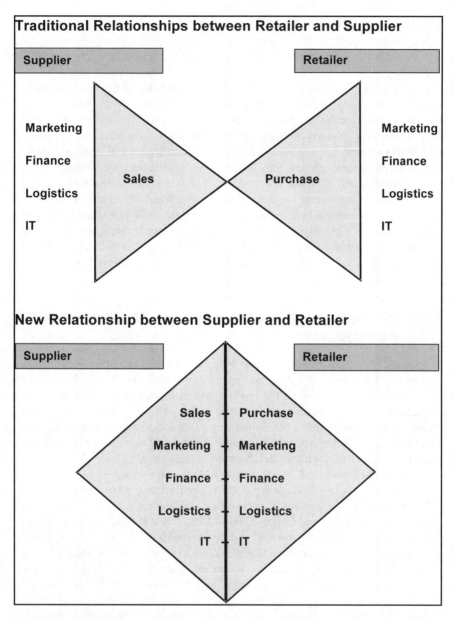

Figure 4.3:   Traditional and Newly Configured Relationship between Manufacturing and Retailing[5]

---

[5] According to Nielsen 1992, p.10; Wiezorek 1998, p.401

Multifunctional teams simplify the search for customer specific solutions, which facilitates synergies in the design of promotions or in the supply chain, and increases the flexibility and responsiveness changing demands on the part of the retailer.[6]

A good example of the implementation of multifunctional teams is the organization of cooperation between Procter & Gamble and Wal-Mart. P&G has been oriented to retailers for some time. Recently though, that firm increased its influence measurably. Instead of the traditional one-on-one communication between customer representative and purchasing agent, multifunctional Customer Business Development Teams stepped into the fray. Representatives from marketing, finance, logistics and IT make up the team. The teams can work relatively independently with the resources at their disposal. The Wal-Mart team from P&G was exceptionally successful in coordinating the strategic goals of both partners. P&G secured a role as Category Captain in important areas and could thereby execute successful co-marketing initiatives. The resulting revenue increases exceeded even Wal-Mart's unusually high growth rate. P&G and Wal-Mart have been intensifying their cooperation ever since.[7]

4.2.2   IT-Infrastructure and Other Structural Arrangements with Customers

In principle, every point of intersection with the consumer can offer an appropriate opportunity for a joint appeal to, and winning of customers. Possibilities exist in the area of sales assistance, in the product, and in service information in the way of product tests. The cooperation discussed in this volume gives an impression of the many possibilities that exist. In the way of structural arrangements, IT infrastructures can be considered which supports the demand side as well as the supply side of Collaborative Customer Relationship Management.

Customer Relationship Management (CRM) is mainly used to acquire and retain long-term, profitable customers. CRM applications, also known as front-office applications, in contrast to back-office applications such as Enterprise Resource Planning (ERP) and Supply Chain Management (SCM), are used by marketing, sales, and support personnel and by executive management to understand and manage critical customer relationships. CRM applications support all of the customer-centric processes within enterprise, mid-enterprise, and mid-market organizations including marketing, sales, and customer support. These systems can also be used directly by customers, partners, and prospects to gather product and service information, obtain pricing quotes and configure complex products, place and track orders, solve product- and service-related problems and questions, and schedule service calls. E-Business applications integrate Internet-based tech-

---

[6] Seifert 2000, p.26

[7] Miroschedji, Schick, Schumann & Soliman 2001, p.29

nology applications to augment the reach of CRM and represent the next evolving phases of CRM application, technology, and best practices.[8]

In the context of Collaborative Customer Relationship Management and Collaborative Planning, Forecasting and Replenishment respectively, the following list represents the cornerstones of an IT strategy for a network of manufacturers, suppliers, retailers and consumers.

- Partnership

- Trust

- Information exchange

- Cooperation

Every vertically and horizontally integrated IT networks require a coordination of corporate strategies of the participants in the value chain. Only under such conditions can a technological platform be so constructed, that customer retention and new customer generation along the value chain can be created between partners on down to the consumer. This Customer Relationship Network (CRN) includes not only the direct relationship between manufacturer and retailer, or retailer and consumer respectively, but rather all relationships between all suppliers, sub-contractors, and so forth. Others have called this expansion XRM for Extended Relationship Management or in an even broader definition, Value Webs.[9] As discussed elsewhere, the central focus of all participants at all times is the consumer in order to maximize the utility for all concerned. All component processes are consistently oriented to the consumer and where necessary redefined so that, a fully new business model in the sense of a paradigm shift forms the basis for the IT platform.

Traditional Business Design

e-Business Design

Figure 4.4:   Restructuring the Value Chain[10]

---

[8] See www.aberdeen.com

[9] See www.forrester.com and www.gartner.com.

[10] Kalakota & Robinson 1999, p.60.

Basically CRN IT infrastructure is a process supporting technology for Collaborative CRM through which bilateral or multilateral win-win situations between partners first become possible or more strongly pronounced (supporting and enabling IT technology). In order to draw the most utility for the customer from the IT infrastructure, several modules are necessary. In addition to the multiplex CRM architecture, an inter-company collaboration or 'extended CRM' must be supported. A functioning CRN system is absolutely dependent on an integrated Enterprise Resource Planning solution (ERP) through which professional Supply Chain Planning and Supply Chain Management first become possible. The combination of Collaborative CRM and ERP is then the backbone of a functioning CRN from the perspective of IT. These sub-systems allow consumer demand to be recognized, orders to be taken and quickly processed, i.e. a seamless integration of front and back office activities coordinated throughout the value chain.

A company can only be successful with a particular campaign, if it is able to react to the individual requirements of customers with tailor-made offerings. The good old corner-shop of yesteryear could be a model for this: such a shop could "tie-in" its customers, because the owner remembered all their particular preferences. A company can have just such a memory: ERP-systems register every order, every cancellation, every transaction between the customer and the company – creating a huge knowledge pool. To be able to use these big amounts of data for personalized communication with the customers, ERP-systems have to be integrated tightly with CRM-applications.[11]

CRM and ERP build on the integration of existing systems, data, and data processing. Of particular interest are

- Data integration: data processing in the sense of extraction, transaction and loading (ETL) in the context of data warehousing technologies including the integration of different databases. Focus is on data processing with XML in contrast however to data arrayed according to content, structure, and presentation, thereby making it portable.

- Enterprise Application System (EAI): the integration of different applications in one system in order to simplify the use of different applications through a uniform user interface.

- Connection of old systems (legacy systems) to new structures. The coupling of hosts to clients is supported by Java technologies (J2EE, Java Beans). Java makes different systems portable and thereby can be integrated.

Parallel to the purely technical requirements for CRN, there are additional preconditions, which can be subsumed under the following:

---

[11] See www.softlab.com: ERP and CRM: Two Worlds are Coming Together

- Business process integration,

- Content management, and

- Team collaboration

Among all partners (suppliers, manufacturers, distributors retailers) and customers within the network. As indicated by this roll call, in the interplay of business process and organization with technology, technical questions must be answered after organizational decisions have been taken. The IT infrastructure has a prominent role, which however is a supporting one. In defining the requirements of an IT structure one can orient himself on the relevant business processes like contract management, customer service management, and supporting organizational things like integrated marketing portals and team collaboration.

Important keywords for a CRN system are integration and flexibility.[12] In other words, this means that every participant should contribute to the simplicity of the system. This will increase the acceptance of the system's user, among both partners and customers alike. The greater the usability and the capacity to integrate, the greater the utility for all partners and customers and the more simply each partner can strengthen his own position and that of the partner network. In this way, the potential for synergies can be raised, through which a barrier to entry for competitors can be created. In particular, the planning uncertainty of individual partners can be reduced through better information management, so that inventories can be minimized, or the liquidity of individual partners improved.

In this context, it seems warranted to mention that individual companies[13] do not rely on only CRN, but are involved with alternatives as well and increase thereby their flexibility even further.[14]

For the integration of a CRN system in the context of CPFR and CCRM, it is of special importance that existing data standards like XML and its derivations continue to remain compatible. Only then will the complexity of integration beyond one company's bounds be controllable in view of the technological challenges and affordable relative to the effort required. In addition to the industry and marketing coordination of the tasks of all partners, it is also necessary to push the modernization and standardization within the IT network through the partnership management. The complexity of the integration must be first reined in, while we are dealing with

---

[12] The latter could also be called 'integratability', because every participant must remain aware of, and flexible in response to market conditions.

[13] Daimler-Chrysler is besides Covisint a member of other networks

[14] Gossain & Kenworthy 2000, p.9

- Different organizations, with

- Different databases residing in

- Different data formats running on

- Different applications.

The realization of CRN then seems best pursued through a phased plan worked out in advance by the partners. A variety of milestones should be incorporated, like for example the step-by-step integration of the different partners in the value chain. This process should be begun with the partners and processes closest to the consumer, while the latter is giving the impulse to the whole value chain.

Another important way to integration along the value chain is collaboration hubs. They try to create one common platform to enable all participants in an industry supply chain to share information, conduct business transactions, and collaborate on different topics like CPFR, collaborative Category Management and strategic/operative planning. If the collaboration hub is based on consumer data, the channel partners – from raw-material providers to distributors – could better match consumer demand, reducing uncertainty in the value chain as well as excess inventories in the channel. Collaboration hubs will force retailer and supplier cooperation, as they improve planning and forecasting capabilities and may include tools like product planning, demand forecasting, replenishment planning, and pricing and promotional strategies.[15]

The following study shows, how the integration of supply chain and customer management activities can help to achieve outstanding results.

References

Bowman, S., McKinney, J. and Morgenstern, R. (2000): CPFR – White Paper with Case Study, CSC, 2 Feb. 2000.

Gossain, S. and Kenworthy, R. (2000): Winning in the Third Wave of e-Business – Beyond Net Markets; NervWire (www.nervewire.com), December 2000

Hahne, H. (1998): Category Management aus Herstellersicht, Lohmar 1998

von der Heydt, A. (1997): Efficient Consumer Response, Wiesbaden 1997

Kalakota, R. and Robinson, M. (1999): e-Business – Roadmap for Success; Reading, MA 1999.

---

[15] Kalakota/Robinson: e-Business 2.0., p.319f

Kurt Salmon Associates (1993): Efficient Consumer Response – Enhancing Consumer Value in the Grocery Industry, Washington 1993.

Miroschedji, S., Schick, S., Schumann, R. and Soliman, P. (2001): Hersteller organisieren ihren Vertrieb um; Harvard Business Manager 4/2001, p.24-33

Nielsen (1992): Category Management-Position your Organisation to Win, Chicago 1992

Seifert, D. (2000): Einzelhandel – wie er strategisch optimieren muss; Harvard Business Manager 4/2000, p. 22-27

Seifert, D. (2001): Efficient Consumer Response – Supply Chain Management, Category Management und Collaborative Planning, Forecasting and Replenishment als neue Strategieansätze, 2. Aufl., München 2001.

Terbeek, G.A. (1996): Hinter ECR läutet bereits die Marketing-Ära, in: Lebensmittelzeitung Nr. 22 vom 31. Mai 1996, S. 38-40

Walker, O. C., Boyd, H. W. and Larréché, J. C.(1992): Marketing Strategy – Planning and Implementation, Homewood/Boston 1992

Wiezorek, H. (1998): Efficient Consumer Response – Kooperation statt Konfrontation, in: Informationssysteme für das Handelsmanagement (Hrsg.: Zentes,J./Swoboda,B.), Frankfurt a. Main 1998, p.385-402.

Zentes, J. (1996). Erfolgsstrategie ECR: Potentiale und Voraussetzungen, in: KSA News –Efficient Consumer Response (Hrsg.: KSA), Düsseldorf 1996, p.4-6.

Case Study: ISCRM – A Study of the Business Benefits Achieved through Integrated Supply and Customer Relationship Management

Scott Hines
CTO JDA Software Group, Inc., Scottsdale, AZ, USA

Overview

Over the past several years, numerous companies have reported reductions in cost and increases in revenue through improvements in the management of both their supply chain and their customer relationships. However, rarely have companies integrated these business processes to achieve significant increases in value to their respective businesses. This case study describes the business benefits achieved by a US specialty magazine retailer and its suppliers through the integration of Customer Relationship Management (CRM) and Supply Chain Management (SCM). By integrating these business processes, both the retailer and the suppliers were able to achieve a number of improvements in their financial and performance metrics that would have been unachievable using only stand alone CRM and SCM techniques. The increases in value achieved by the retailer include:

- Price benefits provided by the supplier in return for the shared information

- Reduced inventory carrying costs

- Increased revenue due to reduced out of stock positions

In addition to the value improvements achieved by the retailer, the supplier also derives value from this collaboration. The increases in value achieved by the supplier include:

- Reduced inventory carrying costs due to improved accuracy of demand

- Increased revenue due to improved product assortment

This example demonstrates that Integrated Supply and Customer Relationship Management (ISCRM) allows each of the stakeholders participating in the value chain to optimize their performance beyond that which can be achieved via the management of each of these business processes individually.

Background

The International Federation of the Periodical Press reports that the consumer magazine and periodical market is a global market estimated at over 50 billion US dollars. The existing magazine/periodical supply chain has a number of periodical publishing companies that sell publications to magazine distributors. The magazine distributors contract with retailers to supply the individual titles that retailers offer to consumers. It is estimated that there are over 100,000 periodical titles available in the world. A typical grocery or convenience store retailer will offer consumers approximately 200 different magazine titles. A specialty bookstore may offer up to 2000 titles. The retailer examined in this study was a specialty "category killer" style retailer that focused primarily on offering as broad an assortment of magazine titles as possible. A typical store product offering could include up to 5000 different titles. In addition to offering magazines, the retailer also offered a small amount of merchandise that was associated with particular magazine categories. There are a number of characteristics that make the magazine/periodicals market particularly applicable to the integration of supply chain and customer relationship management.

- **Allocation**

    When a publisher releases an issue of a particular title, each of the distributors is assigned an allocation of that particular title. The entire publishing run of each issue is fully allocated to the distributors based on historical demand forecasting that can be highly inaccurate. The inaccuracy results because the publisher does not have timely or detailed information on who is buying what titles. Since magazines are perishable goods the retailer typically discards any unsold quantities. The retailer reports any discarded quantities back to the publisher for credit but this often times can take as long as 6 months before the publisher has any knowledge of the sales performance. This results in distribution inefficiencies that cause too many copies to be distributed to some locations and not enough copies to be distributed to other locations. Better knowledge of customer buying habits would provide significant opportunity to optimize the distribution and allocation of titles such that a minimum number of copies could be distributed while maximizing the fulfillment of customer demand.

- **Cover Variation Demand Forecasting**

    Sometimes publishers will print an issue that has several variations in the cover of the magazine. An example of this would be a magazine that focuses on sports. To prepare for an up coming special event, say the start of football season, the publisher of the magazine may choose to offer the issue in a "special edition" that features a different cover for each of the teams in the league. This allows football fans in each region to purchase an issue of the magazine highlighting their favorite team. Additionally the cover variations may inspire some customers to purchase multiple copies of the same issue in order to "collect" the different variations.

Knowledge of customer's buying preferences provides an opportunity to optimize the publication, distribution and allocation of the different cover variations. If the publishers are able to accurately predict the customer demand for each cover variation, they can reduce the amount of inventory in the supply chain as well as improve the 'in stock' position for customers at the point of purchase.

Although the magazine/periodical market offers a number of opportunities to add additional value through ISCRM, there are some characteristics of the magazine/periodical market that make it difficult to apply ISCRM techniques.

- **Bar Code Labeling**

Typically, magazine publishers in the United States print a UPC and ISBN bar code on each magazine cover that allows the retailer to automatically identify the title at the point of sale. However, the bar code does not identify the issue and the cover variation. This makes it difficult to collect the actual demand for a specific title/issue/cover offering. When the bar code is scanned at the POS, the retailer doesn't know which issue or cover variation has been purchased. To overcome this limitation the retailer was forced to print and apply their own labels on each magazine when the magazines were received and put on the shelves. This activity added to the cost of the magazines. In order to add value to the retailer, the benefits of the ISCRM techniques must outweigh the additional costs associated with the additional bar coding tasks.

- **Customer Information**

Many magazine purchases are performed as "cash & carry" transactions. Because of this, the customer usually desires to minimize the amount of time and effort associated with completing the point of sale transaction. Additionally customers are often reluctant to share their personal information with the retailer for what they may view as an intrusion of their privacy. In order to collect information on the customers beyond simple demand the ISCRM techniques must provide enough value to the customer that the customer is willing to share their personal information with the retailer.

Methods

The ISCRM method employed by the retailer in this case involved offering customers a shopper loyalty program that would give the latter an incentive for providing the retailer with personal information. The shopper loyalty program was a point based reward program that offered customers points for each title purchased. Once a threshold of points was achieved, the retailer would offer the customer a free issue of a magazine. The points were tracked in a centralized customer information repository and were integrated with the retailer's point of sale. This allowed real time collection of points and offering of gifts. The real time aspect of the system allowed the store personnel to promote additional items to customers at the point of purchase. Providing the sales person with the current point balance for a customer made it possible for the number of points accumulated on the current transaction, and the number of points needed to achieve the next gift level sales person to inform the customer of the amount of additional items that would be needed to be purchased in order to achieve the next gift level. The customer could then purchase additional items, redeem the accumulated points and receive their gift magazine all in a single purchase. Because of this added value, the customer was willing to register for the program and provide the retailer with their personal information.

In addition to collecting the customer's personal information (basic name, address and telephone number), the system also provided a method for assigning demographic attributes to each customer without requiring the customer to provide this additional information. The retailer assigned a customer attribute to each of the titles/issues/covers offered. An example of this might be a lifestyle attribute. The retailer could create a list of customer lifestyles as shown in Figure 4.5. These attributes could then be assigned to each of the products offered by the retailer. When a customer purchased an item, they would then inherit the Lifestyle Attributes assigned to the products purchased. Thus if the retailer assigned the "Cheese Head" customer attribute to a the sport magazine issue and cover that featured the Green Bay Packers then any customer who purchased that particular magazine would be assigned the attribute of "Cheese Head". This information could then be used to perform targeted marketing analysis to determine what type of products "Cheese Heads" purchased.

Once the retailer was able to collect and categorize the buying preferences and demographic information on their customers, the retailer used this information to collaborate with the magazine publishers to allow the publishers to better align their production, allocation and distribution of titles across their entire supply

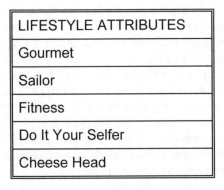

Figure 4.5:   Lifestyle Attributes List

chain. The publishers were provided with an internet portal application that allowed them to view several analytical queries offered from the retailer's CRM system. These queries included a Market Share query that identified the percentage of revenue that a particular publisher achieved within a merchandise category, a Sales Performance query that compared the sales performance of titles over time and a Product Affinity query that described the strength of affinity that a particular title has to other product categories. This information was made available to the publishers within 24 hours of the point of sale transaction. The information was restricted so that publishers could only view the information related to their own product offerings.

This information allowed the publishers to forecast demand for both existing and new titles much more accurately. It also provided them with information such as the differences in demand values for issue and cover variations. From the information obtained with this particular retailer the publishers were able to extrapolate the demand for all of their customers. In exchange for this information the publishers offered price benefits to the retailer that offset the additional activity cost of applying the bar codes, collecting, analyzing, and distributing the information. This provides a clear example of how the integration of Customer Relationship Management with Supply Chain Management can add value for each of the stakeholders participating in the demand chain.

Results

The ISCRM methods employed in this study resulted in a number of improvements in business value to both the retailer and to the publishers. However, it was impossible to measure these results over an extended period of time because the retailer ceased operations for reasons unrelated to this study. Given the short time period the following results were observed. The retailer was able to achieve a reduction in their average purchase price for magazine titles. When normalized against the activity based cost increases this still resulted in an overall reduction in the average cost of goods. The shopper loyalty offering to the customer resulted in an increase in markdowns to account for the products offered as free gifts to the customers but this was off set by an increase in the average purchase per visit. Additionally there was an increase in the average number of visits for customers who participated in the shopper loyalty program. These increase resulted in an increase in revenues and an increase in the gross profit of the company. The retailer estimated that the aside from the activity costs associated with the bar coding of the magazines the costs associated with collecting, analyzing, and distributing the data to the publishers resulted in a relatively minimal increase in their cost of operations. This resulted in a nearly direct improvement to the corporate earnings from the improvements in revenue and gross profit.

In addition to the business value improvements enjoyed by the retailer, the ISCRM methods also resulted in improvements in business value for the publishers. The publishers were able to achieve a reduction in inventory costs while at the same time reducing out of stock events. It is estimated that there is a 30-60% revenue recovery for every reduction in out of stock. If this is extrapolated across the entire US$50B magazine/periodicals market every 1% improvement in out of stock would provide an estimated $150 million in business value improvements across the industry that could be attributed to the ISCRM techniques.

Conclusions

This study clearly demonstrates the significant value improvements that can be obtained through the integration of customer relationship and supply chain management. It is unfortunate that more detailed results could not be obtained from this innovative business model.

In addition to the results identified in this study there are additional potential benefits that could be obtained from this business model. Since the cost to the publisher of printing and distributing the magazines is not increased by the shopper loyalty give away program it is possible that the publisher could offer the gift magazines free of cost to the retailer. This would allow the retailer to improve their average cost of goods. It is also possible that the publisher could distribute only part of the supply of a cover variation issue while maintaining the remainder of the supply without bound covers in the production facility. Then once initial demand information on the cover variations was available the publisher could complete the binding and distribution of the issue with the cover variations aligned with the actual customer demand. This would offer the opportunity for the publisher to reduce their inventory production and carrying costs. At the same time it could result in increased revenue for both the retailer and the publisher by better fulfilling the customer demand. These opportunities for both potential and demonstrable improvements in business value achieved though the integration of supply chain and customer relationship management suggest that the ISCRM techniques outlined in this study will become increasingly utilized by businesses in many different markets.

CHAPTER 5:

The Future of Collaborative Customer Relationship Management: Integrating Demand and Supply Chains

Jim Duffy
Deloitte Consulting, New York, USA

Peter Koudal
Deloitte Consulting, New York, USA

Stephen Pratt
Deloitte Consulting, New York, USA

5.1   Introduction

Consumer businesses that effectively link their customer management and supply chain operations to boost customer satisfaction and profitability are twice as profitable as competitors that do not do so. They are two to five times more likely to achieve superior performance in sales, market share, customer service and other key measures, and much more likely to generate higher shareholder returns (Figure 5.1).

These are just some of the findings of an extensive global study we conducted with nearly 250 major consumer businesses and their executive teams in 28 countries throughout North America, Europe, Asia-Pacific, Latin America, and South Africa.[1]

Companies such as Colgate-Palmolive and Heineken that have linked their supply chain and Customer Relationship Management activities have created what we refer to as "digital loyalty networks" – *digital* in that their demand-generating and supply-chain operations are linked through information technology; *loyalty* based in that higher customer loyalty and profitability is the objective; and *net*

---

[1] The first study in this series, Deloitte Research—Manufacturing Institute, Digital Loyalty Networks: e-Differentiated Supply Chain and Customer Management (New York: Deloitte Consulting and Deloitte & Touche, 2000), was conducted in collaboration with the Stanford Global Supply Chain Management Forum and launched at the joint Stanford-Deloitte executive conference at Stanford University "Creating Digital Loyalty Networks: e-Integrating SCM and CRM," in September 2000.

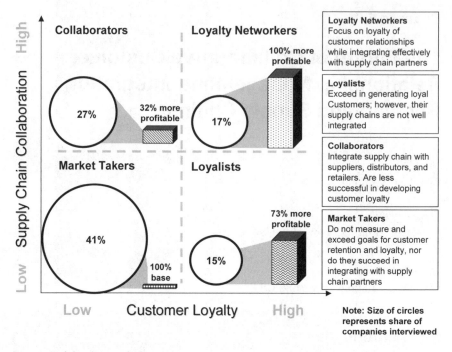

Source: Deloitte Research

Figure 5.1:   Loyalty Networkers and Profitability

works for when a company links its supply and demand-related functions with those of suppliers, customers and other business partners, it creates a virtual network.

Despite the inarguable benefits of digital loyalty networks, only a small number of consumer businesses have been able to build them. The challenges loom large: vastly different cultures between customer relationship (marketing, sales, service) and supply chain functions; hard-to-match information, measurements and incentives; and concerns about constantly accelerating customer expectations.

Nevertheless, our experience shows that these hurdles can be overcome. Here is what it requires:

- Mobilizing the organization toward a clear vision about how to create differentiated and profitable customer experiences.

- Creating a network partnership strategy that creates wins for all stakeholders (customers, suppliers, business partners), particularly between manufacturers and retailers that must collaborate and focus on the ultimate consumer.

- Developing an open business and technology architecture that allows prototyping and linking of disparate operations.

As Dell, Wal-Mart, and General Electric have demonstrated, the rewards for moving quickly and smartly are great. But so are the penalties for being slow at the gate. The PC industry is littered with failed companies that can attest to that. Once the leaders create the dominant digital loyalty networks in their segments, the switching costs for everyone become significant. To get started, managers need to ask a few key questions to understand just how far their organizations are along the path to building digital loyalty networks that generate loyal and highly profitable customers.

5.2   Using Digital Loyalty Networks to Boost Performance in Global Consumer Business

Countless consumer product manufacturers and retailers have overhauled the "back end" of their businesses over the last decade, instituting new supply chain processes and technologies that have lowered costs and reduced time cycles in manufacturing, distribution and procurement. Other consumer businesses have focused on the "front end" through new Customer Relationship Management practices and systems that have boosted retention and profitability. Some companies have been bold enough to launch initiatives on both sides of the house – that is, in both Customer Relationship Management (CRM) and supply chain management (SCM). Only a distinct minority, however, has effectively linked their supply chain and customer operations.

That minority reaps the majority of rewards: our study shows that consumer businesses that have integrated their CRM and SCM capabilities have dramatically and measurably outperformed their competition in virtually every critical financial and operating category (Figure 5.2 and 5.3).

To understand the degree to which companies are linking their supply chain and customer loyalty programs, we asked executives in our study to tell us – on a scale of 1 to 5 – how well-integrated their companies were in four areas: suppliers, distributors/retailers, customers and internally. We call this the collaboration index. A company that was well-integrated in all four areas scored a maximum of 20. We also asked these companies to rate themselves on key customer management metrics (again, on a scale of 1 to 5). Typical measures included customer repurchase rates and shares of purchase. High scores in this area indicated a high degree of customer loyalty that was mapped into a "loyalty index".

We then placed each company that participated in the study into one of four categories (Figure 5.2):

- *Loyalty Networkers* – companies with high degrees of linkage between their supply chain and customer management operations – represented only 17 percent of the sample. (These companies scored 4 or 5 on customer loyalty/retention and 14 or higher on the collaboration index.)

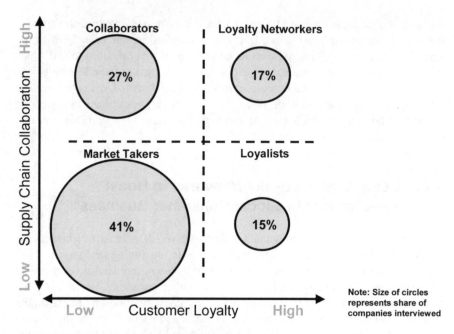

Figure 5.2:   Digital Loyalty Network Quadrant

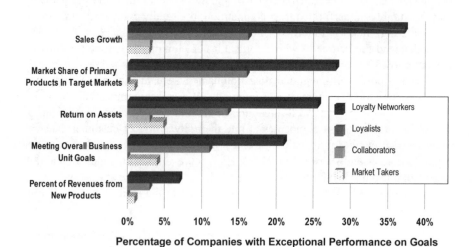

Source: Deloitte Research

Figure 5.3:   Loyalty Networkers and Business Performance

- *Loyalists* (15 percent) had high scores (4 or 5) on the loyalty index but low levels of supply chain collaboration (13 or below on the collaboration index).

- *Collaborators,* comprising 27 percent of the sample, had high degrees of supply chain collaboration (both internally and with their supply chain partners) but low levels of customer loyalty. They scored 3 or less in building customer loyalty (or do not measure it), and 14 or higher on the collaboration index.

- *Market Takers* (41 percent) scored low on both the collaboration index (13 or below) and the loyalty index (3 or less, or do not measure it).

Companies such as Heineken and furniture maker Herman Miller are part of the small-but-growing number of companies that are building digital loyalty networks between themselves and their suppliers and customers. These networks have enabled them to satisfy *different* customer needs with *differentiated* supply chain capabilities.

Heineken, for example, has implemented an Internet-based system that provides distributors access to information on pending orders, forecasting data and promotions. This has allowed the company to cut its order fulfillment cycle by 75 percent and has accelerated its sales growth.

(See Box 1, "The Emergence of Digital Loyalty Networks in the Global Beer Industry")

Box 1: The Emergence of Digital Loyalty Networks in the Global Beer Industry

In the beer industry, companies like Molson and Heineken demonstrate the impact of digital loyalty networks (DLNs). (See Figure 5.4)

To understand the shareholder value impact of DLNs, we looked at how companies performed in customer management and supply chain effectiveness and looked for any correlation with their stock performance. Using asset turnover as a key measure of supply chain collaboration and operating margin as a primary yardstick of customer loyalty, both companies have made major strides in improving customer management and supply chain processes over the last five years – gains that have also correlated with increasing shareholder value.

Take Molson Inc., the 215-year-old Canadian brewer that accounts for nearly half of the beer sold in its home country. Last year the company launched a private online exchange to cut procurement costs – one of a number of initiatives that the $2.5 billion Montreal-based company intro-

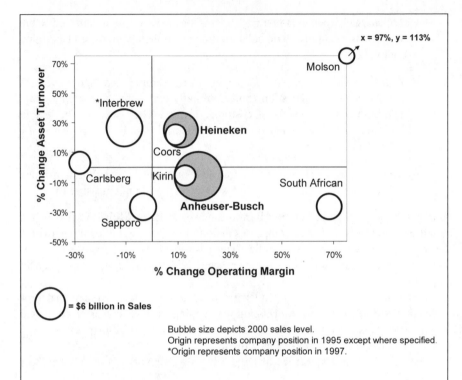

Source: Deloitte Research and HOLT Value Associates

Figure 5.4:   The Emergence of Digital Loyalty Networks in the Global Beer Industry

duced to save $120 million on its $1 billion annual spending in supplies over the next two years. The use of a common procurement system for such items as packaging materials, computer equipment and services, and travel and entertainment will enable Molson to better pool its purchasing clout and streamline purchasing activities. Eventually, the procurement initiative will target expenditures more directly involved in the production of beer.

In marketing, sales and distribution – the customer side of its business, Molson has been working with Coors Brewing Co. to use Coors' vast sales and distribution networks in the U.S. This has helped Molson decrease inventory levels, improve supply planning and better meet customer demand. As a result, Molson's asset turnover and operating margins have improved substantially since 1995 (Figure 5.5).

Investors have responded in kind. Last year, Molson's share price zoomed up by 60 percent, the highest gain in the industry.

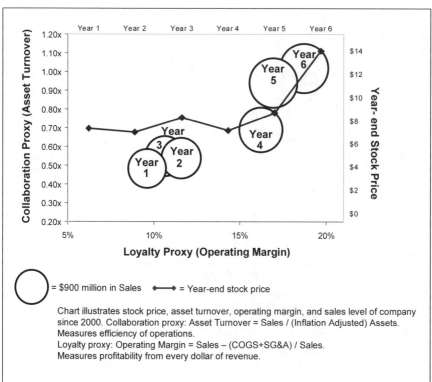

Chart illustrates stock price, asset turnover, operating margin, and sales level of company since 2000. Collaboration proxy: Asset Turnover = Sales / (Inflation Adjusted) Assets. Measures efficiency of operations.
Loyalty proxy: Operating Margin = Sales – (COGS+SG&A) / Sales. Measures profitability from every dollar of revenue.

Source: Deloitte Research and HOLT Value

Figure 5.5:   Performance Measures: Molson, Inc.

Heineken, like Molson, was a technological backwater just a decade ago before it began revamping the demand and supply sides of its business through technology. A decade ago, it took three months (equivalent to half of beer's standard shelf life) to produce beer in Holland and ship it to its large North American operations. Visibility across the supply chain was very limited as well. Even in 1994, the company's U.S. unit, Heineken USA, communicated with customers and suppliers mainly via phone and fax. In 1995, the U.S. operations of the $6 billion Dutch company installed an information system (called Heineken Operational Planning System, or HOPS) that links it to 450 North American distributors.

The system has since dramatically improved communication of order, inventory, and other information. Today, through a Web-based system, beer distributors can get data on Heineken sales forecasts, marketing and promotional deals and order status. The system tailors demand forecasts for each distributor. The impact has been profound (Figure 5.6).

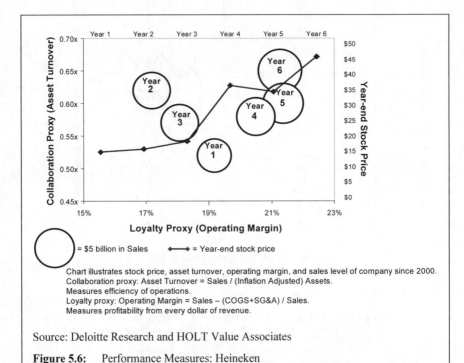

Source: Deloitte Research and HOLT Value Associates

Figure 5.6: Performance Measures: Heineken

Order lead times have shrunk from three months to three weeks. In the year 2000, for the first time in many years, sales growth of Heineken in the U.S. exceeded that of Corona, the No. 1 imported beer in America.

Herman Miller's is an example of a true digital loyalty network in action. They are starting to differentiate products and services for customers according to the value the latter bring to the company. Herman Miller has redesigned its Web pages to target and service its most important customers on the front end. This redesign simultaneously improves operations at the back end, streamlining manufacturing and allowing order information to flow from more than 500 suppliers worldwide. The company has reduced shipment errors by 20 percent. In addition, it has cut a full week off the time it takes to fill most orders and has boosted on-time shipments from 75 percent to nearly 98 percent between 1995 and 2000. These and other capabilities have enabled the company to outperform its peers in stock performance by nearly four times over the last five years.[2]

---

[2] According to Dow Jones & Co.'s DJ Furnishings Index, Herman Miller's five year stock appreciation was about 89 percent (as of October 2001) vs. 23 percent for the other companies that comprise the index.

Loyalty Networkers outperform their competitors because of several strategic capabilities they are developing. For one thing, they are able to identify their most valuable customers and adjust their service based on customer requirements, life-time potential and an intimate understanding of total supply chain cost on a customer-by-customer basis. This enables supply chain managers to know which orders should get preferential treatment based on real-time knowledge about the importance of their customers and the products, services and supply chain capabilities that are most important to those customers. As a result, it is not surprising that Loyalty Networkers are 100 percent more profitable than the Market Takers (Figure 5.1), are two to five times more likely to achieve exceptional performance in sales growth, market share, customer service, return on assets and other goals (Figure 5.3), and are much more likely to meet their goals for generating share-holder returns (Figure 5.7).

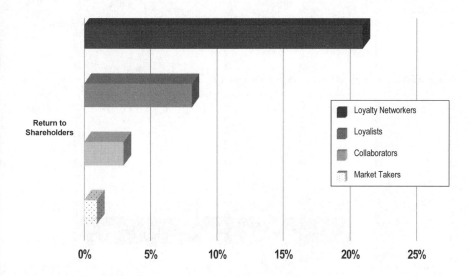

Percentage of Companies with Exceptional Performance on Goals

Source: Deloitte Research

Figure 5.7:   Loyalty Networkers and Shareholder Returns

Furthermore, Loyalty Networkers proactively address emerging customer needs before competitors have an opportunity to discover them. As shown in Figures 8-10, Loyalty Networkers outperform their competitors on most customer relationship goals. In addition, to satisfy their most important customers, Loyalty Networkers are building supply chain operations that can move in lock-step with their suppliers' operations. Some can even alter pricing, product mixes, and offerings in real time.

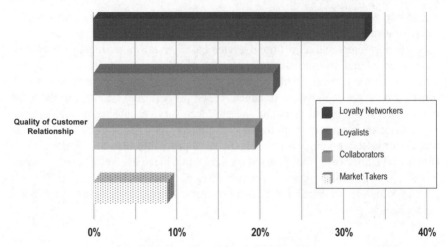

Source: Deloitte Research

Figure 5.8:   Excellence in Managing Customer Relationships

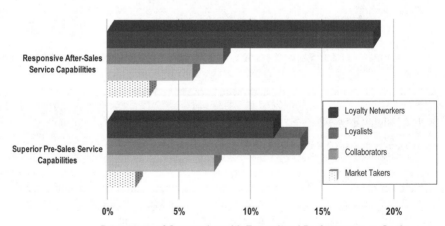

Source: Deloitte Research

Figure 5.9:   Loyalty Networkers and Customer Service

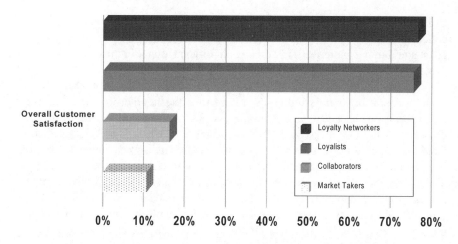

Source: Deloitte Research

Figure 5.10:   Loyalty Networkers and Customer Satisfaction

Quite simply, the impact of integrating demand and supply chains can be profound. Our research shows that Loyalty Networkers are far ahead of their competitors in key measures of supply chain performance (Figure 5.11).

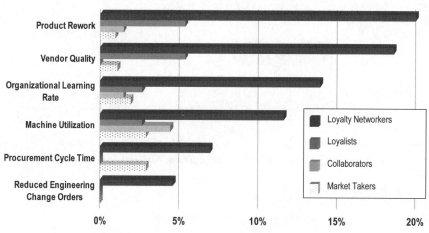

Source: Deloitte Research

Figure 5.11:   Loyalty Networkers and Supply Chain Performance

Unlike most manufacturers, retailers have direct contact with consumers. They can collect detailed sales information and thus are in a much better position to monitor consumer buying patterns. This creates significant opportunities for companies that are vertically integrated and control both the manufacturing and retailing ends of the value chain. Consider one such company: Spanish apparel-maker Zara. A $2 billion unit of Spain's Inditex SA, Zara uses the Internet to gather real-time information on the needs and changing tastes of consumers – changes that are dictated by fashion shifts as well as seasonal transitions. But that information would be of little use if the company didn't control its supply chain. By controlling the entire retail, manufacturing and distribution chain, Zara has been able to design and produce its new clothing lines in five or six weeks, a quarter of the average time its competitors[3] take. That means that Zara can introduce three to four clothing lines every fashion season, compared with one for most of its competitors. This capability has also enabled the company to charge higher prices while being able to better serve its customers at the same time. This has also made it possible for its supply chain managers to better manage their assets. Figure 5.12 shows how a company's focus on loyalty can drive the effective utilization of its assets.

So far, no company – not even Herman Miller or Zara – has developed and fully leveraged its digital loyalty network. This means that a number of opportunities remain – even for the leaders.

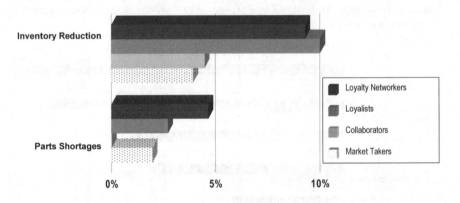

Percentage of Companies with Exceptional Performance on Goals

Source: Deloitte Research

Figure 5.12:   Loyalty Networkers and Asset Management

---

[3] C. Vitzthum, "Just-in-Time Fashion," The Wall Street Journal, May 18, 2001, p. B1.

5.3   Understanding the Barriers to Building Digital Loyalty Networks

The fact that only a small minority of consumer businesses have digital loyalty networks, and that the ones that do are just scratching the surface of their full potential suggests that significant barriers to the creation and success of digital loyalty networks exist. Understanding these barriers is crucial before setting out on the digital loyalty network journey. We have identified three such barriers.

5.3.1   The Divide between Supply Chain and Customer Management Operations

This challenge springs from the big successes many companies have had in supply chain and customer management initiatives. Supply chain managers in most consumer businesses have made significant strides in reducing time and costs in manufacturing, procurement, and distribution, while improving product and service quality. Many have moved up from being Market Takers to Collaborators by using Pareto analysis of suppliers to identify their importance in terms of spending, quality and delivery performance; creating strategic sourcing processes to move away from antagonistic supplier relationships; managing customer inventory; making supplier information available on the Web; and introducing collaborative planning, forecasting and replenishment (CPFR) (See Figure 5.13).

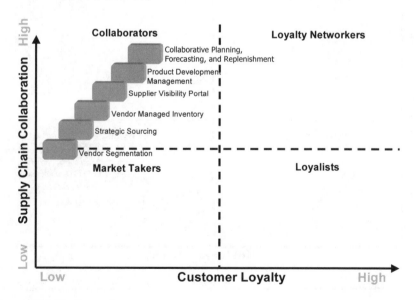

Source: Deloitte Research

Figure 5.13:   Digital Loyalty Network Matrix: Collaboration Usually Comes First

At the same time, managers in customer-facing functions such as service, marketing and sales have been improving customer relationships markedly through CRM initiatives. Through better customer service, capturing and integrating of customer purchasing data, segmenting customers, personalizing solutions and integrating across channels, they have taken steps to become relationship-oriented Loyalists (Figure 5.14).

However, these supply chain and CRM initiatives typically tend to operate independently. In part, this is due to the long-established practice of functional excellence – manufacturing directors, warehouse managers, distribution heads and other executives focus on improving their piece of the overall value chain. They are therefore often sceptic of cross-functional initiatives. They think that tampering with already existing mechanisms that have been refined over time might result in operational deterioration. Further, differences in working styles sometimes amplify the gap between the supply chain and customer sides of the house.

Because they are continually measured on improving the way goods are produced and delivered, supply chain professionals are process-oriented and thus more receptive to diving into operational details and rooting out workflow inefficiencies. On the other hand, marketing and sales teams – while poring over ever more data on customer segments, buying patterns and promotion lifts thrive in a less predictable world of changing customer demands, creativity and experimentation.

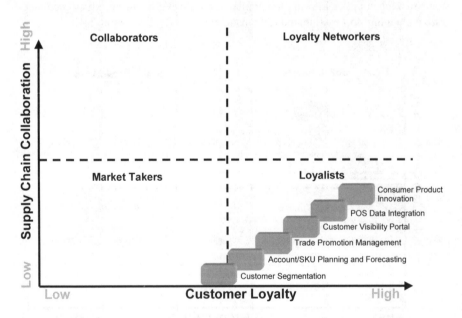

Source: Deloitte Research

Figure 5.14: Digital Loyalty Network Matrix: Customer Loyalty Is Tougher but More Important

5.3.2   Incompatible Information, Measures and Rewards

The information, performance measurement and incentives of supply chain and customer management-related functions often don't match. Manufacturing and distribution managers tabulate and control their own information on customer orders and shipments; marketing, sales and service people keep their own records on those customers in different systems and computer formats that can't be integrated easily with the data that supply chain managers possess. Incompatible information technologies are perhaps the least of the differences. Measurement and reward systems can be so contradictory that both sides won't even broach ways of creating mutual benefits. For example, manufacturing and distribution managers rewarded on achieving rock-bottom costs will view customization of products and delivery options as a threat to their performance. On the customer-facing side, the monthly incentives that drive higher sales also drive huge artificial spikes in demand, which are followed by severe drop-offs as the next cycle gets under way. The result is higher logistics cost and over production in the supply chain.

5.3.3   Continually Rising Customer Expectations

We call this the "customer paradox" (Figure 5.15). The concern is that customers might get overly accustomed to customized products and delivery options, faster delivery times and other key benefits of digital loyalty networks – and continually ask for more.

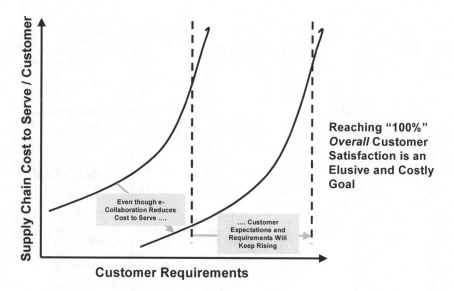

Source: Deloitte Research

Figure 5.15:   e-Collaboration and the Customer Paradox

So despite improving customer service and overall delivery, customer satisfaction may, paradoxically, deteriorate because the basic "table stakes" for service have risen. What was once seen as "great service" can come to be viewed as simply "doing what was promised". Since linking electronically with customers is part of the game, many managers can't fathom giving all customers a perpetually updated scorecard on product quality, on-time shipments and other measures. In having to provide ever more information to customers, managers worry about whether they are handing over proprietary information on costs and other data that might later be used against them for, lets say, wringing price concessions. Thus, to some managers, this appears to be a treadmill that they can never get off.

While the challenges in developing digital loyalty networks are significant, they're not insurmountable. We have uncovered a number of techniques that Loyalty Networkers have used, without disrupting day-to-day operations, in bridging the gap between SCM and CRM and achieving breakthrough performance.

5.4   The Digital Loyalty Network Journey: Seizing the Opportunity

The majority of companies today have launched initiatives to help them more effectively collaborate with suppliers and customers. Collaborative planning, forecasting and replenishment (CPFR) pilots and forays into public or private online marketplaces are two of the most prominent examples. From our research,

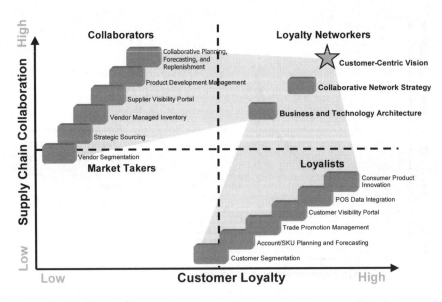

Source: Deloitte Research

Figure 5.16:   The Path to Digital Loyalty … Don't Control

we've found that overcoming the challenges to building digital loyalty networks does not begin with a huge business process overhaul or the creation of a new top-heavy corporate bureaucracy. Rather, it starts with the creation of key linkages between the supply and demand sides of the house (Figure 5.15).

By connecting and sharing collaboration-based performance indicators, supply chain and customer management functions can take several big first steps toward aligning themselves with overall business goals and creating effective digital loyalty networks. Three elements play major roles in establishing and maintaining these CRM-SCM connections: a customer-centric vision, a network partnership strategy and an open business and technology architecture.

5.4.1   Establishing a Consumer – and Customer-Centric Vision

Digital loyalty networks in consumer businesses begin with a clear picture of not only the retailer but also the consumer. This picture shows how to differentiate the product and service offering for different retailer and consumer segments and it is shared across key business functions. As such, customer-centric companies realize that a small number of customers account for a very large proportion of profits. In fact, for individual major customers, the "segment" size may be one.

Customer-centric companies do cost analysis of individual customers or customer segments through Activity-Based Costing (ABC) and other methods. The key to creating and developing digital loyalty networks is in understanding customer requirements that can be served profitably (Figure 5.17 and 5.18).

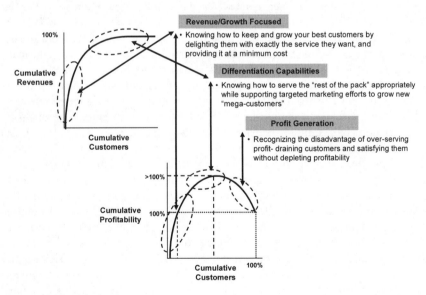

Source: Deloitte Research

Figure 5.17:   A Change of Focus is Needed

Digital Loyalty Networks Resolve the Paradox by Optimizing on Customers':
- *DIFFERENT lifetime values*
- *DIFFERENT costs to serve*
- *DIFFERENT requirements*

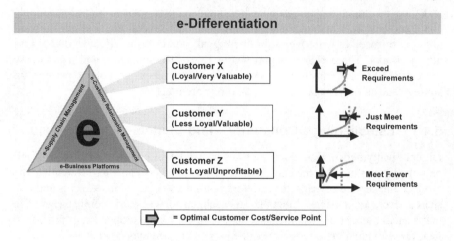

Figure 5.18:   e-Differentiation and the Customer Paradox

Herman Miller is a case in point. The Michigan-based furniture maker provides red carpet service to different customer groups by tailoring its Web pages for them and letting them order at special rates. On the supplier side, Herman Miller has streamlined order processing and accounting via the Internet to speed up delivery time and reduce costs. The company then shares this data with its network of suppliers around the world. Suppliers can minimize their inventory costs and make available just-in-time supplies, materials and parts to Herman Miller for final assembly. Herman Miller has recognized the substantial profit impact and customer loyalty benefits from providing the right offerings to the right customers.

However, catering to the most profitable customers isn't enough. A company must develop and institutionalize a mindset that puts customers' needs first. It can then use that perspective to help shape how the company interacts with its customers. For example, seeking to ride the wave of Efficient Consumer Response (ECR) in the early 1990s, one food manufacturer began revamping its operations by looking at its activities from a customer's point of view. This led to a pioneering CRM implementation that enabled the company to serve its key customer accounts in ways that maximized their profits as well as its own. In another example, cosmetics giant Estée Lauder has started uses its own website, "smart" cards and a massive database to drive customers to department stores that sell its products. This enables the company to spot purchasing trends, better forecast manufacturing requirements and reward its best customers, thereby increasing their loyalty. (See Box 2 "Global Cosmetics Industry Makeover: On the Path to Digital Loyalty Networks?") Such a "customer-centric" mentality is critical to a successful digital loyalty network.

Box 2:   The Global Cosmetics Industry Makeover –
On the Path to Digital Loyalty Networks?

Competition in the cosmetics industry has been fierce over the last five years. However, companies such as Estée Lauder and Avon have made significant operating and financial improvements by better matching supply and demand through digital loyalty networks (Figure 5.18). The stock of Estée Lauder, a $4.3 billion New York-based Company, has outperformed the industry by a wide margin since 1996 – its price has appreciated 70 percent in four years.

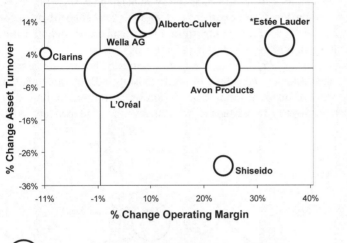

Bubble size depicts 2000 sales level.
Origin represents company position in 1995 except where specified.
*Origin represents company position in 1996.

Source: Deloitte Research and HOLT Value Associates

Figure 5.19: Global Cosmetics Industry Makeover: On the Path to Digital Loyalty Networks?

In order for this to happen, Estée Lauder has made aggressive moves on the customer management side of its business. The company's brands – which include Estée Lauder, Clinique and Aramis – each have developed their own websites. Clinique.com alone boasts over a million users, 28 percent of whom never had used the products before. The site helps customers determine which products they should use, often by asking them questions about their skin (color, degree of oiliness etc.). Online sales are but a tiny sliver of total sales today for the Clinique brand. But the World Wide Web serves a much larger purpose: getting customers to the store. A massive data warehouse enables the company to spot purchasing patterns in days instead of months, and more accurately predict sales and production requirements.

Realizing the power of the Web to connect with women on beauty issues, and their desire for a one-stop shopping experience, Estée Lauder has launched a website called Gloss.com with rivals Clarins and Chanel. The website gives consumers online access to their favorite brands.

Estée Lauder is starting to make strides on the supply chain as well. In the summer of 2001, the company announced a major initiative to build new supply chain systems and overhaul its warehouses. In distribution centers in Pennsylvania and New Jersey, the company has invested heavily in software and business process changes to improve inventory management.Such improvements on both the customer management and supply chain sides of its business have enabled Estée Lauder to outperform many competitors in both asset turn and operating margin improvements (Figure 5.20).

Avon Products Inc., the $5.7 billion cosmetics company, has moved aggressively on both the customer and supply fronts to boost its industry position. On the customer side, Avon is spending $60 million on an Internet initiative to increase consumer loyalty by partnering with its 3 million independent sales

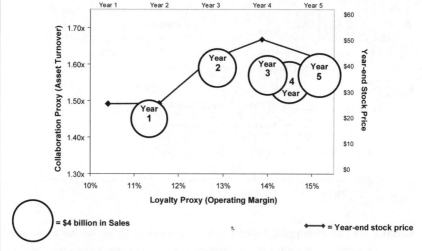

Chart illustrates stock price, asset turnover, operating margin, and sales level of company since 2000.
Collaboration proxy: Asset Turnover = Sales / (Inflation Adjusted) Assets.
Measures efficiency of operations.
Loyalty proxy: Operating Margin = Sales – (COGS+SG&A) / Sales.
Measures profitability from every dollar of revenue.

Source: Deloitte Research and HOLT Value Associates

Figure 5.20:   Performance Measures: Estée Lauder

representatives. Recently, the company launched a website that lets "e-Representatives" place orders, check product availability and order status, and market to new and present customers. The system has slashed the cost of taking an order from $3 to 50 cents. As important, the system relieves sales peoples' frustrations over constantly changing stock codes, onerous order forms and fulfillment delays. By reducing the huge turnover rate of sales reps, Avon's district sales managers can spend more time helping seasoned reps and far less time searching for new ones.

Further, the websites eventually will help Avon build a consumer database enabling visibility of key marketing trends and individual consumer preferences and buying behaviors. If a rep quits, the company can easily pass the names and contact information to another rep in that territory, thus perpetuating consumer loyalty.

Avon recently announced the launch of "Teen Business," a unit that will recruit teenage girls as "e-Reps" and use the Internet and techniques such as viral marketing to establish fierce loyalty with teen consumers.

To reduce lead times and inventory levels, Avon is also overhauling its supply chain by installing advanced planning and scheduling software and an ERP system. Over the last five years, asset turnover has increased while operating margins have improved significantly (Figure 5.21).

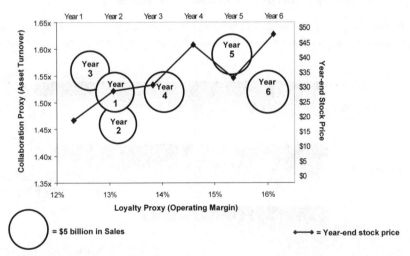

Chart illustrates stock price, asset turnover, operating margin, and sales level of company since 2000.
Collaboration proxy: Asset Turnover = Sales / (Inflation Adjusted) Assets.
Measures efficiency of operations.
Loyalty proxy: Operating Margin = Sales – (COGS+SG&A) / Sales.
Measures profitability from every dollar of revenue.

Source: Deloitte Research and HOLT Value Associates

Figure 5.21: Performance Measures: Avon Products

Over the last decade, the Internet and other technologies have shifted power from manufacturers and retailers to consumers themselves by greatly simplifying their shopping and comparison process. However, some consumer businesses still lack a customer-centric culture. Without this, trying to institute a digital loyalty network is like embarking on an intense exercise program without a profound desire to get healthy. In other words, the program won't "stick." This is not surprising given the high failure rate of CRM initiatives, due in large part to the unwillingness of companies to change the values, attitudes and beliefs of their people around the importance of profitable, loyal customers.

For digital loyalty networks to take hold and thrive within a consumer business and across its customers and suppliers, the company must create a culture of customer loyalty by changing values, performance measures and reward systems. Given that the way a company treats its customers is a function of how it treats its employees, it does not come as a surprise that companies with digital loyalty networks have more loyal, satisfied and higher-skilled employees (Figure 5.22). The rate at which people learn new skills is much higher in these companies, in part because they have been among the first to adopt Internet-based "e-learning" technologies and have, in turn, been able to dramatically increase the speed of deployment and drastically cut the cost of training for their companies.

5.4.2   Creating a Network Partnership Strategy

Very few consumer businesses control every aspect of the value chain from the raw materials up to the finished products that are delivered to retail outlets or

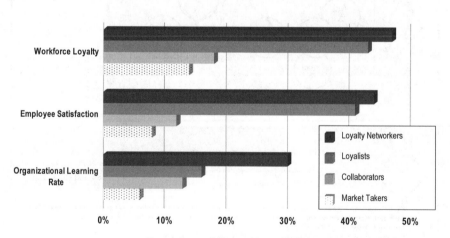

Percentage of Companies with Exceptional or Near Exceptional Performance on Goals

Source: Deloitte Research

Figure 5.22:   People and Organizational Learning

consumers themselves. Even Zara relies on outside suppliers and distributors. To get every critical party to play a role in a digital loyalty network, a company must create a strategy that considers, and provides wins for all players in the value chain.

Consumer manufacturers with digital loyalty networks are partnering with retailers to focus on demand-pull rather than supply-push. In the past, retailer and manufacturer have conducted totally separate inventory-planning activities, often resulting in oversupply or undersupply of products. But with the emergence of digital loyalty networks, replenishment decisions are done through collaborative retailer/manufacturer efforts that balance sales with store and warehouse inventory data.

The importance of such a customer orientation cannot be overstated. Through demand and supply chain integration, digital loyalty networks promise to significantly cut on billions of dollars that manufacturers otherwise spend on trade promotions to even out supply imbalances in the retail supply chain. (See Box 3, "Trade Promotion Management: A Ticket to Digital Loyalty Networking").

Box 3:   Trade Promotion Management: A Ticket to Digital Loyalty Networking

You say you don't know where to start your digital loyalty network journey and how to produce immediate financial results? Well, look no further than an area ripe for taking on – Trade Promotions Management (TPM). With American consumer packaged goods companies collectively spending $470 billion annually and certain firms spending as much as 16 percent of sales, trade spending is larger than the combined gross domestic product of more than half of the world's countries.

Despite this massive investment, the TPM process is wrought with several inefficiencies. Sales and marketing functions are not in synch (sales is focused on volume, marketing on brand equity). Manufacturers lack understanding of consumers and their behavior, and rarely collaborate with retailers in developing more effective joint promotions. Many companies make poor selections in promotion tactics, and fail to evaluate promotions after they are run. Promotions are often not factored into demand planning; and failure to monitor results means that retailers often get discounts without performing according to the terms of the promotion.

These issues have challenged even the best consumer packaged goods companies. However, leaders such as Procter & Gamble, Kraft, General Mills, and Coca-Cola have taken TPM head on and are dramatically improving their capabilities – leveraging the tenets of true digital loyalty network performance. These companies are actively building their capabilities in three distinct areas:

- *Understanding the Consumer.* Through digital loyalty networks, companies are learning to strike the appropriate balance between trade, consumer and advertising spending. They better understand what promotional tactics target which consumer segments. They also know how promotions impact the brand perception of various consumer segments. Further, they are learning how certain promotional tactics cannibalize sales or margins during and after the promotion.

- *Understanding the Effectiveness and Profitability of Promotions.* Companies with digital loyalty networks are more likely to know how well retailers participated in promotions and how consumers responded. Thus, they are much more likely to know if the promotion met their ROI and other goals.

- *Understanding Operational Execution in the Entire Supply Chain.* Digital Loyalty Networks enabled companies incorporate incremental consumer lift projections into their demand planning processes. They are good at collaborating with top customers on incremental demand projections. They are better at coordinating collateral materials with product shipments and merchandising promotional items according to guidelines.

Companies that use advanced technologies and information (e.g., syndicated data, retailer data) to create disciplined, closed-loop processes for TPM (Figure 5.23) are dramatically improving their TPM performance. For example, a leading consumer products company cut trade spending by 10 percent and boosted volume a year after implementing new TPM processes and technologies. The company also augmented its TPM foundation by adding predictive modeling and analysis tools, thereby generating over a 50 percent internal rate of return on the project in 18 months.

Ideally, once TPM foundations are in place, companies can start achieving breakthrough performance. Imagine tailoring promotions at the store level within the same retail chain for the same period of time – e.g., TPM in urban store location vs. end aisle display with no TPM in upscale store location during the same promotional period. In other words, this approach allows companies to achieve true micro-marketing/merchandising and all of the associated benefits – increased volume, enhanced profitability, increased consumer satisfaction and high levels of brand equity in those segments where it counts.

Implementing this model is no small feat. Addressing trade promotion management through "point-in-time" analytics alone will not solve the issues at hand and will not create an advantage that is sustainable. It is the combined principles of digital loyalty networks – namely the focus on the consumer, the integration of operational excellence and the emphasis on measurements and profitability – that allow companies to capture share and profits away from age-old category leaders.

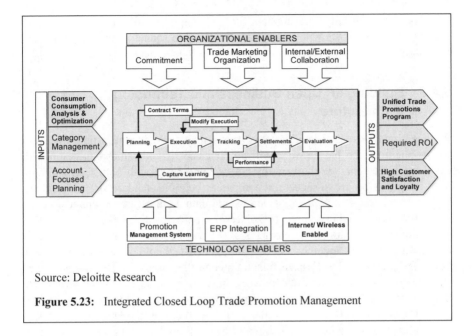

Source: Deloitte Research

Figure 5.23:   Integrated Closed Loop Trade Promotion Management

Examples of such collaborative network strategies are growing by the day. Tesco, UK's largest grocery retailer, makes available to its 1,000 suppliers complete, reliable point-of-sale data from more than 800 stores. Combining point-of-sales data and internal analytics at key suppliers has enabled reductions in forecasting errors and supply chain costs.

Wal-Mart and Procter & Gamble have better balanced demand and supply over the years through electronically stitching together their sales, forecasting and inventory systems.

Kraft Foods allows suppliers like Universal Packaging to peek at its Jell-O sales forecasts so that the box maker can efficiently prepare for future orders.

General Mills uses the Web to collaborate with 20 other companies from other industries that ship products on the same routes. On test runs, General Mills has saved 7 percent on shipping costs – or about $2 million in the first year alone. Heineken's U.S. unit has worked closely with distributors over the last decade to dramatically cut order delivery times and costs. (See Box 1, "The Emergence of Digital Loyalty Networks in the Global Beer Industry")

To get all stakeholders in a digital loyalty network on board, it is important to forecast the outcomes for each participant. The prospect of quantifiable gains for everyone is what increases participation in the network.

The fear that there will be inequitable sharing of benefits is often cited as the most frequent barrier to retailer/manufacturer collaboration. Companies that harbor this fear often see cost reduction as the primary benefit and assume that parties closest to the end customer (i.e., retailers) will capture those benefits. But this view is too narrow. Cost reductions are only a fraction of the total potential benefits. Companies usually find dramatic improvements in fill rates and sales from synchronizing forecasts with promotions and tend to funnel greater spending and new product development efforts to their closest loyalty network partners.

5.4.3   Building an Open Business and Technology Architecture

Participation in a digital loyalty network is a major investment in time for every player. Getting into the network will be far easier if companies can begin with small initiatives and see the benefits before jumping in with both feet. As these pilot initiatives progress, successful companies begin to standardize their policies, business processes, software applications and data architectures to create an open platform that is scalable and secure for network participants.

We refer to these and other elements of the ways companies in a digital loyalty network could work together as the business and technology architecture. In the last year, the prevailing form of this architecture has been private Internet-based exchanges in which a company transacts business with suppliers and customers. Such private exchanges are quickly displacing all but a few of the venture capital-funded public Internet exchanges that proliferated during the late 1990s dot-com boom. As shown in Figure 5.24, Loyalty Networkers have taken a lead in using technology for competitive advantage.

Nevertheless, each of the companies that lead the way in the creation of digital loyalty networks began with small steps. In 1995, Colgate-Palmolive began phasing in its digital loyalty network by standardizing its hodgepodge IT infrastructure and increasing supply chain visibility among its global divisions. It is now in the

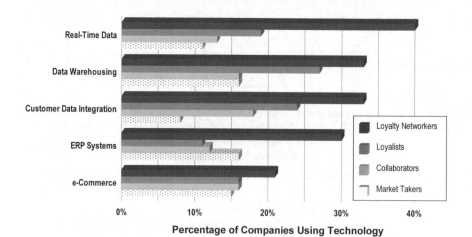

Source: Deloitte Research

Figure 5.24: Loyalty Networkers and Technology Adoption

process of extending this visibility to suppliers and retailers using an advanced planning optimization software. (See Box 4, "How Colgate-Palmolive Brightened its Standing through Digital Loyalty Network Strategies")

Box 4:   How Colgate-Palmolive Brightened Its Standing through Digital Loyalty Network Strategies

The creation of a digital loyalty network has propelled Colgate-Palmolive Co. to new heights. The journey began in the mid-1990s, after the $9.4 billion global manufacturer of such households brands as Mennen, Softsoap, Ajax and Hill's had watched two years of stagnant sales and narrowing operating margins in key North American product lines such as toothpastes, detergents and other personal care products. Its stock price was in the doldrums – below $20 a share by the end of 1995.

Colgate decided it had to overhaul its inefficient supply chain and technology infrastructure. The company wanted to slash $150 million in supply chain costs and reduce manufacturing and delivery times. It was taking an average of 120 days for Colgate to convert raw materials to finished products and deliver them to store shelves – a number that it wanted to reduce by more than 80 percent. To reach those goals, the company had to invest 60 percent of its capital expenditures into revamping its onerous supply chain.

In the end, it took only three years to get its money back and the return has kept on growing. How did Colgate do it? First, it had to radically change the way it manufactured, distributed and accounted for its products – changes that would call for much greater coordination of plants, distribution routes and warehouses and planning activities. This demanded standardized information systems rather than the hodgepodge of systems that could be found in each of the 200 companies in which Colgate operated. As a result, Colgate launched a four-year reengineering initiative that made SAP software the nerve center of a new, streamlined supply chain. A central database let sales forecasts drive materials purchases, production scheduling, labor scheduling and other activities. The movement of finished product was then tracked all the way from plants to the grocery stores through devices such as radio frequency-operated communications in warehouses.

Colgate also moved quickly to improve its customer-facing processes. It was an early participant in CPFR in 1996. From successful pilot projects, it saw the potential payback in linking the customer-related processes of planning and forecasting with supply chain processes of replenishment. Planning became far more precise; errors in forecasts went down from 61 percent to 21 percent. Moreover, case fill rates – a measure of the accuracy of shipped orders – nudged up from 94 percent to 97 percent.

Today, Colgate is thriving. Asset turnover and operating margins have been the highest since five years (Figure 5.25).

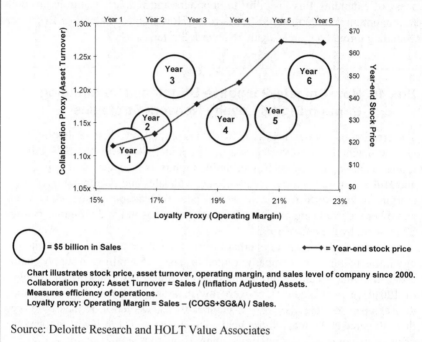

= $5 billion in Sales   ◆——◆ = Year-end stock price

Chart illustrates stock price, asset turnover, operating margin, and sales level of company since 2000.
Collaboration proxy: Asset Turnover = Sales / (Inflation Adjusted) Assets.
Measures efficiency of operations.
Loyalty proxy: Operating Margin = Sales – (COGS+SG&A) / Sales.

Source: Deloitte Research and HOLT Value Associates

Figure 5.25:   Performance Measures: Colgate-Palmolive

Gross margins, which had been flat at 46 percent for a decade, have zoomed to
54 percent. Since the company has reinvested a great deal of its supply chain
savings into promotions and new products, the company has surpassed Procter
& Gamble to regain its lead in the U.S. toothpaste market after 34 years.

Wal-Mart began its digital loyalty network by capturing point-of-sale data. It then
initiated links with suppliers and created CPFR standards that it ran through a
private exchange called RetailLink.

  In the implementation of a 'closed' architecture – where every company has its
own definition of key terms, its own data formats and so on – it is more difficult to
link demand and supply chains.

5.5   Conclusion: The Digital Loyalty Network Effect

If the prospect of profit improvements of as much as 100 percent is not enough to
motivate a company to build a digital loyalty network, the fear of watching companies like Avon Products, Dell, General Electric, Intel and Southwest Airlines
dominate their industries should. Failing to react quickly, many of their competi-

tors are dying a long, painful death of a thousand cuts. Don't believe it? Remember that the PC industry once had dozens of competitors? Today, Dell effectively has reduced the competition to a handful of players and is essentially the only one making money on PCs.

We believe that now is the right time for consumer businesses must to start examining the feasibility of digital loyalty networks. As the network grows in loyalty and the number of participants increases, its value increases exponentially. We call this the "digital loyalty network effect" (Figure 5.26), building upon Metcalfe's Law on the economics of loyalty and supply chain collaboration.

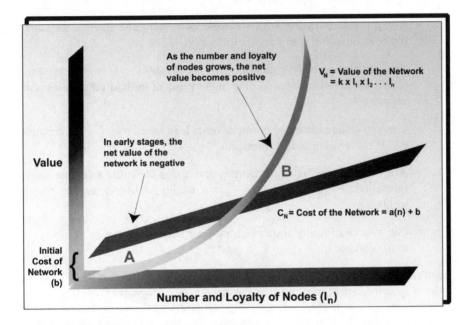

Source: Deloitte Research

Figure 5.26: Digital Loyalty Network Effect

Furthermore, once these network relationships are established and investments made in infrastructure and collaboration, switching costs become substantially higher – as do the costs for late-arriving competitors hoping to mimic the business model. Competitors will always find ways to copy new products and quality standards, new services, individual marketing and sales efforts, supply chain operations, production models and sourcing strategies. However, it will be virtually impossible for competitors to copy the way in which a digital loyalty network differentiates the entire supply chain response for each customer or segment in real time.

Now is the time for consumer business executives to ask themselves some key questions:

- Do you know who your **most valuable customers** are, what their requirements are, and what it costs to serve them well?

- Are your supply chain managers getting customer information on changes in **lifetime value** and customer requirements on a real-time basis?

- Are you leveraging new e-business technologies to manage customer and supplier relationships in real-time?

- Are you **collaborating with strategic customers** and sharing deep customer information with your critical suppliers?

- Are you dynamically committing plants, capacity, logistics, and other supply chain resources according to the **value of individual** customers or segments?

- Can you differentiate and optimize order lead times according to customers' lifetime value and requirements?

- Are you and your network partners optimizing the entire customer value proposition for each customer – price, quality, delivery, service, brand, technology?

- Can you **continually improve** how your network responds to new customer demands?

Answering these questions will reveal to organizations how far they need to go in order to gain the capabilities required for success, or perhaps even survival, as the decade plays itself out. They will also help organizations determine how far down the path of deploying digital loyalty networks they have gone and how much further they need to go.

PART 3:

The Demand Side:
Collaborative Customer Relationship and Category Management

This part extends the subject of Collaborative Customer Relationship Management with two important concepts – individualization and Category Management. We will show in chapter 6, that just as does traditional CRM, collaborative CRM has to be based on the individualization of the solutions offered to a customer as well as on the individualization of the marketing activities in order to build long lasting, persistent customer loyalty. This creates new challenges for managing the relationship between a company and its retail partners, but at the same time, creates new opportunities as well. Chapter 7 focuses on the conditions in which different models of collaboration nets can work profitably. Chapter 8 answers the question: Why is Collaborative Customer Relationship Management necessary?" and describes the role of Category Management. The main goal of Category Management is to focus on fulfilling customers' needs and to jointly achieve it. Category Management therefore is a process-oriented philosophy that puts the customer with his or her wishes and needs at the center. It promotes and even commands co-operation between retailers and manufacturers – and is therefore a basic requirement for successful CCRM. This is also explained by chapter 9, which explains the importance of Category Management in today's marketplace.

CHAPTER 6

Collaboration in CRM: Potentials and Challenges of an Individualization Based Approach

Christian Schaller
Technical University Munich, Germany

Frank T. Piller
Technical University Munich, Germany

Ralf Reichwald
Technical University Munich, Germany

Acknowledgments:

The research for this paper was supported by grants of the "Stiftung Industrieforschung" and the European Community's Fifth Framework program within the "Euro-Shoe" project. We are grateful for the support.

6.1 Challenges of Collaborative CRM – a Case from the Sports Shoe Industry

To introduce this chapter's topic, we will first look at a case study from the sports industry. Through this case study, we will be able to demonstrate the models that can be developed for individualization based Collaborative CRM.

The international sports shoe industry is a textbook example of innovative variant management. The five biggest brands – Nike, Adidas, Reebok, Asics and Puma – no longer do their own manufacturing, but rely on "outsourcing", and often to the same suppliers. Their core competencies are the recognition of market trends and the design and development of new products. Extensive market research activities, lean contract manufacturing systems, sound forecasting skills and good supply chain management along with a strong brand management are seen as the basis for success within the industry. However, even leaders like Adidas or Nike are facing problems. Their brand name is being attacked by new and trendy fashion labels. Consumers are demanding high quality shoes for lower prices and customer loyalty is decreasing fast.

The reasons for these developments can be found primarily in the culmination of increased competitive pressure, technological progress and changes in shopping behavior. Firms, not limited to those in the sporting goods industry, are challenged by an increasing individualization of demand. Explanations may be found in the tendency towards an experience economy, the growing number of single households, an orientation towards design and most importantly, a new awareness of quality and functionality which demands durable and reliable products corresponding exactly to the specific needs of the purchaser. A further influence is the maturing of a brand-literate society that is evolving from awareness to involvement with brands, with members keen to exercise greater choice and influence over what they consume (Crosby/Johnson 2001). In particular, consumers with great purchasing power are increasingly attempting to express their individuality by means of their product choice. Thus, almost all suppliers in the sporting goods industry have been forced to create product programs with an increasing wealth of variants right down to the production of units of one (differentiation by means of variety). In the final consequence, many companies have to process their customers on an individual basis (Glazer, 1999; Kahn, 1998).

"The mass market is dead," said Kotler (1989, p. 47) provocatively when describing the emerging change in marketing philosophy; the evolution from mass marketing to target oriented marketing arriving ultimately at individualized marketing. Since then the individual customer has increasingly become the focal point of research and practice. Numerous studies point noticeably towards a turning away from the one-sided focus on new customer acquisition in favor of a stronger commitment to existing customers (Glazer 1999). For many firms, building long-term relationships with existing customers has acquired a value previously attributed to the pursuit of market share by winning new customers.

Faced with these trends, German sporting goods company Adidas-Salomon AG decided to move into a new form of value creation: mass customization.[1] The objective of mass customization was to produce goods and services meeting individual customer's needs with near mass production efficiency (Tseng and Jiao 2001). The reasons for introducing its new, customizable product range "mi adidas" were, besides the ongoing challenge to differentiate the brand, the explosion of variants due to the growing individualization of demand. This development made forecasting and planning for Adidas more difficult than ever. The consequences were high overstocks, an increasing fashion risk, an enormous supply chain complexity and a need to give large discounts in order to get rid of unwanted products, not to mention lost sales caused by products which had performed better than expected, and were therefore not available in large enough

---

[1] Information on this case is drawn from company sources, own user tests, and extensive interviews with Adidas executives carried out by the authors. The authors wish to express special acknowledgments to Christoph Berger, head of Adidas' mass customization operations.

quantities or the right sizes. Mass customization provided a solution to overcome these challenges.

Adidas-Salomon launched "mi adidas" in 2001.[2] The program made customized shoes available to consumers in specialized retail stores and at selected events. Consumers were given the opportunity to create their own unique footwear to their exact personal specifications in terms of fit, function and design, thus providing a service that until now was only available to football stars like David Beckham or top running athletes like Haile Gebrselassie. The shoes were offered in selected markets world wide at a price that was about 30 per cent above the price of an in-line (standard) product.

By means of a foot scan system, the customer's feet were scanned to determine the exact length, width and pressure distribution of each foot. Together with trained "fitting experts" the customer reviewed the result of the scan. This information, combined with personal fit preferences, was entered into a computer to determine the best-fitting shoe. Once the customer had chosen his or her personalized function and fit, he or she had the opportunity to test the shoes before the final design phase. The customer then got to design the color elements and select his or her material preferences. As a final sign of individuality, the customer could create a uniquely embroidered monogram on his pair of shoes. All these steps were performed with the help of a configuration system – a PC-based sales kiosk leading the customer but also the sales clerk through the whole customization process. The system also visualized the results and connected the point of sale with the fulfillment systems. Once a customer's data was stored, it could be used for easy re-orders on the Internet, via a call center or in retail. All shoes were made-to-order at an Asian factory, and the delivery time was about three weeks.

"Adidas introduced a new business model into the industry, influencing and changing the whole value chain and potentially the sporting goods marketplace, creating a new level of relationship between the consumer and the brand," says Christoph Berger, Project Manager Mass Customization at Adidas-Salomon AG, while describing the marketing opportunities of the system. However, reality is not as simple. While consumer interest and demand is very high, and supply chain issues are mainly solved, relationship and collaboration management has proved to be the biggest challenge. Adidas is facing four demanding areas with "mi adidas" that are typical for many situations of collaborative Customer Relationship Management:

---

[2] Adidas competitor Nike had already started a mass customization program in 1998. However in this system consumers can simply choose some customized design options on a standard model and print their name on it. The "mi adidas" program goes much further as it adds a customization option with regard to fit and functionality.

6.1.1 Transition from Product Marketer to Solution Provider

Within "mi adidas", the product itself ceases to be the central focus in the interaction with the customer. As the final product does not exist during the sales process, demonstrating solution competence in sales becomes one of Adidas' top priorities. This competence is shown on the one hand by the design of the configuration system, but is primarily based on the perceived competence of the interaction expert at the point of sales. Mass customization poses new challenges for brand managers because customers that co-design their products expect to have a different relationship with brands than traditional consumers. They are not satisfied with simple one-way communication, but instead want a true two-way relationship.

Retail is often not prepared for this step. Shoe retailers are used to selling products, not to co-design and co-develop them with their customers. While the involvement of retail personnel in traditional sales channels is already often below manufacturers' expectations, this problem is much more significant in a mass customization system. Experiences from pioneering companies in mass customization show that many suppliers have had to replace the whole sales force within the first year of operation (Piller 2001). Traditional sales clerks have often shown reluctance to change from selling stock items to co-designing a product with a specific customer. Adidas has overcome this problem by sending its own team of experts into the stores on an event-based basis. However, if the "mi adidas" system is going to gain major market share, this solution is far too expensive (even if retailers are paying a fee for this service). But the problem can emerge from the retailer's perspective as well: while selling standard goods, the manufacturer of the product is seen as responsible for quality failures and is responsible for the warranty and product liability. However, as mass customization implies a change from selling a product to providing a service, the retailer will be made responsible much more readily for dissatisfaction with the final product, even if the error is based in the fulfillment system of the supplier. Furthermore, when the product is finally handed over after delivery, it has to be ensured that a competent sales clerk is present to get feedback information and round off the experience, even if the "mi adidas" experts are gone by that time.

Thus, models of collaboration need to address the following questions: How can suppliers motivate retail personnel to participate in mass customization and personalization and address the transition to offering solutions instead of products? What institutions are there to increase the motivation and involvement of the retailers and to prevent biases in retail?

6.1.2 Ownership of Customer Data

One of "mi adidas'" major advantages comes not in the sale of the first pair of shoes, but during the subsequent purchases made by a single customer. Properly implemented, "mi adidas" can become the company's premier tool for increasing customer loyalty. Based on the generic foot scan and the knowledge of fit preferences of a user, this data can be used not only to fulfill the first order, but also to make re-orders very easy. Profiling information regarding the style and comfort preferences of a customer is rather subjective data. Often some effort has to be undertaken in order to obtain reliable information. However, once it has been collected, a re-order can be processed by phone or Internet, without the usual problems connected with distance shopping. Moreover, once Adidas has proved that it can deliver a customized solution in-time, the trust perception is higher. This reduces the risks customers face when ordering customized goods. Thus, cross-selling of different kinds of sporting equipment or selling add-ons or upgrades becomes possible. Often, all these additional sales can be based on the first set of data with just a few additional interactions. If Adidas can maintain control of brand values by listening and responding to their customers to ensure that they do not feel duped into a false relationship, the resulting closer relationship can rekindle brand loyalty, provide a competitive opportunity for differentiation and increase the "share of customer" (i.e. the aggregated profits a firm makes with one single customer).

To fulfill this potential, the configuration process of "mi adidas" has to be designed to get as much information as possible from a customer. Secondly, getting feedback data immediately after delivery is very important in order to extend the knowledge about any one customer. This potential implies a major source of conflict: Who owns the customer data and who will take re-orders? At this point, Adidas would have all the information for selling re-orders in a direct channel, which is much more profitable than using the retailer. Also, from a consumer's perspective, a direct sale is often more comfortable. But why should a retailer invest in getting a customer into the system when the fruits are reaped by the supplier? How can the retailer be motivated to get feedback data (after delivering the goods) and to share it with the supplier? Is the supplier willing to use this information to improve the joint relationship with a customer? Here, new kinds of cooperation and profit sharing have to be implemented to address lost sales for a retailer if re-orders are carried out within a direct channel.

6.1.3 Multi Channel Interaction and Sales Approach

When Adidas' competitor Nike started mass customizing with NikeID (a sports shoe that can be customized with regard to design (color) options only), it decided to offer this product only via its own web site. Apart from lower transaction costs due to the "design it yourself" approach, the main motivation behind this decision was to gain experience with consumers directly via the Internet. To avoid channel conflicts, Nike could argue successfully that the product would be too costly and labor intensive if it were sold offline (Nike just charges a small surplus for the customization option).

Due to the full customization approach, "mi adidas" products need a real life interaction tool. They are sold in special in-store-events in traditional retail outlets as well as at various locations during sporting events. While in the first case, a retailer books an Adidas team as a facilitator and makes the sale within its system, in the second approach, Adidas sells shoes directly to the end user. In the long run, this double strategy has potential for conflict. On the other hand, the system is promoted to retailers as a "retail innovation" – helping participating retailers stress their local store image and sports shoe competence in the market. Thus, the retailer is particularly important for Adidas, as it enables the company to benefit from the existing customer relationships of a retailer. The individual retailer is responsible for marketing the product prior to and during to the event. So what are the instruments that are available to solve or at least lessen multi channel conflicts? We will develop four models for collaboration to address this question in the last section of this chapter.

6.1.4   Synergy of Collaboration

If carried out well, the customer will view the intensive 'customer care' element as being the deciding factor in making a purchase, as opposed to the quality of the standard product. In addition, it's not only the sales assistant who is at the customer's disposal, but also the customer who is at the sales assistant's disposal and therefore, in principle, at Adidas' disposal. By interacting with the end-user, "mi adidas" obtains important market research data by aggregating the data on individual customers through the use of data mining activities (Kelly 1997, Kotha 1995). The results can improve not only the customized line, but also the standard product lines by providing better market research information and more accurate forecasting on customer needs. To plan manufacturing for standard (in-line) products, the mass customized segment provides panel-like market research information without the common panel effects biasing the results. The information gained here can be used to plan and control better existing variants of products made to stock.

Thus, all findings must be checked and consistently evaluated in terms of their relevance for in-line production (e.g. the modularization of production and the definition of country specific color preferences for the product management). Data such as preferred color combinations of a country are important for Adidas in order to improve regional offerings and to improve sales planning and forecasting. However, retail could also use this knowledge to improve an assortment of standard products across brands and it might be interested in sharing this information with other suppliers. The resulting conflict prevents the gain of learning economies and synergies between the customized and the traditional system. Thus, using this opportunity is once again dependent on retail collaboration.

As the Adidas case shows, individualization based Customer Relationship Management offers a large range of opportunities, but demands new forms of cooperation within the whole value chain. The objective of this chapter is to extend the framework of CCRM developed earlier in this book by adding individualization as a major enabler of customer loyalty and by discussing potentials and restrictions of individualization based collaborative CRM.

The organization of the rest of this chapter is as follows: In Section 2, we will take a closer look at the drivers of customer loyalty and present a framework with the most important influencing factors. We will then discuss in more detail how individualization can strengthen relationship management. This framework will be extended in the context of collaboration in Section 3. Collaboration nets will model the basis of individualization based CRM. A brief discussion of the main potentials and restrictions of this approach will finalize this chapter.

In order to elaborate on different strategies of collaboration along the whole chain from the supplier via the retailer to the customer (and back), the next chapter will discuss different models of supplier-retailer-customer collaboration and follow the basics discussed here.

6.2 Customer Relationship Management and Customer Loyalty

"It is the customer who determines what a business is." (Drucker 1954, p.37). Apart from approaching customers individually and producing customer specific products, individual business relationships are increasingly becoming the center of attention in the discussion of a more closely customer orientated approach. Many writers are pleading for a marketing perspective which gives priority to the building up and maintenance of long-term profitable relationships with promising customers, as opposed to the short-term success orientated approach of single transactions in anonymous mass markets (Grönroos 1989; Glazer 1999; Webster 1992).

As a result of the technological developments over the last few years, the final realization of the principle of (individual) customer orientation, which has always been a part of the marketing philosophy, seems to be on the horizon. However, the heart of the matter in the field of Customer Relationship Management is not technology, but rather – as the name suggests – the customer, the business relationship to him or her and (from the supplier's point of view) the possibility of molding this business relationship. In order to define efficient and effective Customer Relationship Management, it is necessary, first and foremost, to establish its central goals. A successful relationship can best be defined in economic goals such as a growth target or target rate-of-return (see for e.g. Diller 1995). Customer loyalty, i.e., the long-term relationship of the customer with the company, is seen as the primary pre-economical goal of Customer Relationship Management (see for e.g. Homburg and Bruhn 1998). Efficient and effective Customer Relationship Management strives therefore primarily to positively influence customer loyalty and to make optimal use of all resources. Customer loyalty therefore does not represent a goal in its own right, but is rather a means of achieving economic targets. The relationship with a committed customer can therefore be seen as an investment.

In the following section, we will discuss a model showing the interaction of the central drivers of customer loyalty and their influencing factors. This argument is supplemented by the conceptualization of the term 'individualization', and the integration of 'individualization' into the model showing the influencing factors of customer loyalty.

6.2.1 Drivers of Customer Loyalty

In order to conceptualize customer loyalty, or in other words, to clarify which characteristics are relevant in describing it, we will use the following layer model with customer satisfaction, trust and commitment[3] as the central determinants:

- customer loyalty = customer satisfaction + trust

- persistent customer loyalty[4] = customer loyalty + commitment

The main antecedent variable is **customer satisfaction**. If we put the focus on the longevity of a business relationship rather than individual transactions, customer satisfaction can be seen as describing the "cognitive and affective evaluation of one's overall experience with a specific provider and its products" (Homburg et al. 1999, p. 177), on the basis of a target/actual comparison between perceived performance (actual) and expected performance (target).[5] Customer satisfaction can be measured by the number of complaints, repeat purchases and the communicative behavior of the customer, all of which are factors which have a considerable effect on customer loyalty.

We see **trust** as the second antecedent variable of customer loyalty. Trust reduces uncontrollable complexity and the risk of opportunistic behavior in a relationship. It is this self-energizing effect (echo-effect) that is important for creating customer loyalty (Diller 1996; Bauer et al. 1999).

The strength of the correlation between customer satisfaction and customer loyalty is further influenced by the so-called moderator variables. In what follows, we will concentrate on **competition intensity** and **exit barriers** as key factors (Herrmann and Johnson 1999; Homburg et al. 1999). The stronger the competitive

---

[3] This concept builds on socio-psychological behavior theories of the marketing science research, see for e.g. Bauer et al. 1999; Diller 1996; Matzler and Stahl 2000.

[4] Unlike German literature, English-speaking literature tends not to make any distinction between the terms ,Kundenbindung' (as being loyal, mainly on the basis of satisfaction and exit barriers) and ,Kundenloyalität' (as being "very" loyal, without the use of exit barriers). Due to the lack of an English synonym to ,Kundenloyalität' we will represent the German term by the phrase "persistent customer loyalty."

[5] This concept relates to the most popular explanation of a target/performance paradigm, the confirmation/ disconfirmation paradigm; see Oliver 1980.

intensity in a market, the weaker is the correlation between customer satisfaction and customer loyalty. On the other hand exit barriers have a positive effect on the relationship between customer satisfaction and customer loyalty, i.e. "the greater the exit barriers, the stronger the correlation between customer satisfaction and customer loyalty" (Homburg et al. 1999, p. 187). Whereas, for example, customers in a monopolistic telecommunication market would remain loyal as a result of exit barriers no matter how dissatisfied they were, in the intensely competitive car industry, there is a clear difference in the loyalty of satisfied and very satisfied customers (Jones and Sasser 1995; Heskett et al. 1994).

A further antecedent variable affecting *persistent* customer loyalty is **commitment**. Commitment is seen as an inner sense of obligation felt by a person towards a specific object. It therefore includes "the wish to develop stable business relationships, the willingness to make short-term sacrifices for the benefit of maintaining a long-term business relationship and trust in the stability of the relationship" (Anderson and Weitz 1992, p. 19). Thus, 'a loyal customer relationship' is created by a high level of commitment by the consumer. In the next section, we will discuss how the concept of individualization affects these antecedent variables.

6.2.2   Individualization and Customer Relationship Management

Measures carried out to foster customer loyalty[6] should take certain principles into account. These include being orientated towards each individual customer, seeking mutual interaction with the customer, and striving to integrate the customer into the provider's value chain (Diller and Müllner 1998; Hildebrand 1997). Individualization can be seen as a major driver of loyalty. In this section the composition of individualization and its influencing factors will be discussed. In doing so we will be able to extend our model introduced above.

Often, individualization is only seen in the context of individualized customer relationships, or more specifically, in personalized communication (relationship level). From our perspective it is fundamental not to restrict the concept of individualization to relationships, but also to include the individualization of products or services (performance level). In the end, most customers are not interested in communicating individually with a company, but in getting products or services that exactly fit their needs and desires. The construct of individualization therefore includes both a relationship and a performance level (see Figure 6.1 adopted by Hildebrand 1997):

---

[6] Despite the differences between customer loyalty and persistent customer loyalty for the sake of simplicity we will use the term loyalty resp. customer loyalty as umbrella term for both in the following.

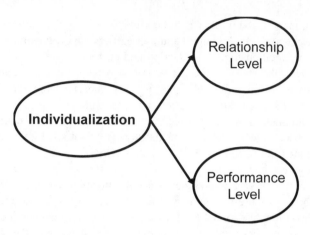

Figure 6.1:   Conceptualization of Individualization

- Individualization on the relationship level is typically modeled by the term **One-to-One-Marketing** (Peppers and Rogers 1997). Personalization is a term often used in connection with the individualization of the communication with the customer using new Internet technology.

- Individualization on the performance level is typically modeled by the term **Mass Customization**. The concept of mass customization refers mainly to delivering physical products or core services according to each customer's wishes with near mass production efficiency (see Piller 2001; Pine 1993; Tseng/Jiao 2001 for an overview).

We understand **individualization** from the supplier's perspective as being a strategic option of activating the market, where the scope for strategic decisions will be shaped by the traditionally antithetic concepts of standardization and individualization. (Hildebrand 1997; Mayer 1993). Between the two extreme positions of 'individualization', seen as an intense orientation towards the individual needs and wishes of each individual customer, and 'standardization', seen as an orientation towards the average demands made by the anonymous mass of customers, lie a variety of combination forms.

From the consumer's perspective, individualization seeks the ultimate possible satisfaction of the individual consumer's preference structures through the performance of the provider. The individual preference structure illustrates the expectations of a consumer (or a combination of performance specifications) that define his or her ideal point of 'optimal performance' (Piller 1998). As shown, this ideal point shows the level of expected performance. Generally speaking, in order to address the aims of individualization in the form of differentiation options and relationship options as efficiently as possible, the performance components, which are significant for the consumer's preference, are individualized and otherwise standardized components are relied upon (Wehrli and Wirtz 1997).[7]

Taking a closer look at the relationship between individualization and customer loyalty, we can identify five main influencing factors following the framework from the last section. Their relationship is described in Figure 6.2. First, the individualization of product and service attributes to customer-specific needs and requirements holds the potential to increase **customer satisfaction**. In the course of individualization, the supplier enters a quasi monopolistic status as its offer is unique and, at least to a certain degree, not comparable with the other products in the market segment (cf. Chamberlin 1962; Piller 2001). Customer satisfaction is based on benefits (value added) such as a reduction in costs of use, an increasing perception of quality, image advantages of customized solutions or the reduction of transaction costs. Thus, customer satisfaction can be considerably strengthened

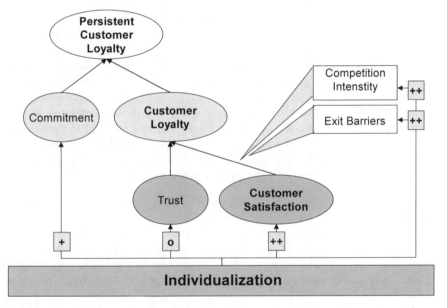

Figure 6.2:   Effects of Individualization on Customer Loyalty[8]

---

[7] One should note, however, "(...) that the individualization of performance only becomes a (customer) success factor beyond a certain level of individualization i.e. when the performance is genuinely cut out to exactly meet the customer's wishes. A wide range of variations which have not been specifically designed for one particular customer have the tendency to be negatively received by the customer and contributes less to customer loyalty." (Hildebrand 1997, p. 174).

[8] The expected extent of the interrelation of the effects is illustrated on a scale ranging from ++ (very positive) to + (positive) to o (neutral).

through the explicit orientation towards an individually defined ideal level of optimal performance.

Trust is not directly influenced by individualization. It may, however, be indirectly and positively affected by the influence of individualization on customer satisfaction.[9] In a relationship between supplier and customer, the self strengthening effects of trust can have positive results on customer loyalty (Diller 1996). But as we will discuss in more detail below, individualization also demands more trust by customers due to the higher risk for an individual when buying a customized product as compared to buying a proven standard solution.

Intensity of competition is considerably reduced through the individualization of performance and relationships. The differentiation potential of an individualization strategy has a market position which is hard to recreate, with competitive advantages as a result (Wehrli and Wirtz 1997).

Exit barriers and switching costs are also positively influenced (i.e. raised) by the individualization of performance and relationships. The relationship potential of individualization as a starting point for a learning relationship represents a valuable instrument for increasing customer loyalty: once the customer has successfully purchased an individual item, the knowledge acquired by the supplier during the product configuration represents a considerable barrier against switching suppliers. Even if a competitor possesses the same individualization skills and offers a lower price, a switching customer would have to go through the procedure of supplying information for product customization a second time (Riemer/Totz 2001; Pine/Peppers/Rogers 1995). Also, he or she is once again faced with uncertainties with regards to the quality and the producer's behavior.[10]

Commitment is also positively influenced by individualization. The main reasons for this positive effect are the potential that individualization has to capture the consumer's enthusiasm and the aim of voluntary loyalty on the basis of considered usage. The consumer should therefore not be bound to a provider as a result of the traditional "create-capture-keep" principle (Clemons 1986) but should voluntarily remain loyal to the supplier because of the perception of the advantages and a

---

[9] Based on an empirical study (Bauer et al. 1999), there is a strong positive influence of customer satisfaction with an business relationship on trust in this business relationship. For reasons of simplicity this direct and positive link has not been integrated in our model here.

[10] But nevertheless one should be careful in seeing exit barriers and locking in a customer as positively influencing the customer's loyalty. An empirical investigation significantly proved that customers who are locked on i.e. ,positively bound' to the company as a result of customer satisfaction behave far more positively in the sense of re-orders and recommendations then customers who are lockend-in i.e. ,negatively bound' in the sense that they are in some way trapped by the company as a result of exit barriers. (Eggert 1999, Bliemel and Eggert 1998).

unique benefit. Here, especially mass customization offers many more possibilities when compared to standard personalization techniques like direct mail, personalized web sites or micro-targeted e-mail campaigns. Furthermore individualization has an indirect but positive effect on the commitment as a result of the very positive effect on the levels of customer satisfaction.

6.3   Collaborative Customer Relationship Management

Management thinker Peter Drucker calls the accelerating growth of relationships based not on ownership but on partnership as the greatest change in the way business is being conducted today (Drucker 1995). The number and scope of inter-organizational collaborations have grown rapidly in many industries. Purchasing co-ops (B2B exchanges) is one sure sign that the rules of business have changed. If fierce competitors like GM, Ford and Daymler Chrysler can cooperate, then so can manufacturers, retailers and customers. Some are even talking of the "collaborative economy" and take it to mean that "supply-chain collaboration will intensify as pressure builds to cut costs, streamline the supply chain and tie sales directly to production" (Mahoney 2001, p. 8).

6.3.1   From Value Chains to Collaboration Nets

Individualization, being a major influencing factor of loyalty, always means collaboration too. Every transaction in such a model implies information and coordination about the customer specific needs and is based on a direct communication between the customer and supplier (Hibbard 1999; Zipkin 2001). While the solution architectures and the range of possible individualization are fixed, the customer is integrated into the value creation of a concrete solution. This relationship between the customer and supplier can be seen as a collaboration providing benefits for both sides, but demanding input from both participants too. The integration of the customer into the value creating activities breaks the traditional view of value creation in a firm (Ramirez 1999). Industrial value production is most often conceptualized in terms of the value chain (Porter 1980). In this concept, value creation is sequential. Value is added from one step to the other (as it is also reflected in most of today's taxation systems, just think of the "value added tax"). The customer is no part of the value chain. Value is finally realized only in the transaction between the customer and producer (purchasing of the final good).

In contrast, individualization means that value is mutually created among the actors on different levels. Customer integration can be defined as a form of industrial value creation where "the consumers take part in activities and processes which used to be seen as the domain of the companies" (Wikström 1996, p. 360). The result is a system of prosumerism, i.e. a company-customer interaction (social exchange) and adaptation for the purpose of attaining added value (Milgrom/ Roberts 1990; Normann/Ramirez 1994; Toffler 1971). The consumer is not destroying value (just think of the term "to write down" products after their purchase) as in the traditional sequential system of value creation, but creates value together with a firm in the course of interaction.

However, to provide individualization, not only do the supplier and customer have to collaborate, but as the example of "my adidas" showed, manufacturers and retailers must as well. The usually implicitly literal interpretation of the term relationship management focuses on relationships between supplier and customer only (as indeed we did in the previous sections). In accordance with the concept of Collaborative Customer Relationship Management (CCRM), we have to extend those inherent individualization based relationships with further partners along the value chain. Additionally, some new intermediaries might come into play. All these actors are integrated in value creation based on a strong collaboration. We will therefore replace the term value chain with the term *collaboration net*. Additionally we will split up the umbrella term *supplier* into the corresponding parties, i.e. manufacturers and retailers (see Figure 6.3):

- Manufacturer we simply define as a business engaged in manufacturing some final product or offering some service (e.g. Adidas; Nike etc.).

- Retailer we define as a business engaged in the sale of goods or commodities as well as services in small quantities directly to consumers (e.g. Foot Locker; Sears, Roebuck and Co.).

- Consumer we define as one that acquires goods or services for direct use or ownership rather than for resale or use in production and manufacturing, i.e. the ultimate buyer and end user of the value chain.

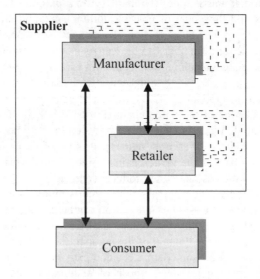

Figure 6.3:   Collaboration Net of Manufacturers, Retailers and Consumer

The objective of a *collaboration net* is to create specific competitive advantages as a result of the increased proximity of its partners and members of other partner networks (Diller 1992). We understand *Collaborative Customer Relationship Management* as an integrated effort to identify, maintain and build up a network with individual partners, including the customer. *Collaborative Customer Relationship Management* also serves to continuously strengthen the network for the mutual benefit of all involved parties, through individualized, interactive and integrated performance and through building communicative relationships over a longer period of time.[11] In the following, we will limit our discussion to the relationships between manufacturers, retailers and customers in consumer goods mass markets.

6.3.2   Collaboration – Why?

The idea of collaboration nets in the context of our analysis breaks with the presumption that retailers would become more and more obsolete. Disintermediation was the word of the day. Disintermediation is a boring word that got people really excited during the heyday of the dot-coms. It referred to the Internet's ability to cut the middleman out of the sales process, allowing manufacturers to deal directly with its end customers [but] disintermediation's devotees overlooked the market dynamics that create and sustain the sales channel. They also downplayed the importance of the selling expertise of channel partners and the knowledge of the customer" (Gonsalves 2001, p. 45). This statement becomes even more accurate as the offer becomes more complex and more consulting dependent. This is particularly true for individualized offers that are not digitalizable (like information goods), as we have already seen above with the example of "mi adidas".

The emergence of new customer channels over time has not led to the displacement of existing channels.[12] However it has made it necessary for manufacturers as well as retailers to re-evaluate their channel-management strategies. According to numerous studies the trend towards a multi-channel approach is growing: based on interviews with 30 executives at bricks-and-mortar retailers that also sold online, 83% said that offering customers multiple channels increased overall sales (Chatham et al. 2000).

The central challenge lies therefore in the integration of these channels, as well as those from partner relationships, into the domain of channel management. For many, however, the comprehensive integration of channels within a company is too much of a hurdle and is rarely carried out consistently in practice. "Despite the overwhelming amount of online/offline customer interaction occurring among the

---

[11] According to (Shani and Chalasani 1992).

[12] A study of 75 large enterprises found that, despite the growth of e-commerce, no traditional channels were eliminated or reduced to any significant extent (Peppers et al. 2000).

traditional stores, print catalogues, telephone and web channels, Jupiter [a consumer research company] found that 76% of retailers were unable to track customers across those channels" (Peppers et al. 2000, p. 5). The reason for this observation was not only that collaborations with external partners were weak, but also that there were obstacles in the internal cooperation between the marketing, sales and services functions of a firm. This disconnected response to customers and the lack of channel integration directly correlated to customer dissatisfaction and lower customer loyalty.

Thus, the goal becomes clear: seamless customer relationships. From the customer's point of view this means individualized, reliable treatment, tailor made to meet her own specific needs in all channels. From the supplier's point of view this forms the basis of persistent loyal customer relationships. "In its most advanced form channel and partner collaboration should make it tough for the customer to tell where the manufacturer leaves off and the retailer picks up" (Allen 2000). Retailers and suppliers should collaboratively maintain customer relationships by sharing customers, margins, and intangibles like brand, as well as jointly planning marketing, merchandising, and sales activities and becoming more like peers than master and servant. From our perspective the individualization based CRM model can be used to study relationships between all partners along a collaboration net. In particular for relationships between manufacturers and retailers, satisfaction, trust and ultimately commitment will be central success factors for a loyal relationship.

6.3.3   Knowledge Gains versus Channel Conflicts: Potentials and Restrictions of Collaboration

Individualization based CRM necessitates collaboration between all partners. The effects of cooperation between the consumer and a supplier during the course of individualization have already been discussed above (see also Duray et al. 2000; Fulkerson/Shank 2000; Lee/Barua/Whinston 2000; Piller 2002; Wind/Rangasmany 2001). With the splitting up of the supplier into its parties and with cooperation between them, the approach of individualization based CCRM yields great potentials. But besides exploiting chances, there is also the need for addressing the according challenges and restrictions.

What are the major potentials of collaborative CRM?

- A fundamental advantage lies undoubtedly in learning from collaboration. The core capabilities of an organization are based increasingly on knowledge-seeking and knowledge-creation. Competition is often best regarded as a learning race. The ability to learn about new opportunities, as well as to exhaust existing ones, requires participation in them. Thus, a wide range of inter-organizational linkages is critical to knowledge creation and diffusion. With this knowledge, manufacturers and retailers can structure the relationships amongst themselves more effectively. Transferring collaboratively gathered information into insights and knowledge about an individual customer's wants and needs is the basis for any persistent loyal relationship.

- Powell (1998) found in an investigation of knowledge generation through cooperation in the field of biotechnology that "in sum, regardless of whether collaboration is driven by strategic motives, such as filling in missing pieces of the value chain, or by learning considerations to gain access to new knowledge.

- Connectivity to an inter-organizational network and competence at managing collaborations have become key drivers of a new logic of organizing" (Powell 1998 p. 231). The study also proved internal capabilities and external collaborations to be complementary. Internal capability is indispensable in evaluating ideas or skills developed externally, while collaboration with outside parties provides access to news and resources that cannot be generated internally. This is also true in the field of relationship management: Alliances provide firms with a unique opportunity to leverage their strengths with the help of partners.

- Collaboration can also raise entry barriers. To the extent that the capabilities of organizations are based in part on the qualities or capabilities of those with whom they are allied, collaboration increases the admission into a field for competitors (Powell 1998). Thus, collaboration may itself become a dimension of competition. Collaboration will become the basis of a strategy that strives not only for seamless customer relationships, but also for competitive advantages through the building up and extension of knowledge about the individual customer needs (Hamel et al. 1989).

- There are still a few more challenges to meet on the way to becoming a CCRM champion. The most substantial hurdles are those of channel conflicts and trust.

- A recent Forrester study in which 50 manufacturers were questioned (25 of whom currently sell online and 25 with sites without transaction capability) reports that 66 per cent of the firms said that conflicts with their retail partners is, by far, their largest problem (Allen 2000). As consumers appear to support the move by manufacturers to sell directly, this conflict will be intensified.[13] Although manufacturers and retailers share the same

---

[13] "While many retailers have supplemented their offline businesses with online sales, manufacturers should also venture into the direct-sales arena" (Peppers et al. 2000, p. 13). Like Peppers et al., there are many voices saying that it is absolutely critical that manufacturers learn how to sell directly to consumers, in particular to address the seg-

interests in part, at the same time there is also competition over the distribution of responsibilities and sales margins of a product. Fundamentally this conflict of interests lies in the desire on both parts for profit respectively the highest possible proportion of the sales margin, and independency from the other party. In the traditional model, the wish of the manufacturer is to 'guide' its product through the retail stage with minimal restriction, and to build up high market entry barriers, whereas the interests of the retailer lie in maintaining the marketing leadership and benefiting from low entry barriers and competition amongst the manufacturers themselves.

- With regard to individualization in the context of CRM, the relation between the manufacturer and the retailer demands a new quality which efficiently and effectively allows both parties to manage a close collaboration. Here, channel conflicts occur if there are varying demands made on the ability to deliver experience and meet the high customer expectations connected with individualization. This goes hand in hand with the qualification of sales clerks and the demand for a steady quality of service at the point of customer interaction. Conflicts are also sometimes based on different approaches to brand representation. CRM (in general) and individualization approaches (in particular) often aim at strengthening the brand preposition of a supplier or a retailer, depending on who is the driving force behind these activities. Thus, the different brand names of the retailer and the supplier may compete and cannibalize themselves.

- The hurdle of trust in a collaboration net lies largely in the information asymmetry i.e. in the unequal distribution of the information between the collaborating parties. The partner working under contract (e.g. the retailer) often has an information advantage and can benefit from behaving opportunistically. This was a major reason why many manufacturers decided to reach their end consumers via online media. By getting closer to the end consumers' needs, manufacturers wanted to acquire knowledge which a retailer in general already had. In the context of the principal agent theory, a distinction is made here between different forms of risk and measures for overcoming these risks (Eisenhardt 1989; Fama/Jensen 1983; Wigand/Reichwald/Picot 1997). Suitable incentive systems could certainly help here, as could an improved information system. While advancing technology has given companies more opportunities to interact

---

ment of customers who would not necessarily go into retail channels. Manufacturers that fail to go online would then give up business from traditional store shoppers who have migrated to the Web and from a whole new computer generation that prefers shopping online.

with consumers, it has also allowed companies to improve communications with their channel partners. This is being discussed under the concept of 'partner relationship management, i.e. systems to facilitate comprehensive partner integration. But as is so often the case, technology alone will not solve the problem.

Ultimately, it might still seem that the right strategy to exploit chances and address challenges can be formulated straight forward as Chris Mahoney, Senior Vice President of UPS, said: "Building a collaborative network ... requires applying many elements of a good marriage: communication, vulnerability, and trust. After all, you have to share sensitive customer data with your supply chain partners, and you have to trust them to do their part to help you serve your customers" (Mahoney 2001, p. 8). But who would claim that it is easy to be happily married? To build the basis for your journey to becoming a CCRM champion, we dedicate the next chapter to introducing and discussing CCRM approaches and applicative models.

6.4 Conclusion

The current economic challenges and alterations within society, along with the technological developments, are leading to far-reaching changes in the competitive conditions of many industries. The individual customer is, once again, the center of attention. Loyal and profitable customer relationships are becoming the central success factor for competitive advantage and individualization based collaborative CRM a most appropriate means of achieving this.

Persistent customer loyalty, i.e. the long-term relationship of the customer with the company based on benefits for both sides, is seen as the primary pre-economical goal of Customer Relationship Management. Efficient and effective Customer Relationship Management strives therefore primarily to positively influence customer loyalty, and to make optimal use of all resources. Measures carried out to foster customer loyalty should take certain principles into account: being orientated towards each individual customer, seeking mutual interaction with the customer and striving to integrate the customer into the provider's value chain. All these aspects can be addressed by the individualization of products, services and relationships on the basis of the individual customer's needs. Individualization can be seen as a major driver of loyalty and a key success factor for efficient and effective Customer Relationship Management.

Individualization necessitates collaboration. The aim from the customer's perspective is clear: seamless Customer Relationship Management. That is to say, individualized, reliable treatment, tailor made to meet the consumer's individual and specific needs in all channels. This, however requires collaboration and ideally not only between supplier and consumer, but between all partners involved in value creation. For this reason we no longer talk of the value chain, but rather of collaboration nets. So we get to the point where individualization is the basis for efficient and effective Customer Relationship Management and collaboration is the best-suited means to provide seamless and individualized relationships via all channels. The model of managing your customer relationships needs to be extended to one managing all your partnerships in the collaboration nets you are participating in.

Besides being the basis for individualized CRM collaboration offers further potentials and chances as well as the need for addressing the according challenges and restrictions. There are potentials such as knowledge gains on the one hand, but restrictions such as channel conflicts on the other. But if fierce competitors can cooperate within supply chains, why should manufacturers and retailers not do the same? Yet, all too often dependency strategies still dominate the relationships between manufacturers and retailers and prevent that partners work together to exploit potentials that one alone couldn't utilize on his own.

How should one start one's journey to becoming a CCRM champion? There are numerous options on the way to be effective and efficient, i.e. individualization based collaborative CRM. The next chapter will focus on the conditions in which different models of collaboration nets can work profitably. The suggestions for action found there should not be understood as generic strategic patterns, but rather as a starting point for questions on where success in individualization based collaborative CRM can begin.

References

Allen, L. (2000): Channel Conflict Crumbles. Cambridge, MA: Forrester Research, Inc.

Anderson, E., and Weitz, B. (1992): The Use of Pledges to Build and Sustain Commitment in Distribution Channels. Journal of Marketing Research, 29, 62-74.

Bauer, H. H., Grether, M. and Leach, M. (1999): Relationship Marketing im Internet. Jahrbuch der Absatz- und Verbrauchsforschung, 45. Jg., H. 3, 284-301.

Bliemel, F. W. and Eggert, A. (1998): Kundenbindung – die neue Sollstrategie? Marketing – Zeitschrift für Forschung und Praxis, 20. Jg., 37-46.

Chamberlin, E. H. (1962): The theory of monopolistic competition, 8. ed., Cambridge.

Chatham, B. et. Al.: The Customer Conversation, Forrester Research, June 2000

Clemons, E. K. (1986): Information system for sustainable competitive advantage. Information and Management, 11. Jg., H. 3, 131-136.

Crosby, L. A. and Johnson, S. (2001): Technology: Friend or foe to customer relationships. Marketing Management, Vol. 10, No 4 (Nov./Dec. 2001), p. 10-11.

Diller, H. (1992): Vahlens Großes Marketing Lexikon. München: C. H. Beck; Vahlen.

— (1995). Beziehungs-Marketing: Wirtschaftswissenschaftliches Studium, 24. Jg., 442-447.

— (1996). Kundenbindung als Marketingziel: Marketing – Zeitschrift für Forschung und Praxis, 18. Jhg., H. 2, 81-94.

Diller, H., and Müllner, M. (1998): Kundenbindungsmanagement. In A. Meyer (Ed.), Handbuch Dienstleistungs-Marketing (pp. 1219-1240). Stuttgart: Schäffer-Pöschel.

Drucker, P. F. (1995): The Network Society. Wall Street Journal, March 29, 12.

— (1954): The Practice of Management, New York: Harper, 1954.

Duray, R. et al. (2000): Approaches to mass customization: configurations and empirical validation, Journal of Operations Managements, 18: 605-625.

Eisenhardt, K. M. (1989): Agency Theory: An Assessment and Review, Academy of Management Review, Vol. 14, No. 1 (January), pp. 57-74.

Eggert, A. (1999): Kundenbindung aus Kundensicht: Konzeptualisierung – Operationalisierung – Verhaltenswirksamkeit. Wiesbaden: Gabler.

Fama, E. F. and Jensen, M. C. (1983): Separation of ownership and control. Journal of Law and Economics, Vol 26, No. 2, p. 301-25.

Fulkerson, B. and Shank, M. (2000): The new economy electronic commerce and the rise of mass customization, in: Michael Shaw et al. (Hg.): Handbook on electronic commerce, Berlin: Springer, p. 411-430.

Glazer, R. (1991): Marketing in an Information-Intensive Environment: Strategic Implications of Knowledge as an Asset. Journal of Marketing, 55, 1-19.

Gonsalves, A. (2001): Customers In Demand. Informationweek, Nov. 19, 45-51.

Grönroos, C. (1989): A Relationship Approach to Marketing. The Need for a New Paradigm. Helsingfors, Finnland: Swedish School of Economics and Business Administration.

Hamel, G., Doz, Y., and Prahalad, C. K. (1989): Collaborate With Your Competitors – and Win. Harvard Business Review, 11. Jg., H. January/February, 133-139.

Herrmann, A., and Johnson, M. D. (1999): Die Kundenzufriedenheit als Bestimmungsfaktor der Kundenbindung. Zeitschrift für betriebswirtschaftliche Forschung (zfbf), 51. Jg., H. 6, 579-598.

Heskett, J. L., Jones, T. O., Loveman, G. W., Sasser, W. E., and Schlesinger, L. A. (1994): Putting the Service-Profit Chain to Work. Harvard Business Review, 16. Jg., H. March/April, 164-174.

Hibbard, Justin (1999): Assembly online: the web is changing mass production into mass customization, Information Week, April 4, 1999: 85-86.

Hildebrand, V. G. (1997): Individualisierung als strategische Option der Marktbearbeitung. Wiesbaden: Gabler.

Homburg, C., and Bruhn, M. (1998): Kundenbindungsmanagement – eine Einführung. In C. Homburg (Ed.), Handbuch Kundenbindungsmanagement: Grundlagen – Konzepte – Erfahrungen (pp. 4-35). Wiesbaden: Gabler.

Homburg, C., Gierling, A., and Hentschel, F. (1999): Der Zusammenhang zwischen Kundenzufriedenheit und Kundenbindung. Die Betriebswirtschaft (DBW), 59. Jg., H. 2, 174-195.

Jones, T. O., and Sasser, W. E. (1995): Why Satisfied Customers Defect. Harvard Business Review, 17. Jg., H. November/December, 88-99.

Kelly, S. (1996): Data Warehousing: The Route to Mass Customization, Chichester: Wiley 1996.

Kotha, S. (1995): Mass customization: implementing the emerging paradigm for competitive advantage, Strategic Management Journal, 16, special issue, p. 21-42.

Lee, C.H. S., Barua, A. and Whinston, A. (2000): The complementarity of mass customization and electronic commerce, Economics of Innovation & New Technology, 9(2): 81-110.

Ludwig, M. A. (2000): Beziehungsmanagement im Internet. Köln: Lohmar.

Mahoney, C. (2001): Global Supply Chains. Executive Excellence, August, 8-9.

Matzler, K. and Stahl, H. K. (2000): Kundenzufriedenheit und Unternehmenswertsteigerung. Die Betriebswirtschaft (DBW), 60, 626-641.

Mayer, R. (1993): Strategien erfolgreicher Produktgestaltung: Individualisierung und Standardisierung, TBW.

Milgrom, P. and Roberts, J. (1990): The economics of modern manufacturing: technology, strategy, and organization, The American Economic Review, 80(6): 511-528.

Normann, R. and Raminez, R. (1993): From value chain to value constellation, Harvard Business Review, 71(4): 65-77

Oliver, R. (1980): A Cognitive Model of the Antecedentes and Consequences of Satisfaction Decisions. Journal of Marketing Research, 17, 460-469.

Peppers, D., and Rogers, M. (1997): Enterprise one to one. New York u.a.

Peppers, D., Rogers, M. and Skinner, S. (2000): Channel Management: Consumer and B2B (pp. 1-32). Norwalk: Peppers and Rogers Group.

Piller, F. T. (1998) : Kundenindividuelle Massenproduktion – Die Wettbewerbs- strategie der Zukunft. München, Wien: Carl Hanser.

— (2001): Mass Customization, 2nd ed., Wiesbaden: Gabler.

— (2002): Customer interaction and digitizability, in: Rautenstrauch, C. et al (ed): Moving towards mass customization, Berlin et al: Springer, p. 45-68.

Piller, F., Reichwald, R. and Möslein, K. (2000): Mass Customization Based E- Business Strategies, Proceedings of the SMS 20th International Conference 2000, Vancouver, British Columbia, Canada.

Pine, B. J. and Gilmore, J. (1999): The Experience Economy, Boston: HBSP 1999.

Porter, M. E. (1980): Competitive strategy, New York: Free Press.

Powell, W. W. (1998): Learning from Collaboration: Knowledge and Networks in the Biotechnology and Pharmaceutical Industries. California Management Re- view, Vol. 49, No. 3, 227-240.

Ramirez, R. (1999): Value co-production: intellectual origins and implications for practice and research, Strategic Management Journal, 20(1): 49-65.

Riemer, K. and Totz, C. (2001): The many faces of personalization, In Tseng M. M. and Piller F. T. (ed.): Proceedings of the 2001 world conference on mass customization and personalization, Oct. 1-2, 2001, Hong Kong: Hong Kong University of Science and Technology.

Shani, D. and Chalasani, S. (1992): Exploiting Niches Using Relationship Market- ing. Journal of Consumer Marketing, Vol. 9, No. 3, 33-42.

Tseng, M. and Jiao, J. (2001): Mass Customization, in: Gaviel Salvendy (ed.) Handbook of Industrial Engineering, 3 rd edition, New York: Wiley, p. 684- 709.

Webster, F. E., Jr. (1992): The Changing Role of Marketing in the Corporation. Journal of Marketing, Vol. 56, 1-17.

Wehrli, P. and Wirtz, B. W. (1997): Mass Customization und Kundenbeziehungsmanagement. Jahrbuch der Absatz- und Verbrauchsforschung, 50. Jg., H. 2, 116-138.

Wigand, R. T., Picot, A. and Reichwald, R. (1997): Information, Organization and Management. Chichester: John Wiley & Sons.

Wind, J. and Rangaswamy, A. (2001): Customerization, Journal of interactive marketing, 15(1): 13-32.

Zipkin, P. (2001): The limits of mass customization, Sloan Management Review, 42(3): 81-87.

CHAPTER 7

Building Customer Loyalty with Collaboration Nets: Four Models of Individualization Based CCRM

Frank T. Piller
Technical University Munich, Germany

Ralf Reichwald
Technical University Munich, Germany

Christian Schaller
Technical University Munich, Germany

Acknowledgments:

The research for this paper was gratefully supported by grants from the "Stiftung Industrieforschung" and the European Community's Fifth Framework program within the "Euro-Shoe" project.

7.1   Challenges of Individualization Based CCRM

The previous chapter established a general framework of individualization based collaborative CRM. We showed that "collaboration nets": collaborative forms of joint value creation between manufacturers, retail partners, intermediaries and customers[1], replace the traditional value chain. This chapter focuses on the conditions in which different models of collaboration nets can work profitably.

When sports goods manufacturer Adidas-Salomon introduced its "mi adidas" program for mass customized footwear, the company faced strong challenges of managing all actors within their collaboration net. As shown in the previous chapter, "mi adidas" offers plenty of new opportunities for Adidas to increase loyalty

---

[1] Like in the previous chapter, we will again use the term „supplier" as an umbrella term for all actors providing an individualized solution for a customer. The terms „manufacturer" and „retailer" differentiate specific kinds of suppliers along the supply and distribution chain. Note that "manufacturer" is used generically and relates also to the production of services, and not only of physical goods.

of its end-consumers and to gain knowledge about their desires and needs that can be used for continuous improvement of all product lines. But the underlying concept of mass customization – building the foundation of these relationships – requires completely new functionalities from all actors (a definition of mass customization and individualization is given in the previous chapter).

While the requirements of a manufacturer of customized goods or services have already been discussed to some extent (e.g., in the works of Agrawal/Kumaresh/ Mercer 2001; Sahin 2000; Piller 2001; Pine 1993; Tseng/Jiao 2001; Zipkin 2001), the perspective of retail and other channel partners has not yet been evaluated. Traditionally, the competitive advantage of a retailer is based on its ability to provide a fitting assortment for the targeted market segment and its capabilities in distribution. By bundling supply and demand, retail is lowering transaction costs. When providing customized solutions, however, assortment, efficient stock keeping and distribution are no longer the driving sources of competitive advantage.

As the case of "mi adidas has demonstrated, consultancy, interaction skills and matching capabilities of a solution set with the needs of a specific customer are becoming the most important success factors of a retailer. However, this change is not simple but connected to many challenges. Thus, it may not be the traditional retailers that provide these functions, but new players and intermediaries. Thus, new models of organizing and operating collaboration nets emerge. The objective of this chapter is to discuss possible forms of collaboration. Collaboration nets are differentiated from each other by the different allocation structures of information, knowledge, risks and profits. Before we describe our four models of collaboration within individualization based CRM, the next section will establish a framework to evaluate these models.

7.2   Characteristics of Collaborative CRM: A Framework for Evaluation

Individualization based CCRM can be organized in various forms and models. Before describing these models, we will establish a framework for their evaluation. To discuss their particular strengths and weaknesses in comparison to each other, we will draw on four evaluation parameters:

(A) Integration Capability and Risk of Channel Conflicts

(B) Addressing Needs for Interaction

(C) Realization of Economies of Integration

(D) Realization of Economies of Relationship

(A) Integration Capability and Risk of Channel Conflicts

As discussed in the last chapter, the integration of the customer creates a collaboration net which supersedes the traditional value chain. Companies successfully pursuing individualization build an integrated knowledge flow that not only covers one transaction but also uses information gathered during the fulfillment of a customer-specific order to improve the knowledge base of the whole collaboration net. The representation of these processes in a knowledge loop model (Figure 7.1) stresses the importance of an interconnected and integrated flow of knowledge. All these functionalities have to be delivered in an integrated, streamlined way, starting from the point of interaction where information required for individualization is surveyed and processed in order to create a customized offering. Finally, activities that deepen the relationships and create customer loyalty are undertaken. All the communication with a customer has to be individualized too, following the concept of personalization. Furthermore, the model of collaboration has to be able to realize synergies between individualization and concurrently operated mass production (standard activities). Not only does the information about the customer need to be collected, but the internal processes need to be improved as well.

Different models of collaboration nets share these activities among a different number of actors, or group them all around one supplier. Different models may also have diverse capabilities of integrating these tasks or breaking down interface problems, and have diverse potentials to reduce and prevent channel conflicts (also discussed in the previous chapter): Often, manufacturers wish to market their product in retail with minimal restriction to consumers, and to build up high switching costs to increase loyalty. On the other side, the interests of a retailer lie in maintaining the marketing leadership and benefiting from low entry barriers and competition amongst the manufacturers. Further, individualization in the context of CRM drives channel conflicts if there are varying demands made on the ability to deliver experience and meet the high customer expectations connected with customization. This goes hand in hand with the qualification of sales clerks and the demand for a steady quality of service at the point of customer interaction. It is one of the primary demands made of specific forms of collaboration to prevent or reduce these channel conflicts.

Hence, collaboration has to be able to create an integrated knowledge loop, the benefits of which are not counterbalanced by new channel conflicts. Therefore, questions for the evaluation of different collaboration nets include:

- How strong is the integration of all actors along the knowledge loop? Does the model create new interface problems, or is it able to solve existing ones?

- Which kinds of channel conflicts might possibly appear? Are they related to the products or services in question, or are they related to different sectors or segments?

- What instruments arise from this form of collaboration that could be used to solve channel conflicts?

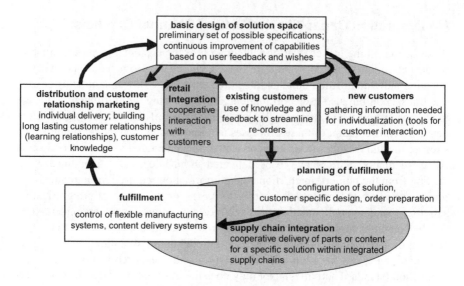

Source: Adapted from Reichwald, Piller, Möslein 2000

Figure 7.1:   The Knowledge Loop of Individualization Based Collaborative CRM

(B) Addressing Needs for Interaction

Interaction between a customer and the supplier is a cooperation providing benefits, but demanding input from both sides too. The benefits are two-fold: saving
potentials and value added. From a supplier's perspective, the benefits contain
both the possibility to ask for premiums and to realize new saving potentials based
on customer integration. The latter will be described as economies of customer
interaction and economies of relationship in the following paragraphs.

Prior to this however, we will take the customer's point of view. Getting a
product or service that exactly fits one's need is the premier benefit of individualization for a customer. To gain this benefit, the integration of the customer is required primarily to configure a product or service according to her needs. This
also includes ascertaining the information required for personalized communication. While being a core functionality of individualization, major obstacles are
rooted here as well. They consist of the uncertainties and risks from the customer's point of view during the configuration process (Huffman/Kahn 1998;
Gilmore/Pine 2000). In consumer markets in particular, customers often do not
have sufficient knowledge for the definition of a solution that corresponds to their
needs. As a result, customers may experience an increasing uncertainty during the
transaction process. Comparison processes are more difficult because of smaller
transparency of supply compared to standardized goods or services. Uncertainty
about the behavior of the supplier exists as well. The newer and more complex the
individualization possibilities are, the more the information gaps increase. These

processes are characterized by an asymmetrical distribution of information a typical principal agent constellation:[2] A customer (principal) orders (and pays in advance) from the supplier (agent) for a product he or she can't evaluate and has to wait days or even weeks to receive it. Without a clear reference point for the definition of optimal performance, it is also difficult to judge whether a case of warranty arises or not. This is much less difficult when purchasing standardized goods or services.

These uncertainties and factor transfers can be interpreted as additional transaction costs of a customer arising from individualization. One of the most important tasks of the supplier is to ensure that the customer's expenditure is kept as small as possible, while the benefit he or she experiences has to be clearly perceptible. Companies have to implement strong instruments to build trust and reliability in order to reduce the risk seen by prospective customers in an individualization process. Thus, models for collaboration have to be able to provide a sufficient interaction system to perform these tasks and address the change of providing a solution instead of just selling a product. Questions for evaluation include:

- Does the interaction system of a specific collaboration net address the change from selling products and services to providing a solution?

- Does it offer a dedicated set of options and tools that allow the customer to collaboratively create (co-design) her specific solution? This may imply also the availability of specific and efficient tools like scanners or design kiosks.

- To what extent does the system succeed in creating trust and reducing the complexity and risk perceived by a customer? How is this task shared between the manufacturer and the retailer?

(C) Realization of Economies of Integration

The main economic drivers of collaboration and customer integration are new kinds of saving potentials, which we will refer to as *economies of (customer) inte-*

---

[2] A collaboration net can be seen as a net of principal-agent relations. Principal-agent theory tries to explain how different actors behave in situations that are typically characterised through asymmetrically distributed information and uncertainties about the occurrence of certain environmental situations as well as the partner's behaviour (Eisenhardt 1989; Fama/Jensen 1983; Wigand/Reichwald/Picot 1997). The principal (the ordering party) assigns a task to an agent. Doing so, he has no full information about the capabilities, but also the willingness of the agent to fulfil this task. Whoever holds the position of the principal, respectively the agent, meaning who is the "poorly" or the "well" informed transaction partner, can only be judged according to the particular situation. For example someone being the principal in one relation might be the agent in another relation.

gration and *economies of relationship*. These economies supplement economies of scale and scope and provide the economic benefits of individualization based CRM (and thus a main incentive for firms to apply these forms). Their gains are generated by all partners collaboratively, but also have to be shared among them.

Economies of integration describe cost saving potentials as a result of the direct interaction between each customer and the firm in the course of individualization. They go beyond the differentiation advantages of individualization, which are expressed in the price premium. Economies of integration represent the efficiency generated when a firm establishes value processes that eliminate waste on all levels. More concretely, economies of integration are formed by a bundle of cost saving potentials in two classes.

First, they are the result of the build-to-order approach for individualization concepts following mass customization. Mass customization postpones some stages of fulfillment until the order has been placed. Here, economies of integration occur due to the reductions in inventory, decreasing planning complexity and fashion risk, better capacity utilization and stability, and the avoidance of lost sales in retail due to out-of-stock items and the prevention of discounts at the end of a season. The savings from these effects can be huge. Industry analysts estimate for example in the car industry that if customers bought a majority of cars built to order, the industry could capture as much as 70 percent of the capital locked up in the present system lost when inventory becomes obsolete following a change in models, production processes, and assembly structures, or locked up in metal and components kept on the shelf to meet unanticipated demand. By capturing this capital and by reducing discounts offered to move inventory, carmakers could realize total savings (reckoned by capital spent) of $65 billion to $80 billion a year (Agrawal/Kumaresh/Mercer 2001).

The second class of economies of integration is based on the aggregation of customer knowledge to better perceive market information, and can be achieved by all forms of individualization. Peppers and Rogers (1997) call this principle the "learning relationship" between a company and its customers. The self-configuration by the buyer allows access to "sticky local information" (von Hippel 1994, 1998). Sticky information rises when the costs of information exchange between two different actors are higher than the cost of processing this information within one unit. They originate in location specific costs like technological and organizational activities of decoding, transmitting and diffusing the information. For example, it is very difficult for a customer to accurately and completely convey information about novel product or service needs to a supplier. One reason is that customers are often interactively developing the need and the solution at the same time. We can argue that often customer specific information is sticky in that sense. Tastes, design patterns and even functionalities are rather subjective and difficult to describe objectively. By interacting with a customer in the course of individualization, a firm may get easier access to the sticky information. Customers tend to find it easier to develop the product themselves than to accurately and fully tell the supplier what they want. A configuration tool (just think of the "mi adidas" interaction kiosk described in the last chapter) makes it easier for customers facing sticky information to innovate for themselves (von Hippel (1998) calls this idea "toolkits for innovation").

Individualization provides access to sticky information. It may be used to intensify a relationship to one particular customer, as described in the last chapter. Additionally, new product development and continuous improvement of existing products can benefit greatly from this information (Fowler et al. 2000). Economies of integration are demonstrated by the saving potentials in obtaining this information by other means of market research, and also the savings by providing better fitting products and minimizing the risk of flops of new products. The firm can transfer sticky information into explicit knowledge. Note that this class of economies of integration results from the sheer possibility of interacting. The information gains are not exclusively based on actual sales, but only on information tracked from interacting with the users by using an interaction tool. Questions for the evaluation of different forms of collaboration (with regard to economies of integration) include:

- At what stage within a collaboration net will economies of integration occur? Who has the main responsibility for their realization, and who is most likely to benefit from them?

- Is the collaboration model able to decouple knowledge gained by interacting with its customers in order to deepen and re-direct market-driven and technological competences?

- How can waste be reduced along the whole collaboration net? Can interface problems counterbalance the new saving potentials?

(D) Realization of Economies of Relationship

Economies of relationship are closely connected with economies of integration and are based on the same source: interacting with a customer during the course of individualization. However, while economies of integration describe capabilities to improve the efficiency of fulfillment activities and are based either on the postponement of value creating activities until a specific order is placed or on aggregated knowledge from fulfilling these orders and interacting with the customers, economies of relationship relate to cost savings connected with the loyalty of one specific customer. Economies of relationship reflect in this sense the experience of a company with a customer (Vandermerwe 2000).

The prerequisite for economies of relationship is the ability of individualization to establish long lasting customer relationships (an aspect that was also discussed in our general model of CRM in the previous chapter). Individualization fosters customer loyalty, as a defecting customer risks to lose the net-benefits of the current relationship. During the previous interactions, a customer should have established trust towards a supplier and its capabilities to meet promised quality and individualization levels. The familiarity of a customer with a configuration tool or the knowledge about the modular structures of an offering can be seen as relationship specific "investments" of a customer (Riemer/Totz 2001). Once the customer has successfully purchased an individual item, the knowledge acquired by the supplier during the product configuration represents a considerable barrier against switching suppliers. Even if a competitor possesses the same individualization skills and offers a lower price, a switching customer would have to go through the procedure of supplying information for product customization a second time (Pine/ Peppers/Rogers 1995). Also, he or she is once again faced with uncertainties with regard to the quality and the producer's behavior.

However, contrary to the traditional principle of "create-capture-keep" (Clemons 1986) connected with switching costs, customers should not be "locked-in" to a collaboration net, but rather remain loyal because of the perception of the advantages and a unique benefit. Here, individualization, and mass customization in particular, offers many more possibilities when compared to traditional personalization techniques like direct mail, personalized web sites or micro-targeted e-mail campaigns.

Once the relationship to a customer is assured, the partners of a collaboration net can stretch their activities into other revenue-generating opportunities (in regard to this customer) at relatively low cost. They have no acquisition costs and low marginal costs, because information, knowledge and relationships have already been established (Peters/Saidin 2000; Vandermerwe 2000). Cost saving potentials arises additionally from using the information from a first sale for further sales. While often the first sale process is rather time consuming and requires a high intensity of information exchange, and is thus cost intensive, additional sales can be performed more quickly and easily. A firm can draw on its existing customer base to produce additional value for customers at little or no extra cost. The flexible capabilities and the increased knowledge about the needs and desires of every customer offer the opportunity to serve existing customers with new activities. By enhancing all this knowledge about a single customer in a continuously learning relationship, customers can be served better. The ability to retrieve such information represents a huge potential for shortening learning cycles and therefore contributes to cost reductions which we will summarize with the term economies of relationship.

A premier example for this principle is provided by San Francisco based Reflect, a sister company of Procter & Gamble (P&G). Reflect offers customized cosmetic products. Once a customer has individualized his or her very own cosmetic line that exactly meets his or her needs and desires, he or she is often literarily "subscribing" the products as Reflect can offer a unique solution that gets further fine-tuned with every further order, based on the knowledge from the previous orders. The firm can also easily cross-sell additional products fitting into the previous orders (in regard to ingredients, composition, fragrance etc.). We will explore this case in further detail in the next section.

With regard to economies of relationship, questions for the evaluation of different forms of collaboration include:

- At what stage within the collaboration net will economies of relationship occur? Who is most likely to benefit from them?

- Who has the main responsibility for their realization, i.e. which collaboration partner has the largest capability to gain and use the knowledge about one customer? And who has the responsibility to foster and strengthen the relationship with the customer?

- How is the relationship seen from the customer's perspective? With which player does a customer feel herself to be in a relationship? Are multi-level relationships possible?

7.3 Models of Collaboration for Individualization Based CRM

This section will discuss four models of collaboration for individualization based CRM. They describe an evolutionary path of development; starting with new kinds of collaboration between the customer and the manufacturer, moving directly on to collaboration with new partners in retail and arriving at models including additional players and intermediaries. Using the framework of the last section we will evaluate all models with regard to their ability to deliver the benefits of individualization based CRM, while preventing the drawbacks.

7.3.1 Consumer Direct Manufacturer Managed Pure Play

To avoid channel conflicts, eliminate the channels themselves and sell directly. This is the approach many companies are taking when entering the field of individualization based CRM. Many of the prominent examples of mass customization and personalization rely on direct sales strategies. Consumer goods companies like Mattel, Levi Strauss, P&G or Nike, which normally use multi-level retail channels, sell their mass customized products efficiently via the Internet in direct interaction with their consumers. Theory also backs up this approach. For individualized goods and services, transaction cost theory recommends, at first glance, direct interaction between manufacturer and buyer. Configuration and purchasing should be fulfilled without any intermediaries (Williamson 1989). A retailer would do nothing more than transfer the product specification to the manufacturer where each order would be checked, planned and processed separately. Thus, a retail channel would just add an additional (transaction) cost-generating level, especially today, where electronic commerce has allowed manufacturers to communicate and trade with large groups of consumers directly and efficiently.

Take the example of P&G's Reflect, which offers customized cosmetics on the Internet. Using interactive software, visitors to the site can create their own cosmetic line, mix and match various options like colors, scents and skin-care preferences to create a unique product at off-the-shelves prices. A facility in upstate New York manufactures the product and a "concierge service" in Cincinnati handles follow-up interaction with customers. The company is a premier example of how to gain the benefits of individualization based CRM. Reflect allows customers to redesign a product as many times as they want. In doing so, it intensifies the knowledge about any one consumer, establishes switching costs and increases customer loyalty. Many customers are already "subscribing" to their own cosmetic line (economies of relationship). Furthermore, the made-to-order approach does not only decrease inventory, but also, as mentioned earlier, minimizes the problem of new product development flops. But above all, Reflect generates knowledge for the whole company (economies of integration). The site acts as a "life panel" for all P&G cosmetics operations without panel effects. Its customer base contains more than one million buyers who create their own cosmetics and thereby formulate dermatological needs, evaluate new scents, bundle products, choose packages and develop new products. The customized order specifications are matched with the socio-demographic profiling information of each customer and the feedback or change of specifications after the sale. For P&G, Reflect is reported to be one of the most efficient market research tools (Warner 2001). Recent empirical research also reports that consumers are willing to give permission to use this data as privacy concerns are being counterbalanced by the value of personalized products or services (Gardyn 2001).

In order to reap the benefits that this offers, P&G decided to sell directly, thus bypassing the retail channels that usually distribute their products. Although big retailers watched Reflect very carefully, they realized that this model is not possible in a normal retail channel. Transaction costs would be far too high if a sales clerk went through all the customization options with a consumer. Thus, when launching Reflect, P&G realized that the largest challenges of the model would not be retail, but internal conflicts with the existing business model. In a wise move, they decided to partner with a venture financier and operate Reflect as a separate company, totally independent from the normal operations. This is, in our opinion, one of the model's major success factors.

Reflect's management has now realized that they need further contact points with the consumers in order to grow in new market segments. Many consumers are not willing, or are not able to customize cosmetics online. An online channel can never address all the sensual and tactile attributes involved in shopping for cosmetics. So recently Reflect announced the opening of its own stores where consumers can interact more closely with the system, learn about the products and create their first order. However, to make re-orders, customers are encouraged to use the Internet in order to manage transaction costs.

Taking into account the four fields of evaluation discussed above, dealing with the consumer directly prevents channel conflicts simply by not integrating any channel partners and establishing no collaboration on the retail side at all. Moreover, interface problems do not occur. However, conflicts may derive from outside the system if the manufacturer still sells goods and services that are sold in traditional channels. In this case, selecting products for the direct channel that do not cannibalize traditional channels is crucial. Manufacturers can also argue that innovative forms of individualization strengthen the whole brand with innovation leadership and therefore can create benefits for the retailers too.

This is the argument Nike used with its retailers when it started selling customized sneakers through a direct channel on the Internet. The firm prevented channel conflicts by choosing a product that was not made available through traditional retail. On the other hand, Levi Strauss failed with its direct channel on the Internet, since big retail chains felt attacked when Levi started selling exactly the same products as were available in the stores.

Economies of integration can be realized reasonably well in this fully vertically integrated approach. Information gained from the customers is not biased and can be related smoothly with fulfillment activities. Furthermore, the responsibility for realizing economies of relationship is set clearly. From a customer's point of view, there is only one contact name and no confusion as to who is responsible for reorders, feedback or complaints.

However, in the consumer goods industry, interacting with end consumers is a completely new task for many manufacturers, especially if one takes the large requirements of a mass customization system into account. Manufacturers often lack the capabilities to interact with consumers and have to invest heavily in sufficient interaction systems. Many concepts of individualization have failed as manufacturers did not have the capability to close the knowledge loop described above. This is especially true if not all communication can be carried out on the Internet and traditional offline retail channels are needed (as we saw in the "mi adidas" case above). Here, the cooperation with an established retail chain often becomes crucial.

7.3.2 Manufacturer-Driven Collaboration

Nevertheless, the hour of retail is not over. Within individualization based collaboration nets, retailers have to acquire new skills. They have to build up new knowledge and capabilities necessary for interaction with a customer. In doing so, the inclusion of a retailer in a collaboration net can provide added value. Many customers do not have the necessary know-how to specify an individualized solution that corresponds to their desires. While, for example, more and more users nowadays have learnt to configure a PC online, only a few may be able to configure a new suit, for example, on their own. Therefore, providing assistance to customers in the configuration process becomes an important task for retailers. Consider again the case of "mi adidas" introduced in the previous chapter. To provide customization and to acquire the knowledge that will become the base for the relationship with users, scanning data has to be recorded. As Adidas has no retail chain of its own (apart from some flag ship stores), this requires a physical presence at a point of integration, and therefore cooperation with retailers.

However, Adidas is the clear leader in the whole collaboration. Retailers have more or less their traditional role of a distribution partner and that of providing the point of sale, extended by a new set of interaction functionalities. The advantages, which can be gained by a manufacturer if retailers are included in individualization based CRM concept, are mainly based on saving potentials from such collaboration. This saving has to counterbalance the additional transaction costs (and smaller margins) resulting from the inclusion of a retailer. More specifically, a manufacturer can profit from decreasing costs in three categories:

- *Outsourcing of Customer Interaction:* As already mentioned, the proximity of retail to customers can provide substantial value in terms of more accurate and timely information about needs and market trends. This better understanding of the customer also leads to a more efficient handling of the configuration process on behalf of the manufacturer. Another advantage is simply the ability of retail to bundle customer interaction, therefore reducing internal complexity.

- *Outsourcing of Information Processing:* Collection and storage of customer data, system security and administration etc. are basic activities connected to individualization which require very specific knowledge, but do not represent core competences of many manufacturers. Retailers may realize substantial economies of scale and scope by providing this service for multiple manufacturers, therefore reducing the costs of these activities.

- *Economies of Speed:* New solutions may start on a higher level of reputation if they use a retailer's market name. Especially when selling online, the adoption of technologies and higher levels of attention paid to an established retail web site allow significant economies of speed during market introduction, also providing faster ways of entering into relationship building and thus increasing loyalty at a greater speed.

These aspects heavily support the market entry of individualization based CRM approaches. However, the problem of managing different contact points, and the sharing of gained knowledge challenge them. Normally, manufacturers deliver the same product to competing retail chains. Thus, a "mi adidas" customer purchasing her first pair of shoes with retailer X would expect to make re-orders with retailer Y as well. This, however, would include knowledge sharing about the customer within a horizontal network quite a challenging task. Furthermore, fully integrated IT systems are in practice often still more a wish than a reality. But these systems are needed in order to provide customer information at every stage and to balance the offerings with the actual availability of materials or colors.

Another problem is the motivation of sales personnel. Many retailers are characterized by a high turnover of sales clerks, low levels of education, and a lack of understanding of the need of relationships. This has proved to be one of the most serious problems of all companies following new collaboration based CRM models that we have studied. Incentive models have to be adjusted, and educational programs have to be installed to address the change from selling products and services to providing solution capabilities. The motivation levels of retail management to invest in corresponding programs is especially low if it is not clear who will benefit from the relationship and profit from economies of relationship. Often new contracts between manufacturer and retail have to be installed that honor the efforts of a retailer to establish a customer relationship during a first sale, even if additional sales within this relationship are performed directly with the manufacturer (provisions for the use of customer data).

Economies of integration can become a key incentive for retailers to participate in an individualization concept. Decentralized retail networks are the major winners of reductions in inventory, decreasing fashion risk, and the prevention of discounts at the end of a season resulting from customization. But it is a manufacturer's part to enable these savings and to promote these possibilities to its retail partners. Here, much internal marketing effort is still needed.

7.3.3   Retail-Driven Collaboration

Retail can become the initiator of new forms of individualization-based collaboration with its suppliers, too. Being closer to the customer, retailers are often able to realize needs and evolve trends faster and more precisely than manufacturers. In many highly competitive markets, price competition reaches its limit where further pressure to lower margins on the suppliers is no longer possible. In order to find new ways of differentiation, retailers try to upgrade their offerings by becoming more service orientated. Take C&A, a leading European apparel discounter, for example. At the end of the 1990s the firm was, to use Porter's (1980) phrase, "stuck in the middle". Its brand portfolio and product range was neither fashionable enough to compete with emerging low-price trend stores like H&M or Zara, nor could it become the clear cost leader due to expensive inner city retail locations, large floor spaces, and huge overhead costs. In this situation, going into individualization was seen as a chance to upgrade its service. C&A developed a new in-house brand that is now offered in some 20 plus locations in Europe, selling mass-tailored men's clothes (at off-the-rack prices). The whole fulfillment system was outsourced to two supply chain partners, a clothing manufacturer that offered mass tailoring, and a consultancy that was responsible for the process engineering and operational management. However, from the end consumers' perspective C&A is the only visible partner in the collaboration net, and it is C&A that has full and only access to all customer information.

Otto Versand, the owner of catalog order houses like Spiegel or Eddie Bauer provides us with another example. The company recently took the first steps to implement mass customization within the European market. The foremost objective is to decrease return rates dramatically. Returns count for as much as 40% of all orders in some product categories in the catalog order business. By partnering with a German pioneer from the shoe industry, Otto was able to offer customizable shoes on their web sites. However, as print catalogs are still the major source of inspiration for most of the companies' customers, the shoes were integrated into the catalogs as well. Customers could order standard models there, but were advised to use the web site for further features and customization. But even standard pairs were manufactured made to order using the flexible capacities of the supplier, giving Otto the opportunity of economies of integration such as a total inventory cut, and a strong reduction of the planning risk. In the market, the shoes were sold under the brand name of the manufacturer. This supplier was also responsible for handling service requests and interacting with the consumers. However, in order to prevent direct sales and re-orders, which bypassed Otto, Otto got the exclusive distribution rights for the German market. The supplier accepted this strong limitation as the sheer trust and brand name of Otto provides it with acquisition power in other European and international markets.

With this model, in order to change supply on a large scale, a mail order company like Otto with more than 10 million customers alone in Germany would need new and more stable relationships with its suppliers. Manufacturers are mostly based in Asia and work on a contract basis only. In order to develop these companies into mass customizers, it would be Otto's task to provide consultancy and training to the suppliers, as has been seen in the automotive industry. This is a new management task for many retailers. While channel conflicts are fairly low in this model of collaboration, a major problem could occur if a retailer has invested into a supplier to enable this company to become a mass customizer, and then the supplier would offer its new individualization capabilities to other (competing) retailers as well, or would even go into direct interaction with end consumers.

With regard to the degree of integration of all actors along the knowledge loop retail dominated systems provide benefits for functions related to the consumer interaction. Also, this model may be strong in inspiring trust in the consumers, if a retailer has proved in the past to deliver service and offer consultancy. The concept of experience shopping as a strong contribution to the need of delivering solutions instead of pure products will be in most cases triggered by a retail driven model of collaboration, too (Pine/Gilmore 1999). The objective is to create a point of experience rather than a point of sale. This metaphor should express the fact that experiences often become the dominant part of a business. Retailers may also create easier economies of learning and increase efficiency by providing individualization for whole sets of different products from different sources, if they are able to transfer experiences from one category to another. This aspect will be discussed in greater detail in the next section.

Nevertheless, failures like that of Custom Foot from the USA (Reichwald/Piller/Möslein 2000) show that frequently retailers may have strong capabilities to understand the needs of a CRM program or customer interaction, but lack the capabilities to control the supply and manufacturing chain. Here, the manufacturer driven model may provide advantages. A manufacturer can concentrate on delivering all activities related to an individualization based CRM system and focus on these tasks. Finally, getting market research information and relating this to the development of new offerings will be more difficult in the retail based model than in the manufacturer driven model, as there will be more filtering and loss of information.

7.3.4 Intermediary Based Models of Collaboration

When Nike introduced its NikeID program selling consumer co-designed shoes via the Internet, the company was forced to limit its mass customization program to 400 pairs per day, due to restrictions imposed by leading retail chains that were afraid of loosing their profits. However, as discussed above, established retailers are sometimes neither willing nor able to deliver the new capabilities required for individualization based CRM. But at the same time, many manufacturers are typically not set up for close contact with end-consumers. Here the inclusion of an intermediary may avoid channel conflicts if this broker acts as the visible market player. The same is true for internal conflicts between the individualization processes and the old sales force or between business units. The inner structure of many manufacturers often impedes a seamless and comfortable interaction process, since customer-orientation is not anchored in the company's culture. Compared to direct online sales of mass produced goods, individualization based CRM demands an even stronger customer relationship. It took mass customization pioneer Levi Strauss four years to establish a relationship management program for its "Original Spin" program in order to lock-in first-time customers into its system. Here, the collaboration with a specialized intermediary which understands the relationship processes of individualization could have sped-up this practice rapidly (Piller/Reichwald/Lohse 2000).

For the clothing industry, Possen.com, a Dutch company, may become such an intermediary. Acting as a scanning broker, the company takes three dimensional body scans of its clients in main street "scanning" shops as well with a mobile scanning truck. Supplemented by personal fit and style preferences, the data is stored on a central database and delivered to its own retail outlets and participating, but independent retailers selling made-to-measure clothes. Clients can also log in to the firm's web site and order clothing (given that a client's body shape has not changed too much since the last scan). The body scan data goes directly to different workshops in Europe, where mass customization technology manufactures the individual clothes. Even though the company strongly leans on the application of the Internet, it is not the most important sales channel. "You can use the

Internet as an instrument, but selling clothes through the Internet does not work. It is all about the service for your customers. And my clients always need personal contact," founder and managing director Bas Possen says.

The company's major business objective is becoming the central body data broker for the industry, enabling many more retailers to sell made-to-measure clothing without having to invest heavily in scanning equipment or needing to employ skilled tailors to do the measurements. Possen will earn a provision every time a body data set is used, and will provide the value added service of processing the raw body data into a customized cutting pattern, the technically most difficult part when mass customizing clothing.

The business idea behind Possen offers a premier example of the benefits of intermediaries for a collaboration net. They can improve individualization based CRM in several ways:

- *Economies of Scale and Enhanced Efficiency:* For many retailers the reuse of one configuration system (like the 3D body scanner in the case of Possen) decreases the cost per use and enables these technologies to break even much faster. Intermediaries can also enhance competitive pressure on the whole collaboration net by forcing manufacturers and retailers to design their processes more efficiently (for example by choosing only the best mass customizer from one product category).

- *Economies of Specialization:* Brokers like Possen have core competencies in configuration, selection and assisting the customers in finding the product that really fits their particular desires. By specializing in these individualization specific tasks at the customer interface they may be able to foster these activities on a much higher performance level at lower costs. Also, learning curves will be faster.

- *Shared Reputation:* Brokers may be asked to rank and assess new manufacturers and retailers in order to create shared reputation backgrounds of different suppliers. Customers don't have to rely purely on direct personal experiences, which is both inefficient and perilous since one will only discover untrustworthy partners through one's own hard experience (Kollock 1999). Reputation can reduce uncertainty and guide the decision of whether to trust the supplier. Great gains are possible if information about past interactions is shared and aggregated within a group. Here an intermediary may add new value too (Raub/Weesie 1990; Yamagishi 1994). By bundling a selected group of suppliers under "one roof", the broker assists a prospective customer in finding her particular supplier. If an intermediary offers own guarantees for order fulfillment, it will only cooperate with suppliers that have high quality standards decreasing the uncertainty for the customer.

As described before, a major enabler of customer loyalty by individualization is the knowledge acquired from the first purchase process of any particular customer. While for new customers an individual profile has to be constructed (connected with additional transaction costs), for existing customers the present configuration makes re-orders easier (time- and money-saving). For example, the last configuration may be presented and customers simply asked for variations. A collaboration net of different suppliers around one intermediary enables new possibilities as similar data can be shared. A customer of one supplier can be served on the level of an existing customer by a second supplier if an intermediary enables the joint use of one customer data set while securing privacy and secure transmission (Piller/Reichwald/Lohse 2000).

RealAge, Inc., a San Diego-based intermediary in the pharmaceutical industry, shows another benefit of intermediary based collaboration nets (Peppers 2002). Building long-term relationships with customers is a recurring challenge for pharmaceutical companies. A main problem of CRM in the pharmaceutical industry is interacting with customers to build the learning relationships necessary for repeat purchases and long-term revenue growth. By helping pharmaceutical companies engage consumers in targeted dialogue, RealAge provides a solution. The firm communicates with its highly segmented, 3.4 million members. Each week the health marketer typically sends between eight and ten million personalized email messages to members, including educational content, a bi-weekly newsletter, an opt-in "Tip of the Day", and no more than one promotional message. All information is fully personalized for each member based on various health and wellness assessments that the firm is offering on its web site. The firm also provides an important incentive mechanisms for its members to participate in the suggested recommendations and to report continuously one's health status (as the quality of the individualization – being the main driver of member loyalty – is depended of the accuracy and timeliness of each member's data set): the so called "real age score". This score indicates the "wellness status" and risk of diseases of a user by quoting the difference between the chronologically age and how spry one is biologically, depending on lifestyle, health history, and personal habits. Even if this might sound like a silly marketing trick, it seems to work in practice.

In an industry with plenty of privacy concerns and consumer-needs often fulfilled by different products made by different companies, the concept of an intermediary provides additional value. RealAge interacts between members and advertising partners to connect the users with those advertisers who are most likely to provide products and services of interest to them. All advertising is screened and targeted to make sure that it is relevant to the recipient. RealAge is also bundling information of various sources and about various pharmaceutical products for each member. In this collaboration net, RealAge is the actor that establishes the relationship with the members and is performing the individualization, not the manufacturers. An intermediary like RealAge can secure privacy more trustfully and deliver value-added much better than pharmaceutical companies. RealAge has one of the highest privacy ratings on the Web, having been one of the few health sites to earn a four-star (the highest) rating in Enonymous.com's privacy rating guide.

Who could become these intermediaries? Firstly, there is still a chance for new-comers and start-up businesses. However, as many of the business models of this kind are dependent on network effects, start up entrepreneurships may not have sufficient funds to establish these networks and achieve critical mass. Also, they face problems of building up trust and guaranteeing commitment to manufacturers and retailers. Thus, established companies may seize the opportunity. We see three groups of companies that are particularly dedicated to this kind of service:

- *Logistic Service Providers:* In many supply chains, logistic providers are closest to the customer. The trend of providing integrated services along the whole value chain like packaging, labeling, stock management, or handling returns can be supplemented by CRM related services. Logistic providers are also capable of handling interfaces IT and organizational ones between different partners and of handling complex data, constituting two of the premier capabilities of such a collaboration broker. Finally, nowadays these firms already act as clearinghouses and trusted agents between suppliers and manufacturers. These services may be extended to end consumers, too.

- *Telecommunication Companies* need to upgrade their offerings into more value added services. They have intense capacity to handle data, and also provide millions of touch points with their existing customers. Many firms in this industry also provide already billing and value-added services to third parties. But most of all: In the age of the cell phone why doesn't a telecommunication carrier provide scanning booths (for customized apparel and footwear) instead of telephone booths?

- *Integrated Media Networks* like TimeWarner or Bertelsmann do not only own some of the most valued and trusted brands, but also have direct channels via book clubs, Internet services or magazine subscribers to millions of customers. Take the example of a fashion magazine: The Vogues of this world are selling fashion advice and trend spotting rather than printed-paper. Such a company could become a valuable provider of brokerage tasks in the clothing industry.

While providing many benefits, there are several drawbacks connected with this form of collaboration net. First of all, the intermediary has to have a strong understanding of the whole knowledge loop and how to manage the seamless integration of all partners. From a transaction cost point of view, the introduction of a further player brings additional communication costs that have to be counterbalanced by new savings. Furthermore new channel conflicts can appear if an intermediary gains so much knowledge that it is able to integrate vertically in value activities performed formerly by manufacturers or retailers.

With regard to economies of integration, an intermediary in principle has a good position to decouple knowledge gained by interacting with its clients in order to deepen and re-direct market-driven and technological competencies. But the probability of data sharing related problems may become even higher in such a model. Now a third party, the intermediary, claims ownership of jointly generated customer knowledge. In addition, if a broker cooperates with horizontally competing partners, privacy and ownership of information becomes hard to guarantee.

7.4   Thinking Collaboratively

Much like the dichotomous choice presented by Porter's (1980) low cost and differentiation framework, managers must avoid getting stuck in the middle which may occur if they reach for old economies without understanding the full new cost and profit structure arising from individualization and collaborative CRM. Individualization must be included to a greater extent as a serious option in corporate strategic considerations in order to meet today's competitive challenges. Likewise, opportunities are being thrown away by companies that, by interpreting individualization and CRM as no more than a new trend that should not be missed, merely provide some of their customer interfaces with a veneer of innovative and individual measures.

Many practitioners still think of individualization only in terms of traditional direct marketing including direct mail, personalized web sites or micro-targeted e-mail campaigns without considering the effects on the whole value chain. In doing so, they fail to change the entire value creating activities in an integrated manner towards the customer. But only if the knowledge loop of individualization is followed along the whole collaboration net – including the customer – will all its advantages will come and stay alive. In this, more attention of top management is needed. As demonstrated by the examples of pioneering companies like Adidas, P&G's Relfect, Possen or Real Age, individualization-based CRM can change ways of doing business totally and hold new profit potential.

Meeting the challenges and solving the problems of individualization not internally within one firm but collaboratively with partners offers many opportunities to foster customer loyalty and increase customer knowledge. So start thinking collaboratively! We have presented and discussed four possible models of collaboration nets for individualization based CRM: manufacturer managed pure play (consumer direct), manufacturer-driven collaboration, retail-driven collaboration and the intermediary-based model. All models have their own distinctive demands and requirements (see Figure 7.2 for an overview). They are rich with advantages, but hold challenges that must be met.

The ideas we have presented here provide food for thought and perhaps will stimulate exploring the potentials of individualization for *your* business. But there is no one best way. The suggestions for action found here are not generic patterns, but rather are ideas as to where a successful concept of individualization based CCRM can begin. Never forget: Individualization has to be individualized, too.

	Consumer direct	Manufacturer-driven collaboration	Retail-driven collaboration	Intermediary based models
Benefits	• no direct channel conflicts • absence of interface problems • clear interaction partner for customer • clear owner of relationships and customer knowledge	• use of existing experience of interacting with consumers efficiently • cost savings by outsourcing of customer interaction and information handling to retail • use of existing sales channels and known interaction points	• close proximity to customer, existing experience of interacting with consumers efficiently • low level of channel conflicts • experience shopping • reduction of market uncertainty on the manufacturer side	• possibility of avoiding internal conflicts and channel conflicts • economies of specialization • economies of scale and enhanced efficiency • shared reputation, exchange/re-use of customer data
Challenges	• often insufficient capabilities to deal with consumers • high investments required to build up interaction system • possibility of indirect conflicts if standard products are still sold through traditional channels	• need to acquire new knowledge and skills necessary for customer interaction may demand investments of manufacturer into retail partners • motivation of sales personnel • managing of different contact points • ownership of customer relationships and sharing of gained knowledge	• need to acquire ability to be able to control supply and manufacturing chain • often weak understanding how to manage and integrate all activities along the knowledge loop • difficulties in realizing full benefit of better market research information	• very strong understanding of whole knowledge loop required • additional transaction costs • growing complexity of ownership of information and relationships • increase in filtering may result in loss of information

Figure 7.2: Advantages and Challenges of Collaboration Models for Individualization Based CRM

References

Agrawal, Mani and Kumaresh, T.V. and Mercer, G. A. (2001): the false promise of mass customization, The McKinsey Quarterly, 2001(3).

Clemons, E. K. (1986): Information system for sustainable competitive advantage. Information and Management, 11. Jg., H. 3, 131-136.

Eisenhardt, K. M. (1989): Agency Theory: An Assessment and Review, Academy of Management Review, Vol. 14, No. 1 (January), pp. 57-74.

Fama, E. F. and Jensen, M. C. (1983): Separation of ownership and control. Journal of Law and Economics, Vol 26, No. 2, p. 301-25.

Fowler, Sally et al. (2000): Beyond products: new strategic imperatives for developing competencies in dynamic environments, in: Journal of Engineering and Technology Management, 17. Jg. (2000), S. 357-377.

Fulkerson, B. and Shank, M. (2000): The new economy electronic commerce – and the rise of mass customization, in: Michael Shaw et al. (Hg.): Handbook on electronic commerce, Berlin: Springer, p. 411-430.

Gardyn, R. (2001): Swap meet. American Demographics, Vol. 23 (2001), No. 7 (July), pp. 50-55.

Gilmore, J. H. and Pine, B. J. (2000): Customization that counts. James H. Gilmore/B. Joseph Pine (Hg.): Markets of one: creating customer-unique value through mass customization, Boston: Harvard Business School Press 2000, pp. vii-xxv.

Huffman, C. and Kahn, B. (1998): Variety for sale: mass customization or mass confusion, Journal of Retailing, Vol. 74, No. 4, pp. 491-513.

Kelly, S. (1996): Data Warehousing: The Route to Mass Customization, Chichester: Wiley 1996.

Kollock, P. (1999): The production of trust in online markets, Working Paper, UCLA, 1999.

Peppers, D. (2002): A prescription for CRM pharma karma. Inside1to1, online newsletter of Peppers&Rogers Group, 11.02.2002.

Peppers, D. and Rogers, M. (1997): Enterprise one to one. New York u.a.

Peters, L., Saidin and Hasannudin (2000): IT and the mass customization of services: the challenge of implementation. International Journal of Information Management, Vol. 20, (2000), pp. 103-119.

Piller, F. T. (2001): Mass Customization, 2nd ed., Wiesbaden: Gabler.

Piller, F. T. (2002): Customer interaction and digitizability, in: Claus Rautenstrauch et al. (ed): Moving towards mass customization, Berlin et al: Springer, p. 45-68.

Piller, F. T., Reichwald, R. and Lohse, C. (2000): Broker models for mass customization based electronic commerce, Proceedings of the AMCIS International Conference 2000, Vol. II, edited by Mike Goul/Paul Gray/H. Michael Chung, Long Beach: Association for Information Systems (AIS), pp. 750-756.

Pine, B. J. and Gilmore, J. (1999): The Experience Economy, Boston: Harvard Business School Press.

Pine, B. J. (1993): Mass Customization, Boston: Harvard Business School Press.

Porter, M. E. (1980): Competitive strategy, New York: Free Press.

Raub, W. and Weesie, J.: "Reputation and efficiency in social interactions: an example of network effects," American Journal of Sociology, 1996, pp. 626-654.

Reichwald, R., Piller, F. and Möslein, K. (2000): Information as a critical success factor for mass customization. Proceedings of the ASAC-IFSAM 2000 Conference, Montreal.

Riemer, K. and Totz, C. (2001): The many faces of personalization, Proceedings of the 2001 World Conference on Mass Customization and Personalization, Oct. 1-2, 2001, edited by Mitchell M. Tseng and Frank T. Piller, Hong Kong: Hong Kong University of Science and Technology.

Sahin, F. (2000): Manufacturing competitiveness: Different systems to achieve the same results, Production and Inventory Management Journal, 42(1): 56-65.

Tseng, M. and Jiao, J. (2001): Mass Customization, in: Gaviel Salvendy (ed.) Handbook of Industrial Engineering, 3 rd edition, New York: Wiley, pp. 684-709.

Vandermerwe, S. (2000): How increasing value to customers improves business results, Sloan Management Review, 42 (1): 27-37

von Hippel, E. (1994): Sticky information and the locus of problem solving, Management Science, 40(3): 429-439.

von Hippel, E. (1998): Economics of product development by users, Management Science, 44(5): 629-644.

Warner, F. (2001): Girl, interpreted. Fast Company, No. 49, Aug. 2001, pp. 134-139.

Wigand, R. T., Picot, A. and Reichwald, R. (1997): Information, Organization and Management. Chichester: John Wiley & Sons.

Williamson, O. E. (1989): Transaction cost economics. Richard Schmalensee et al. (Ed): Handbook of industrial organization, vol. 1, Amsterdam, pp. 135-182.

Yamagishi, T. et al. (1994): Prisoner's Dilemma Networks: Selection Strategy Versus Action Strategy, Social Dilemmas and Cooperation, edited by U. Schulz et al., New York: Springer, pp. 233-250.

Zipkin, P. (2001): The limits of mass customization, Sloan Management Review, 42(3), pp. 81-87.

CHAPTER 8:

Collaborative Customer Relationship Management from a Market Research Viewpoint

Matthias Groß
A.C. Nielsen, Frankfurt, Germany

Jens Ohlig
A.C. Nielsen, Frankfurt, Germany

8.1 Why Is Collaborative Customer Relationship Management Necessary?

- Why is the concept of focusing on clients still a topic for manufacturers at the beginning of the 21st century? Should it not have been incorporated into daily business for some time?

- Although most companies have in their "vision" guidelines like "The goal is to satisfy customer needs and solve customer problems optimal", for the most part the offered product is still at the centre of marketing and sales strategies. How effectively is the idea of "focusing on the client" really anchored in companies' goals?

- Should satisfying the customer's needs not be at the heart of every action a marketing based company takes? More often than not it seems that internal structures within many companies have not been adapted to accommodate the change from a seller to a buyer's market.

Consumer expenses for convenience goods have been stagnating for years. This means that continuous growth for manufacturing companies can only be realised by competing for customer lifetime value. A variety of efforts in handling markets are necessary to optimally attract consumer expenditures. How can this be done?

Winning customers is the first step in the customer lifetime value; it's not the most difficult but certainly the most costly step. As a rule the costs attributed to winning customers are 5 to 8 times higher than the costs for managing existing clients and increasing their loyalty. Despite this, many companies still invest more into acquiring new customers than managing existing ones.

Current practice for product launches makes this especially clear. Investments in a new product (or brand) are reduced or stopped altogether once a satisfactory distribution level and the aspired trial purchase rate is reached. From this point on it is "do or die" for most new products, and many of them do not survive this phase. They do not manage the transition from being in the consumer's "Accept Set" (products considered) to the "Evoked Set" (preferred products). They never reach the evoked level in the consumer's relevant set. Next to the fact that the product did not live up to its promises, the main reason for this failure is a lack of investment to promote customer loyalty.

When are customers loyal? When they feel that their needs and wishes are taken seriously. Naturally these needs and wishes change over time. If products are not adapted to meet these changes, customers become disloyal again. This is generally a slow process. Formerly "loyal" customers start testing other similar products. At this point there is a high potential danger to customer loyalty. A further decrease in customer satisfaction leads to less and less barriers to product/brand switching. Customers without specific product/brand preferences are essentially dissatisfied customers with no potential for brand/product loyalty. Moreover during this phase customers clearly focus more on prices. The customer is definitely "lost" and switches to another product if this other product can meet his needs and wishes more effectively.

Companies can prevent or stop this process if they interpret customer loyalty as a continuous service to clients who have to be won over anew every day. Even 90% customer satisfaction can be too little.

Why is it so hard for many companies to incorporate a focus on customer satisfaction into their daily business? Generally it is not for lack of good intentions. However, there is a causal link between lack of knowledge about consumers' usage and buying behaviour and non-existence of direct customer contact in the fast moving consumer goods industry (FMCG). This clearly distinguishes this trade from capital goods industries. FMCG manufacturers use the retail trade as a mediator between themselves and the end user, and thereby transfer a key function to a third party. Although this brings many advantages – mainly with regard to cost – there are also many disadvantages:

- Manufacturers lose direct contact with their customers (end users) as buyers

- Manufacturers cannot independently fix retail prices

- Limited influence on product presentation

- Limited influence on point of sale activities

Evidently these disadvantages can only be compensated for via close co-operation between retail trade and manufacturers. The means that on the one hand both trade and manufacturer have to share information, and on the other hand the strategy on how to fulfil customers' needs and wishes has to be co-ordinated.

The retailer pursues 3 objectives
- Increase of penetration
- Increase of expenditures
- Increase of loyalty

for his outlets

 The manufacturer pursues 3 objective
- Increase of penetration
- Increase of expenditures
- İncrease of loyalty

for his brand

The retailer does not care which manufacturer assists him to achieve his objectives.

The manufacturer does not care which retailer assists him to achieve his objectives.

Contradictions & losing of efficiency

Figure 8.1:   The Conflict between Retailer and Manufacturer

The reality is that this has only been practiced insufficiently. This is mainly due to the fact that manufacturers and retailers define their goals differently (Figure 8.1).

The retailers' objectives can be deduced from the same three elements as the manufacturers' objectives:

- Increase of penetration

- Increase of expenditure

- Increase of loyalty

While for retailers the focus is on their outlets, the manufacturers focus is on their brands. In the past strategies were very rarely coordinated. Often both sides even worked knowingly or unknowingly against each other.

8.2   The Role of Category Management within the Collaborative Customer Relationship Process

The main goal of Category Management is to focus on fulfilling customers' needs and to jointly achieve it. Category Management therefore is a process-oriented philosophy that puts the customer with his or her wishes and needs at the centre. It promotes and even commands co-operation between retailers and manufacturers.

The Category Management process (Figure 8.2) can be split into three different areas:

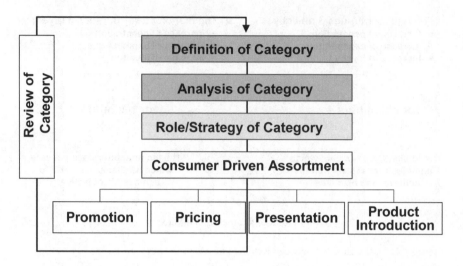

Figure 8.2:   Category Management Process of ACNielsen

Analytical Part

- Definition of the category

- Analysis of the category

Strategic Part

- Role of the category

- Strategy of the category

Tactical Part

- Category tactics (Consumer Driven Assortment, Promotion, Price, Presentation, Product Introduction)

- Review of the category

A category is managed through knowledge about target groups, distribution channels, customer potential and buying motives. At the same time companies have to take into consideration the fact that there is only a limited potential to individualise offers and supervise distribution channels in the FMCG industry. This increases the need/demand for a modular structure of products, measures, and service offers.

A coordination of point-of-sale (pos) activities – *the* point of contact with the customer – can achieve synergies that result in distinct advantages for the customer (in terms of satisfying his needs) as well as improving results for retailers and manufacturers. Therefore the advantages of Category Management are obvious:

- Develop a clear structure of work routines
- Give guidance to master the complexity of the subject
- Provide a way to eliminate inefficiencies
- Obtain an opportunity to get deeper insights into customer needs
- Generate a way to differentiate one's company from the competition
- Enjoy a chance to increase customer loyalty

Category Management offers another considerable opportunity: the opportunity to use the customer information generated in the process to strengthen and expand customer loyalty in the longterm. Customer oriented Category Management is not another leadership philosophy alongside Marketing, but is rather, a return to the original marketing objectives.

A focus on customer needs represents the largest possible common denominator in the co-operation between retailers and manufacturers. It also lays the foundation for a new quality and climate in the collaboration between both parties. Therefore Collaborative Category Management not only creates new impulses for the horizontal customer relationship between manufacturers and consumers, but also for the vertical relationship between manufacturers and retailers.

8.3   Which Requirements Have to Be Met to Ensure a Successful Collaborative Customer Relationship Management?

An important factor to differentiate one's company from the competition via a customer relationship management program is the quality of information and the way in which it is made available. This "new" customer relationship management takes the place of a management that was built on intuition and improvisation. Intuition and improvisation are the most appropriate definitions for the prevalent way in which co-operation between the sales organisation (manufacturer) and the buying organisation (retailer) was handled in the past.

The objective is to intensify the customer relationship by moving it from a simple association to a proactive partnership. This is supported by a coordinated/ synchronised handling of the market. It is necessary to continuously collect and update information on consumers and customers as well as to systematically analyse it. It is important to be able to respond to the dynamics in customer relations and the resulting questions. Therefore, one basic requirement is to build an efficient infrastructure which gains, selects and interprets relevant consumer data.

Today data management is essential for customer relationship management. The goal is to provide the customer with what he or she needs. And how does one know what customers want? From the customers themselves!

In order to gain relevant data, companies equally use both quantitative and qualitative market research. Only the combination of both approaches results in a comprehensive understanding of the consumer.

The selected data should include information on objective market conditions (such as sales volume, number of customers, demographics) as well as subjective market conditions (such as social values, rating of products). A third aspect is motivational research (needs, desires, inclinations).

It is important that the data and its interpretation meet the information requirements of those responsible for the customer relationship management. It is important for the data to be as precise as possible to ensure that the right decisions are being made. Furthermore, it should help to absorb the "customer lifetime value". A market research service (internal and/or external) that provides well-founded advice can be a deciding competitive advantage in this case.

As mentioned before, successful customer relationship management requires that all departments within a company be brought into line with the market and customer requirements. Therefore organisations have to create an infrastructure that will synchronise the strategies of different departments accordingly (Figure 8.3 example for three departments: category management, sales and marketing).

■ **Integration of Category management activities in department or corporate strategies**
  ● Which objectives are pursued with Category management?
  ● Which influence has this on other divisions?

Category Management Strategy
-Which categories und retailers
-Which timing?
-Which results are expected?

Sales-Strategy
-Integration in sales-strategy
-Integration in customer plans
-Consideration to aim system
 of the account management

Marketing-Strategy
-Integration in marketing-strategy
-Integration in brand-/category-strategy
-Consideration to aim system of the
 marketing management

Corporate-Strategy

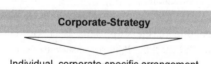

Individual, corporate-specific arrangement

Figure 8.3:   Development of Policies & Procedures – How the Infrastructure is to be Formed?

The basic orientation for the company and with it the company strategy are clearly defined:

8.4   To Consequently Satisfy Customer Needs

Understanding has to be reached within the organisations and strategies of both partners (retailer and manufacturer) and steering mechanisms have to be defined and co-ordinated. If this is realised, it's the method that promises the most success at overcoming seemingly build-in conflicts which are due to different interests or allocations that reach the level of Collaborative customer relationship management.

The initial resulting benefit usually generated through a closely grown collaboration on category management project is primarily non-economic. It cannot be measured in euros and cents. Because there is no economic measurement of its success, however, it may be very difficult to justify Category Management activities inside a company. But Category Management should also be adopted from the manufacturer's side to create more satisfied customers, whether they are retailers or consumers.

8.5   What Is a Market Researcher's Role within the Collaborative Customer Relationship Management?

Category Management is an important part of Collaborative Customer Relationship Management and is defined as a process that runs between one or more manufacturers and a retailer. For both parties the perceptions, wishes, and motives of the retailer's customers are at the centre of their considerations. The final objective is to satisfy customer needs in the most effective way possible.

How can this be done? By offering customers the products they expect to find in the retailer's outlets, at an acceptable price, attractively presented, and supported by point-of-sale activities that appeal to them. The objective, based on the outlet, is to reach as many customers as possible (purpose: penetration), who like to return to the store (purpose: loyalty) and satisfy the majority of their requirements there (purpose: expenditure).

We already mentioned one vital premise to ensure a successful Collaborative customer relationship management – the quality of information. This poses the question as to which dimension determines the quality of information. One fundamental factor for quality is pertinence of the information used. There is often a misconception that simply large masses of data are needed to successfully carry out the Category Management process. However, it is much more important to ensure that the available data is suitable to give concrete answers to the very specific questions within the Category Management process. A 70% answer to a question based on information that is only partly relevant is definitely not sufficient. Yet the sole presence of relevant information does not determine its quality. It is necessary to analyse the available data from a neutral, objective viewpoint as a basis to draw the right conclusions.

Market research companies can support the Collaborative process between manufacturers on one side and retailers on the other side (Figure 8.4). An essential requirement is that market research companies managed to overcome its past role as simple data providers and can now deliver real "added value" through an integrated consultancy service.

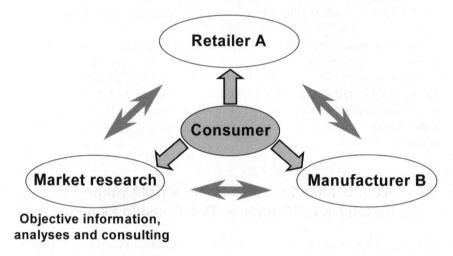

Objective information,
analyses and consulting

Figure 8.4:   Positioning of Market Research Category Management Project
Retailer B & Manufacturer A

8.5.1   How Does a Market Research Company Support the Category Management Process?

To answer the question of how a market research company can significantly support manufacturers and retailers, it is necessary to know which questions the partners in the co-operation process have to answer. These questions must generate "consumer insights" and satisfy customer needs in the best way possible through appropriate measures. Exact answers to these questions are the deciding benchmark to evaluate the relevance of the information.

Since the majority of relevant data is generally not readily available, one central role is to generate, analyze, and interpret the information. Here the combined use of quantitative as well as qualitative methods is essential.

The subsequent paragraphs outline the different questions within the Category Management process and address the potential market research methods that could be used in order to effectively answer those questions.

8.5.1.1   Category Definition

It is necessary for manufacturers and retailers to jointly define the category in order to ensure a common understanding. This definition is based on consumer buying motives on the basis of subjective perceptions as well as actual buying behaviour. The research on buying motives analyses usage situations where defined products can be used jointly or alternatively. This is done through focus groups, in depth interviews in combination with accompanied shopping, or interviews of consumers at the point of sale. Traditionally the main focus here is on the pragmatic question as to what extent new product innovations or niche products are part of a larger category or a specific segment. One of many possible examples is a toothbrush for dental prostheses, for which it had to be decided whether they belonged into the "toothbrush" or the "dental prosthesis care" category. Consequently products are placed at different locations within an outlet depending on customer preferences. Recently the topic of oriented category definitions has come to the forefront in many countries. This is clearly visible for everyone doing his or her shopping in stores that offer shopping "worlds" such as "baby centre", "wellness" or "ethnic food" areas. The success of a category definition based on consumer requests largely depends on the combined efforts of both partners. On the one hand, the manufacturer's category know-how is indispensable, but retailers on the other hand have to be willing to actually realise the respective category definitions, even if this creates rather "revolutionary" results.

Based on the defined product group, the category is then segmented further again looking at consumer behaviour, or more specifically, buying behaviour, at the point of sale. Who makes the purchase decision? Where is this decision made? How long does this process take? What are the main purchase criteria (decision making hierarchy)? These are typical questions that must be answered. In order to gain solid insights, it is mandatory to interview customers as soon as possible (directly) after they made their purchase decision and respectively observe them during the process. This should be done in the outlets of the retailers that are part of the co-operation project.

8.5.1.2   Category Analysis

Part of the strategic analysis is to prioritize categories and retailers in order to be able to focus the available resources on the greatest potentials. This decision is based on consumer related information regarding market shares, customer potential, loyalty and lost expenditures for different retailers. The objective is to identify those retailers with customers that are interesting (i.e. customers that generally spend large amounts on the category) but not loyal to the retailer's outlets. Although these "heavy users" for the category already frequent the outlets, they spend the money on the category in question at other retailers. The "simple" task is to implement suitable measures to ensure that these customers actually purchase the category in that particular retailer's outlets.

Moreover the category analysis identifies "key drivers" for the category as well as customer potentials through market segmentation. This is again based on consumer and trade oriented retail and household panel data .

8.5.1.3   Category Role and Strategy

In order to deduce the role and strategy for a category, it is necessary to compare the retailer's current customer structure with its defined target group to determine to what extent this target group is already being reached. Comprehensive category analyses based on retail panel information studies the importance of different categories for particular target groups, the company, and competitors. The objective is to determine which categories are best suited to distinguish the manufacturer with the retailer's defined target group and differentiate this specific retailer against the competition.

8.5.1.4   Consumer Driven Assortment

Once the general framework has been set, the first step is to determine the optimal assortment. How many separate items are necessary in a category, which products should be included in the assortment? These are the central questions that have to be agreed upon by the project partners.

In order to calculate the number of items required in a category, an analysis specifies the number of skus (shelf keeping units) that are necessary to reach a given quantity of consumers in a shop type with this assortment. This analysis is based on the status quo for the individual retailer. The role/strategy of the category determines the desired penetration/coverage.

As soon as the number of required items has been determined, the project partners have to decide which individual articles should be included in the assortment. This is done through a category-scorecard based on a multidimensional rating of every single item. This method ensures that the evaluation/rating uses all relevant parameters that can help to achieve the objectives of the Category Management process. The use of a rating method based on points also reduces the amount and variety of information. The results are individual assortment recommendations that take into consideration the role of the category as well as the manufacturer's category know-how.

Retail as well as household panel data are used as information sources in determining the Consumer Driven Assortment.

8.5.1.5   Promotion

An optimisation of point-of-sales activities has to aim at creating a promotion plan that is tailored to different shop types. The following questions are important in this context:

- How much attention do consumers pay on promotions?

- What kind of promotions do consumers favour?

- How efficient are different kinds of promotion types?

- What is the effect of promotions on the total category?

- How much gross profit and contribution margin does a promotion generate?

- What happens in the weeks following the promotion?

- How profitable are promotions for the retailer?

- How do promotions affect shop- and brand loyalty?

Two methods are used to answer these questions. One involves customers who are interviewed at the point-of-sale, and the other includes the promotional effects evaluated using trade and consumer oriented information.

8.5.1.6   Pricing

After analysing the effect of price changes on sales volumes, the main objective is to determine price barriers and optimise pricing distances between competitors.

- Which prices do different retailers set?

- Which sales impact do changes to baseline prices have?

- How important is pricing for the category?

- How do sales develop after a change to "every day low price"?

- Do price barriers exist and where are they?

- Which is the optimal price difference between competing products?

Weekly retail panel data is mainly used to answer these questions.

8.5.1.7   Presentation

Within the Category Management process, it is always necessary to actually implement the optimal assortment with a corresponding product presentation at store level. The objective is to present the products at their best in the outlet. Three steps are needed to ensure this, based on consumer wishes and buying behaviour.

- Definition of the optimal category environment within the shop

- Deduction of rules for shelf layouts

- Implementation of shelf layouts into planograms

For the first two steps, interviews and observations of customers in the store as well as an analysis of sales volumes for different shelf layouts are used. Space management software is applied to generate planograms.

8.5.1.8   Product Introduction

A Collaborative new product introduction certainly is a step within the Category Management process that has only been realised in parts so far. New product development is still a main focus for manufacturers and one they will not give up in the near future. This is due to the fact that in many categories success or failure for a manufacturer depends on the consumers' acceptance of the new products. Manufacturers therefore are very worried that the competition could get hold of relevant information if they co-operate with retailers on new product introductions, which would limit their competitive advantage.

Although a joint new product development is not on the agenda right now there are many possibilities to measure the success of recently launched products using retail- and consumer panel data. The development of sales for a new product is tracked primarily in a fixed group of shops where the product was distributed early on, in order to evaluate consumer acceptance without the interference of effects due to distribution gains.

8.5.1.9   Category Review

After the steps to optimise the situation at the point-of-sale have been taken, the effects have to be measured over time. This should start a continuous process that considers changing customer needs over time.

The revision of the measures taken should be done through a scorecard that checks against the objectives set in the Category Management process. The development of this score card can be initiated by the manufacturer, but is in a number of cases defined by retailers and has to be updated on a regular basis by both partners.

8.6   Effective Customer Relationship Management Based on Consumer Data for a Given Category

The first step to develop an effective customer relationship management is an analysis of the status on customer loyalty. This is an ex-post view that naturally can only partly provide information on future customer behaviour. However, looking at past customer behaviour can at least provide the direction in which the company has to move in order to achieve higher customer loyalty. Analyses based on a household panel are ideal to analyse past customer behaviour. E.g., the AC Nielsen Homescan-panel consists of 55,000 representative households, which regularly scan their purchases on convenience goods using a handheld scanner. The objective is to study the consumer behaviour of private households in the USA.

8.6.1   Who Buys What, Where, When and How

This allows statements on socio-demographics, brand and shop loyalty, parallel usage, brand switching and buying frequencies.

- The following example for a category X shows an approach how to operationalise and measure customer loyalty. The insights can be used to develop measures that help to increase customer loyalty continuously.

- The first step is to analyze which strategy regarding trade channels should be pursued for category X. The focus is on mass merchandisers. Based on buying and consumption behavior the second step deduces a product-portfolio strategy for the category that will lead to an increased use of brand D's potential within category X.

8.6.2   Trade Channel Strategy

Customer potential and customer loyalty can be measured and operationalised using two specific indicators. The example clarifies the approach for category X and trade channel of retailer 1 (i.e. named chains such as Wal-Mart, K Mart, Ralphs etc.).

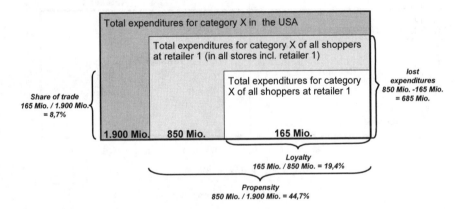

Figure 8.5:   Strategic Category Analysis as well as Analysis of Retailers/Manufacturers Based on Loyalty, Propensity, Lost Expenditures and Share of Trade

The total household consumption for category X is 1,900 Mio. $ per year. The households spend 165 Mio. $ in stores belonging to retailer 1. Consequently the market share for retailer 1 in category X is 8.7% for the USA.

Ultimately the market share is not an indicator that can determine the real potential for retailer 1 in this category or the loyalty of customers buying at retailer 1 stores to this retailer.

The real potential for retailer 1 is defined by the total category expenditures of retailer 1's customers in total. The expenditures amount to 850 Mio $. Therefore the potential for retailer 1 is 44.7% based on the total expenditures for category X. In other words, retailer 1 could reach a market share of 44.7% if all its customers would buy category X in retailer 1 outlets. Since this is not the case, retailer 1 customers spend 685 Mio $ in other stores.

How strong is the customer loyalty for retailer 1 in category X? Retailer 1 manages to utilise 19.4% of its customer potential. In other words, customers of retailer 1 only spend every fifth dollar in retailer 1 outlets. This definition for the indicator "loyalty" provides a behaviour oriented dimension that allows customer loyalty to be quantified and measured. The obvious question is whether 19.4% customer loyalty is a good, average or bad result for retailer 1. For a definite statement the results for retailer 1 (potential and customer loyalty) have to be compared with those of other mass merchandisers.

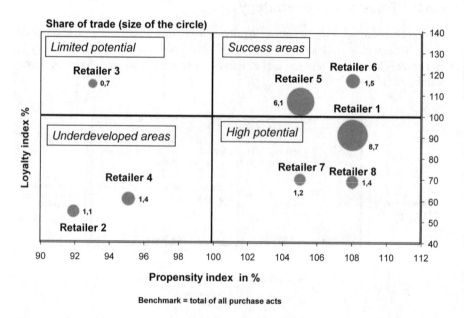

Figure 8.6:   Strategic Retailer Analysis Category Based on Loyalty, Propensity, Lost Expenditures and Share of Trade

Based on customer potential for different mass merchandisers and the loyalty of their customers it is possible to categorise the performance of the trade channels analysed:

Success areas: The individual trade channel profits from a higher disposition to buy among its customers and their high degree of loyalty.

Limited potential: Customers in the individual trade channel show a low degree of disposition to buy but are loyal to the retailer.

Underdeveloped areas in the individual trade channel show a low degree of disposition to buy and purchase the goods elsewhere.

High potential: Customers in the individual trade channel show a higher disposition to buy but purchase the goods at other retailers.

Figure 8.6 shows that retailer 1 has an above-average potential in category X. In other words: customers of retailer 1 generally spend more on category X that the average US household. However, they do not spend it at retailer 1 outlets. The customer/shop loyalty is below average. The customers of retailer 1 do not seem to be satisfied with the offered package (assortment, price, promotion, presentation). Other trade channels use more suitable methods to increase shop loyalty and as a result show higher figures.

The next step for retailer 1 and manufacturers in category X should be to search for opportunities to increase shop loyalty for retailer 1. Suitable measures could include shelf optimisation, assortment optimisation or joint promotions.

8.6.3   Product-Portfolio Strategy

An analysis on the product-portfolio strategy for brand D should answer the following questions:

- What kind of general buying behaviour do customers show for category X?

- Which different groups of consumers can be identified in brand D's competitive environment?

- Which brands are direct competitors?

- How can these different groups of consumers be handled selectively?

Consumers buying category X do not show a strong brand loyalty, they rather use different brands parallel or alternately. On average they buy four different brands per year and spend 2.8\$ on every purchase. "Heavy buyers" for category X even buy five different brands or ten single items respectively. As a consequence manufacturers have to find ways to increase customer loyalty to their own brand or alter their product portfolio in such a way as to minimise customer disloyalty.

In order to develop successful strategies to intensify customer loyalty one crucial question has to be answered: Which other brands are direct competitors and therefore are direct substitutions? Another aspect is the fact that category X consists of very diverse market segments that target various customer groups (e.g. low fat, fat free, natural-, regular segment), and almost all brands offer products for the different segments. This means that it has to be taken into account to what extent the general competitive situation is reflected in the different category segments.

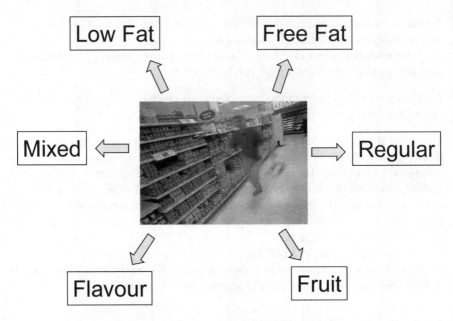

Figure 8.7:   Segmentation of the Category Determination of the Segment Structure According to the Consumer Decision Process

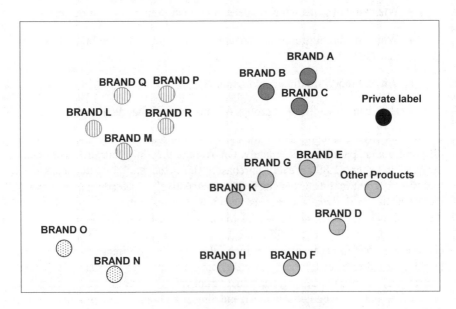

Figure 8.8:   Positioning of Brands – How Can Several Sub-segments be Positioned to Each Other Based on Affinities? Which Clusters Result from This Positioning?

Corresponding information can be generated through a parallel-usage analysis based on household-panel data. It answers the question: Which brands are used parallel to a great extent and are therefore substitutes or complementary. Parallel-usage affinities indicate whether for certain brands the parallel usage is above average (index > 100) or below average (index < 100). Figure 8.8 visualises these indices between different shower brands. The closer different brands are together the higher the affinity index (i.e. high parallel usage) and vice versa. As a result it becomes clear that brand D is generally in a cluster with brand E, G, F, H and K and this strong competition can also be found in the different category segments. Potential customer loyalty strategies for brand D should especially consider this competitive situation.

Which options does brand D have to develop specific measures in order to increase customer loyalty through the brand's own customers or customers of the direct competitors? The approach used in Figure 8.9 combines customers within the defined competitive environment for brand D into different groups (clusters). This cluster analysis is based on actual buying behaviour. The customers within the defined groups are as similar as possible, while the different groups are as diverse as possible. Based on a description of the buying behaviour for each group specific measures to increase customer loyalty for brand D can be developed. The result for the above mentioned analysis shows seven different buyer groups.

In a next step the clusters are analysed to ensure an effective market activities for brand D (Example: Analysis of cluster 1):

Cluster 1 consists of customers who have bought the competitor brand G within the low-fat segment but have not bought brand D. Brand G is especially strong in this segment, 4 items of this brand are among the top10 low-fat products. Which options does brand D have to become more attractive for consumers in cluster 1

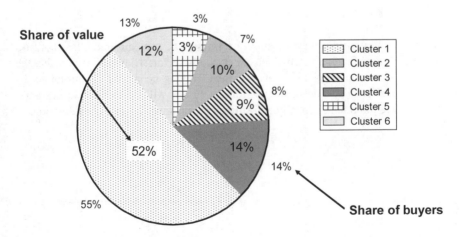

Figure 8.9:   Cluster-Analysis Summary

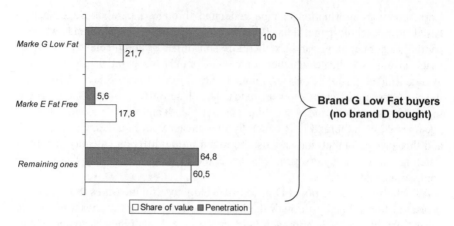

Figure 8.10:   Cluster-Analysis Description of the Cluster 1 (52%)

and cause them to switch? One option would be to replace existing variants with new and current flavours on a regular basis (especially during the season) in order to increase brand D's competence within the segment. Another option is to specifically target consumers in cluster 1 in their primarily frequented shopping outlets. This information is available from the household panel, since it not only provides product-related data (what do consumers buy) but also data on different shopping outlets (where do consumers buy). In this case, the best approach would be to specifically target consumers at the hypermarkets of retailer 5, since consumers in cluster 1 prefer these outlets. Point-of-sale activities that centre on brand D variants for the low-fat segment could generate trial purchases for brand D.

8.7   Outlook

Internationalisation and globalisation are prominent strategic trends for both retailers and manufacturers in the consumer goods sector. They seriously affect the design of customer relationship management. Buying behaviour can no longer be viewed only locally. The challenge for the future will be to analyse customer needs and requirements globally and still take local specifics into consideration.

CHAPTER 9:

Category Management: Why Now?

Peter Barrenstein
McKinsey, Munich, Germany

Stefan Tweraser
McKinsey, Vienna, Austria

Experts have been preaching the wisdom of systematic category management for the last 10 years or more, but with limited success. The time has now come for producers and retailers to give this new, cooperative marketing approach another chance: here's the why and the how.

Everybody is supposed to win with category management. Producers and re-tailers enjoy increased sales and market share, while customers enjoy products and product presentation that speak to their needs. Everything is optimized: Processes and structure on the supply side, product line and marketing mix on the demand side. Category management is to be an economic dream come true.

The dream, however, appears to be only a dream. In a recent review of category management activities, we found a far less glowing picture. In general, companies are analyzing product lines and procedures almost exclusively with a view toward cost efficiency. Only rarely do consumer preferences enter into the assessment, and even more rarely do product lines or organizations emerge in some way redesigned.

What is the main reason? Retailers' continued preoccupation with short-term margins, hence price. This focus remains a major barrier to experimentation with marketing tools and at the same time creates impatience with programs requiring extended implementation.

Producers also tend to be skeptical, sometimes even fearful, about designing category management strategies from a demand-based perspective. The danger that their joint efforts could end up in a reduction, or even elimination, of their product offering is, in their minds, simply too great. The game thus becomes de-fending their hard-won shelf space, whether it makes sense from the customer's point of view or not.

Another common problem is the narrow database that companies use for devel-oping their category management strategies, a database so limited that it barely supports the need to develop them in the first place. Companies also often fail to calculate profit contributions for their product lines and even products on a full-cost basis, and many do not have any detailed information on customer reach and loyalty achieved by their competitors. If a company does collect information about customer preferences in terms of product presentation, promotion or brand choice, it is usually only done once at the beginning of a category management project, but not as an ongoing effort. In short, continuous, systematic efforts aimed at achieving greater proximity to the customer remain more the stuff of marketing textbooks and consultants' presentations than of commercial reality.

9.1   Why Category Management?

Even in the consumer goods industry, large market segments stagnate and decline. Many consumer durables, for example, have reached a clear point of saturation. With 40,000 to 120,000 products in a store, some perceptible structure is necessary. In addition, basic needs have become less important in many product groups: Customers are demanding more value and this requires the use of a broader array of selling tools and approaches.

Strong brands are often able to create customer loyalty, build image and shield products from the cold light of direct price comparisons. But most FMCG companies tend to be focused on the bottom line, on improving profit margins. The top line – sales growth – is at best only secondary in importance.

Category management helps companies focus on both profits *and* growth. It is grounded in a deep understanding of the attitudes, expectations, motivation and behavior patterns of both existing and potential customers, and as such, enables a company to design a product offering that truly maximizes value to them. The customer's point of view is thus the integrating force in category management, a perspective that drives decisions on customer approach, in-store presentation, pricing and product line and also includes the supply chain to ensure uninterrupted market presence. A category management program is, in itself, an integrating force, joining producers and retailers into a common effort to improve performance.

9.2   A Huge Potential

The problem of poor implementation is not so much on the supply side. On the supply side, producers have long since moved out of the pilot phase and are now realizing on-going savings in cost and throughput time as a result of improved supply chain management, automatic reordering and automated factoring and payment, as well as through optimized logistics. With category management, they have also been able to close gaps in market presence and offer seasonal and fresh goods more in line with customer needs.

On the demand side, progress has not been as strong. The potential, however, is clearly there: With more effective product presentation, more optimal shelf and placement policies and generally fewer brands and products, retailers and consumer goods companies in a variety of industries have been able to increase results significantly (Figure 9.1).

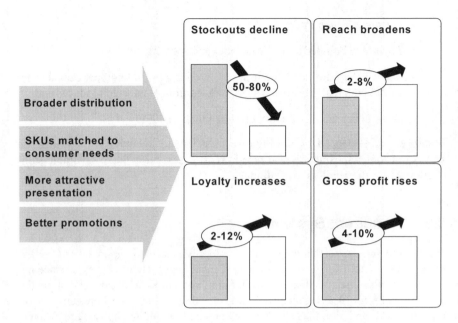

Source: McKinsey

Figure 9.1:   CM Advantage Retailer

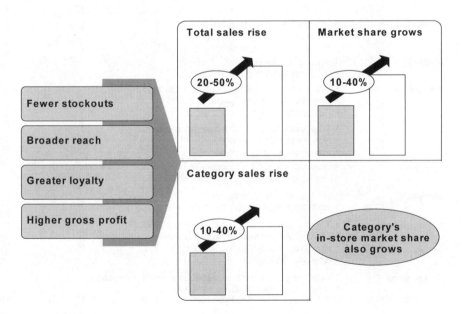

Source: McKinsey

Figure 9.2:   CM Advantage Producer

- *Customer reach* by 2% to 8%,

- *Loyalty* to branded and private label goods by 2% to 12%,

- *Market share* for newly defined core products by 10 to 40 per cent, as a result of both real growth and share pick-up from eliminated products, and

- *Sales* in the whole category up to as much as 40%.

Moreover, as evidenced by the increase in sales and loyalty and confirmed via survey, customer satisfaction also rose in most cases, providing a favorable spill-over effect for the retailers' overall image.

9.3   Required: System!

Essential to success of this magnitude is a highly systematic approach, as well as the courage to act from a more customer-centric perspective. Our experience has shown that this means, first of all, defining categories and category strategies *creatively* (Figure 9.3). It means finding the delicate balance between ground-breaking differentiation ideas on the one hand and the limits imposed by customer habits and the point-of-sale itself on the other. Creative new categories could be, for example, those built around:

Product	• What product groups to include? • Product line breadth? Depth? • How tailor offering to target customers?
Price	• Price range and image? • Individual pricing of brands/products?
Promotion	• Promotion types for different products/lines? • Promotion pricing for products/offers? • How optimize investment?
Store	• Where and how to place category/products? • How much space needed? • How improve overall presence?
Suppliers	• How many suppliers to include? • Appropriate terms/depth of cooperation?
Logistics	• How often to receive goods? • How optimize inventory/handling?
Consumers	• Today's customers, tomorrow's target groups? • Strategy for increasing reach and loyalty? • How raise purchase size, frequency? • How get/use feedback?
Competition	• How react to competition, especially in price/promotion? • How ensure lasting differentiation?

Source: McKinsey

Figure 9.3:   Key Questions in Designing Creative Category Strategies

- Seniors or singles,

- Babies and toddlers,

- Target ethnic groups, or

- Themes, such as garden/leisure, breakfast needs and so on.

Within a category, it may also be useful to break down the products and product lines further. In one of our projects, for instance, a retailer targeting the "Urban Family" included these product segmentations:

- *Attention-getters*, through which the company attempted to increase traffic and build image with the target customer group. Here it was clear that the company had to strongly differentiate itself from the competition. It therefore chose a fairly broad line of new – and also high-margin – products and ensured it was serviced with the utmost care.

- *Standard Goods*, where the company sought to satisfy known customer needs, in contrast to stimulating new or additional ones, as was the objective with attention-getting products. In this category, the retailer did not try to be ahead of the competition. Equal footing was felt to be sufficient.

- *Occasional Goods,* which were by definition less important to the customer. With these goods, the retailer did not feature them across the board, but instead created special highlights. As with attention-getters, the featured products had to stand out as superior to those of the competition.

- *Commodities,* where the objective was not to lose economic ground and to meet the basic needs of the customer. Here there was no attempt to differentiate the products from those of the competition.

In theory, retailers could segment all products in their stores in creative ways like this, but this or any strategy makes sense only if there is a good fit with the expectations, attitudes, experience and resulting behavior of their customers and special target groups.

Customer Relationship Management systems (CRM), which help companies build customer loyalty, can be very useful in determining if there is such a fit. Customer cards, surveys, direct marketing, customer panels and similar tools provide not only a sound basis for designing the product offering, but also for adapting marketing strategies to the changing needs of their customers over time. Because of the investment required to use such tools and the upside potential in efficiency and loyalty they offer, it makes sense to set up CRM not just for key product categories, but for all of them across the board.

In the customer-centric marketing of new categories, pricing plays a special role. This role, however, differs decidedly from that of the traditional one in most retail businesses in two ways:

1. Together, producer and retailer must follow a step-by-step pricing process from the consumer back to production. Dividing up the resulting pool of category profits is the most difficult task of this exercise.

2. Pricing becomes a more dynamic activity, not only because of the more systematic analysis of price/cross-price elasticities, but also because of the "customer-specific" pricing developed as a part of CRM.

Successful category management also requires some form of organizational structure to support it. Depending on its culture, a retailer could go as far as to give special category teams responsibility for all the essential functions, from marketing to purchasing, ordering and supply chain management. In this case, a critical interface to manage would lie between the category team and the various outlet managers. More commonly, retailers charge their category teams with a clear marketing mission and have them report in parallel, as well as in a matrix sense, with existing purchasing and/or supply chain management teams.

There is also a need for organizational adaptation on the part of the producers. Their product developers and product management, for example, are generally still organized by "technical" product segments, rather than those defined by customer value. In addition, a change of mind set is needed. Producers should for example help the retailer in the building of categories by suggesting related products that would fit into the larger whole, but which they themselves do not offer.

Another major area of adaptation is in information and systems support. Most important here is to ensure the continuous collection and analysis of data on price sensitivity, promotion success and other strategic relevant input. Over time then, companies can adjust their strategy to reflect any changes in customer behavior.

Last but not least are new managerial requirements. On the retail side, it is primarily a matter of expanding skills beyond purchasing. As many U.S. and English retailers have demonstrated, skilled cross-functional teams spanning marketing, logistics, purchasing and finance generate amazing energy when they work together to forge an optimal solution. Whether it means bringing in people from the outside, as some of these retailers probably did, or relying on internal capabilities, the key is pulling together a group of people highly skilled in their particular function.

As for consumer goods producers, we see the task as not only to become more customer-centric, but also to try to have more understanding for the needs, strengths and weaknesses of their retailers. This includes calculating competitive profit contributions for their products and product lines that are both analytically sound and fair.

9.4   The Best Way: Joint Pilot Project

Although a producer or retailer can of course launch a category management initiative independently, working together helps ensure that all the potential benefits
are realized. The best way of learning and mastering the process (Figure 9.4) is
through a joint pilot project.

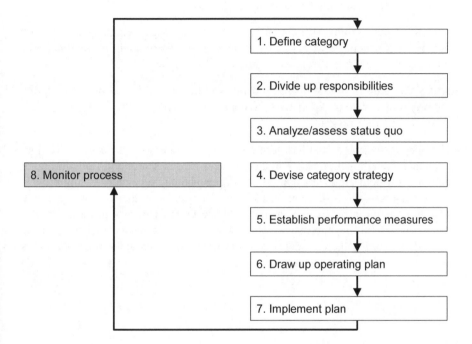

Source: ECR-Europe

Figure 9.4:   Planning Process

Absolutely essential to success in these projects is, we have learned, for producer
and retailer to:

Create transparency, combining and analyzing their different perspectives and
relevant data.

Establish a practical measurement system made up of clear, simple performance indicators of a quantitative type (e.g., sales, margins, market share), of a
qualitative type (e.g., customer satisfaction) and specifically for tracking processes
(e.g., throughput time, out-of-stock).

Build a solid, even new understanding of target groups and their needs, using tools like scanner analysis and primary market research (e.g., customer surveys, in-store observation).

Leverage the full range of marketing tools to ensure coverage of target groups – e.g., redesigning shelf space, "staging" the surrounding sales floor, creating supporting promotions and developing direct marketing campaigns on the basis of loyalty program data, scanner analysis or other sources.

Mobilize store employees – the all-important "sales front" bringing them into the process in a structured way, i.e., by training them, distributing information, providing motivation, organizing work groups and the like.

Allow the team to break rules, to change within reasonable, risk-weighted limits the way things have traditionally been done at the retailer or the producer; it bears repeating: no risk, no gain.

Category management that has been done "right" increases customer satisfaction, stimulates new buying needs, builds sales and market share, and leads to higher earnings for both producers and retailers. This should be enough reason to overcome any reservations or other obstacles that may stand in the way. While it may take time before a project can be declared successful, category management declared successful the impressive results we have seen achieved indicate that the rewards are clearly there. Patience and a near obsession about the consumer that's what it takes to make everybody win.

PART 4:

The Supply Side: Collaborative Planning, Forecasting and Replenishment (CPFR) as a Tool to Support CCRM

Part 4 deals with the collaboration between retailers and suppliers in supply chain management. Joint supply chain management is one of the key opportunities to meet the needs of the consumer. CPFR (Collaborative Planning, Forecasting and Replenishment) promises to achieve the physical integration of the demand and supply chain. Investment in recent supply chain technologies is aimed to get optimal results: a better supply chain performance in terms of inventory reduction, a reduction in out of stocks, better forecasting and promotion planning and a higher speed of new product introduction. To improve supply chain performance, it is critical to use both joint consumer relationship management and supply chain cooperation. Enhanced consumer relationship management leads to greater consumer insight and higher information sharing concerning buying patterns, consumer behavior, in-store measurements etc. This creates a more accurate representation of demand and enhances responsiveness of the supply chain to changes in demand. CPFR is about collaboration in the field of business planning with the use of data from both sides. Based on that data, production, delivery, warehousing and promotion get aligned between all relevant parties. With the help of sophisticated IT systems, the replenishment gets driven automatically. CPFR is also about a paradigm shift in the collaboration between trade and industry. In the past, the exchange of point of sale and forecast data was clearly restricted. With CPFR and extensive information sharing, both parties are better off in terms of cost structure and revenue stream.

In Chapter 10, Peter Hambuch, CPFR & Demand Process Excellence Manager at Procter & Gamble, shares his experiences with CPFR and suggests several best practices. He explains "Supplier, Internal and Customer CPFR " in detail and describes the goals and the business model of CPFR. He also provides some insights on recent CPFR projects with major retailers.

In chapter 11, Georg Engler – Manager with Accenture and a specialist in CPFR-related consulting, shows the long and winding road from pilot stage towards scaled application of CPFR. By asking "How scalable is your CPFR Solution?" he pinpoints success factors of cooperation between all relevant players in the supply chain and gives guidelines for the CPFR implementation. He also describes different CPFR implementation stages and technological requirements to start CPFR.

CHAPTER 10

CPFR – Views and Experiences at Procter & Gamble

Peter Hambuch

Procter & Gamble, Schwalbach, Germany

CPFR is an idea that is not just simply discussed by retailers and manufacturers worldwide, but one in which the first movers are beginning to implement. This means CPFR has become an internationally recognized and supported concept. One can describe CPFR in the following way:

Based on commonly formulated business plans, a production level is jointly defined as one which

- is responsive to collaboratively determined demand, particularly with respect to production and warehousing

- governs the constituent flow of goods between individual participants in the supply chain

- considers the consumer to be central to these cooperative efforts.

In addition to explaining the CPFR concept in general and the presentation of actual cases, this chapter will serve to eliminate confusion of terminology whenever possible. An attempt has been made to place the terms category management, efficient consumer response, CPFR and e-Commerce in their proper place with respect to one another.

10.1 The Objective of CPFR

CPFR is an inter-industry attempt to improve the relations between business partners in the supply chain through cooperative planning and information exchange. The following diagram shows in simplified form the interplay between participants in the process. The term 'Customer CPFR' refers to the collaboration between customer teams (CBD for customer business development), and the retailing concerns. The flow of information upstream continues via the collaboration of CBD with demand planning, which we call internal CPFR, ending in production planning via manufacturing. Supplier CPFR stands for the collaboration between manufacturing and suppliers. An improved information flow (customer demand) upstream allows a synchronized flow of raw materials, packaging and end products downstream, resulting in the efficient fulfillment of consumer demand.

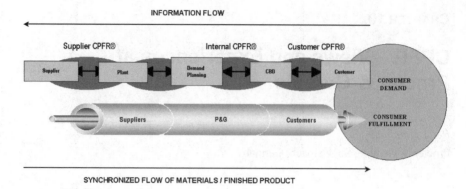

Source: Procter & Gamble

Figure 10.1:   The Flow of Information and Finished Products in the Supply Chain

The improvement of the relationships between partners is sought because in the contemporary supply chain the individual participants operate in relative isolation from one another.

- Communication is insufficient and discontinuous.

- Planning is not coordinated.

- The planning process of retailing is primarily focused on revenues at the POS.

- The planning process of manufacturers is primarily focused on the size of deliveries made to the retailer's central depot.

- Planning is based on assumptions

- Supporting systems do not exist (e.g. IT-systems)

- Because of uncertainty, overly large safety stock strains the supply chain, a consequence of inaccessible data on the expected demand of all other participants.

The results of a study by Benchmarking Partners in the US make this clear. In the year 2000, retailers achieved revenues of 3.2 trillion USD. In any event, 1.1 trillion dollars worth of goods and services were held in reserve in the supply chain during that time. This corresponds to a surplus equivalent to a 4.1 month supply.

Let us look more closely at the unsatisfying and costly inventory situation on both sides of the equation. The reasons why the so-called safety stock is maintained at unnecessarily high levels is because of uncertainty and inefficiency in the process.

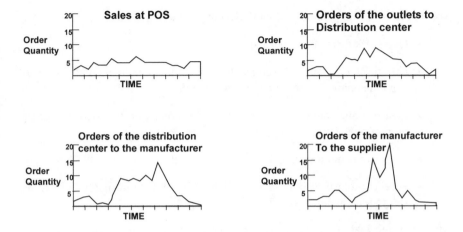

Source: Lee, Stanford University/VICS (1998)

Figure 10.2: Increasing Fluctuation of Orders are Responsible for Increased Stocks in the Supply Chain

- Uncertainty about consumer demand

- Uncertainty about the supply process relative to production and logistics

- Inefficiency in the process between the participants

The diagram above illustrates the consequences of the above mentioned problems. Although consumer demand in this example is relatively stable (upper left graphic), uncertainty and inefficiency causes observable swings in the flow of goods between

- warehouses and retail outlets (upper right graphic)

- the central depots of retailers and manufacturing (bottom left graphic)

- and on the production side between manufacturers and suppliers of raw materials and packaging (bottom right graphic)

Manufacturers and retailers pursue the same goals.

- Both see potential for the reduction of inventories in outlets, warehouses and at their suppliers

- Both want to increase the availability of their product throughout the supply chain

- Both want to increase revenues and reduce costs

Nonetheless, we find a number of inefficiencies in the supply chain

- Overstock throughout the chain

- Unsatisfactory delivery service from manufacturer to retailer, but also from the retailer's central depots to the POS

- Lost revenues through unavailability of a product on the shelf, or during promotional activity

- Deficient communication between participants

- Frequent and cost intensive 'firefighting' in the form of rush orders or short term changes in production planning

All of the information necessary to reach these common objectives is already in existence but it is scattered and not available in the required measure for all of the business partners. This is hindered on a worldwide basis by the closed systems on both sides and in particular through the attitude of the business partners and their corporate culture.

This is where CPFR is instrumental – in eliminating the absolute boundaries, so that a complete solution for the common good can be sought. Through CPFR and supporting technologies, it is possible that:

- relationships between business partners improve

- projections for future sales and orders become more precise, thereby reducing inventories, improving delivery service and avoiding shortages

- transparency is achieved through standards of measurement, which allow the monitoring of progress towards the goals which have been set

It is also important to know what CPFR is not. The concept is not only beneficial to large corporations, but is also useful for mid and small-sized companies. CPFR is not a software solution that is simply installed on the computer. Even when technology plays a significant role in the exchange of information, this is only one aspect of what makes CPFR possible. It is by no means a replacement for efficient consumer response. The concept lives through the commitment of participating retailers and manufacturers and the conviction of involved employees on both sides.

The "Centrale für Coorganisation", Germany's pendant to the VICS committee, refers to the following figure as the ECR house. Up until now, the ECR house has been a duplex. In both halves, different measures were used in order to meet the objectives of ECR in order to offer the consumer more value.

One side concentrates on the supply side. It concentrates on increasing the efficiency in the supply chain by introducing new logistical concepts and new supporting technologies like Electronic Data Interchange. Supply Chain Managers and IT-experts work together on this side. The other side concentrates on the de-

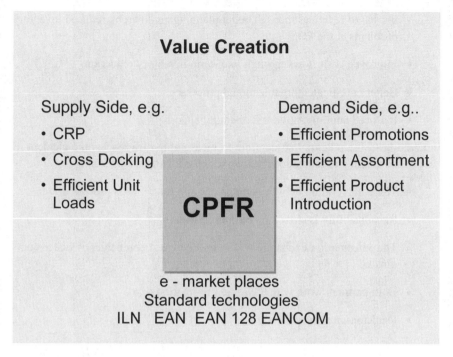

Source: Centrale für Coorganisation, Germany

Figure 10.3:   CPFR and the ECR-House

mand, ergo the consumer and for that purpose uses Category Management. Here people from departments like Purchase, Operations and Marketing work together.

The two sides work relatively separate from one another. CPFR integrates existing ECR solutions of supply and demand, previously employed in isolation, into a comprehensive approach. The core of a CPFR implementation is the willingness of the business partners to jointly control the planning, forecasting and ordering processes. This means coordinating and linking strategic, tactical and operative planning in pursuit of common goals.

In the lower region of the ECR house can be found the so-called enabling technologies. Like those for product identification (EAN), the EANCOM standards for data exchange via EDI or the offers becoming available in e-marketplaces help organizations to communicate in a more efficient way. E-marketplaces have the advantage of not requiring that every participant have implemented his or her own complete in-house CPFR solution, but rather can obtain this information through the Internet. Thereby, e-marketplaces will act as pacemakers for the implementation of CPFR.

The essential elements of CPFR with potential for both manufacturer and retailer are:

- Increased revenues through better planning and thereby reduced inventory problems at the POS

- Improved cash flows through long-term inventory reduction

- Better coordinated organizational processes

- Reduced administrative and operational costs

In addition to the potential susceptible to measurable differences, the element of "better coordinated organizational processes" has a particular meaning.

- The collaboration between companies and functions is process driven

- Responsibility is shared by business partners

- The information exchange within and between companies is better coordinated

- Both partners work with the same information

- Decisions are made jointly

10.2   CPFR – a Learning Process

CPFR is a learning process, which means that lessons learned and information gathered flow continuously into the control process. The gap analysis of the joint business plan also belongs to this process, which is essentially an analysis of the precision of the forecasts or an analysis of completed promotions and the flow of those insights into future forecasts.

In particular, the collaborative evaluation of the results of completed promotions vs. forecasts offers important understanding and enables the comparison and use of historical data for future planning. The effects on the targeted sales are influenced by

- price;

- type and quality of promotional support; and

- season and weather.

The CPFR commission of ECR DACH, together with representatives from retailing and manufacturing, developed the following depiction of the CPFR business model as a learning process.

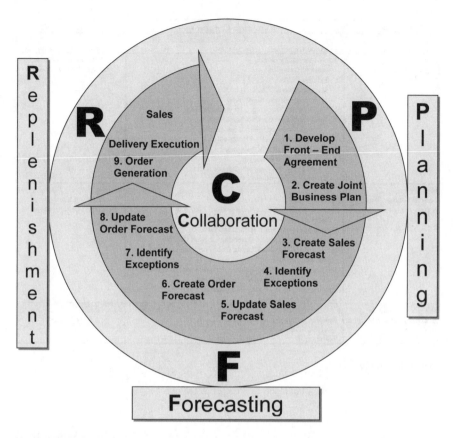

Source: Centrale für Coorganisation, Germany

Figure 10.4:   CPFR as a Learning Process

CPFR as a learning process is reflected in the collaboration with our customers in North America. The following example (see Figure 10.5 below) is a simplified illustration of the CPFR work plan that Procter & Gamble CBD (Customer Business Development) developed together with a customer and shows what has happened over the span of one year:

- The frequency of the individual steps (yearly, quarterly, weekly)

- The expected results of the individual steps (business planning, target performance comparison)

- The responsibilities (from senior management to analysts)

Frequency	Expected Outcomes	Responsible
Annually		
Renew Team Charter	Corporate Objectives / Expectations	Customer / P&G Senior Mgt.
Review / Renew Joint Business Plan	A) Joint Category Goals: - Role of Category - Pricing Plans - Merchandising Plans - New Item Introduction Plans B) Joint Results Tracking & Review Process: - Develop Score Card to Track Results - Confirm Gaps between Goal and Target - Exception Resolution Process - Schedule Quarterly Reviews C) Joint Alignment Process: - Verify Goals/Results will Deliver Corporate Objectives Charter	Account Manager & Buyer: Lead Process
Quarterly		
Joint Business Plan & Gap Analysis	- Review Score Card / Gap Analysis - Review Merchandising Results from Previous Quarter /Gap Analysis Plan - Develop / Revise Merchandizing Plans Volume Forecast and Calendar for Next Quarter - Review Base Volume Results from Previous Quarter and Gap Analysis - Develop / Revise Base Volume Forecast for next Quarter - Develop Plans to Resolve Volume Gaps - Review and Revise Exception Criteria - Document CPFR Wins	Account Manager & Buyer: Lead Process
Weekly		
Exception Management / Review Actuals	- Resolve critical Exceptions - Revised POS and shipment - Forecast	Data Analyst

Source: Procter & Gamble

Figure 10.5: CPFR Work Plan Used by Procter & Gamble

Taken collectively, the CPFR business model can be broken down into the following three base processes:

- The business planning between manufacturer and retailer

- The forecast of expected sales and delivery sizes

- Inventory control from production and distribution through to POS.

10.3 Collaboration – The Core of the Concept

CPFR is a business model, which breaks with superseded behaviors and processes. It offers a comprehensive solution, draws the customer into its considerations and connects the demand side with the supply side. The core of the concept is the 'C'. The relevant business processes involved are coordinated and synchronized across company lines. The prerequisite for this is the willingness of the business partners to collectively guide the planning, forecasting and supply processes. The 'C' for Collaboration is a necessary condition for integration. Business functions, which were previously isolated, are being bound together through CPFR. The quality of 'C' becomes apparent through the fair handling of exceptional situations. When, for example, the development of business does not follow as expected, solutions must be jointly sought. The more strongly 'C' is present, the higher the quality that will be achieved in the dimensions of 'P', 'F' and 'R'.

The 'C' fosters a cooperative culture, builds trust, aims for communication and information exchange and creates win-win relationships between business partners. It is proactive and not reactive.

The development of joint business plans and the measurement of results throughout the supply chain is based on a cooperative process. Cooperative processes support continual improvement.

Cooperation enables the necessary changes in organizational structures towards creating multi-functional teams, whereby the necessary training and the selection of appropriate criteria for measurement support the formation of efficient team structures.

Technology that supports cooperation is being implemented and supports the entire CPFR process. Integrated systems will close the gap between processes and technology.

CPFR leads to tangible and intangible advantages, which have been evaluated through pilot projects between manufacturers and retailers (Source: Transora):

- Improvement of forecasting accuracy $10 - 40\%$

- Inventory reduction in the supply chain $10 - 15\%$

- Improvement in service $0.5 - 2.0\%$

- Growth in revenues $2 - 25\%$
  (through reduced out-of-stocks on shelf and during promotions)

- Reduced warehousing and transport costs $3 - 10\%$

- Improved relations between business partners

- Better internal communication/planning

Around the globe, a tremendous effort is being made to prepare for the implementation of CPFR. Manufacturers and retailers are at the same time busy validating the advantages within pilot projects. These projects also seek to play a formative role in defining the CPFR service functions of the electronic marketplace (GNX, WWRE, CPG, Transora). Based on input from the real world, the tools are being improved and enhanced further in collaboration with their respective software developers. In the same way, the respective organizations (GCI, VICS, EAN/UCC) are working on the standards which will be necessary to support data exchange over the Internet.

10.4 Collaboration through the Entire Supply Chain at Procter & Gamble

Since we are taking the entire supply chain into consideration, the topic of CPFR is not complete without a discussion on collaborations between P&G and its trading partners. The collaborations continue internally, in order to ensure that the information flow between company divisions thrives. Essentially, this means collaboration between the CBD teams and demand planning on forecasting and product availability. The constantly updated forecast from demand planning is the basis for production planning in the factories. Logically, the CPFR concept is useful in the collaboration between the plants and the suppliers of raw materials and packaging.

Procter & Gamble has begun projects across the entire supply chain in order to bring CPFR to realization:

- Between CBD teams and retail companies

- Internally, between CBD teams and demand planning

- Between factories and their suppliers

10.4.1 CPFR with Retail Organizations

Whole arrays of projects are underway with our partners in retail, primarily in North America and in Europe. The goal is to evaluate the potential of CPFR and to jointly test and improve the necessary tools in the field and to bring P&G in a position to implement CPFR on a large scale. With reference to the technology, we use Syncra software and the tools of the e-markets: GNX and WWRE. We also have pilot projects, which are serving the development of tools for building extranets for retailers. In Europe, the focus of CPFR cooperation is on the optimization of business processes related to promotions. This begins with joint planning (product, week, advertising support etc.) and continues with forecasting, sales tracking and inventory monitoring during the promotions. The success of the common business is then measured on the timeliness and sufficiency of material at various places along the supply chain (frequency of out-of-stocks and surpluses). Short-term firefighting in the form of costly rush orders should also be avoided. Concrete results from cooperation with Danish retailer Dansk are shown below.

- Forecast accuracy for promotional revenues

- Improved 83 – 98.5%

- Inventory reduction in Dansk's central depot

- Reduced from 2.1 to 1.9 weeks reserve

- Product availability in Dansk outlets

- Improved from 98.36 to 99.38%

- Rush orders

- Reduced 20%

The pilot project with Metro AG in Germany also addressed the insufficient planning of promotions. Through collaboration, the following problems were identified:

- Inadequate communication in planning

- Insufficiently defined business processes

- Responsibilities not clearly defined

- Differing evaluation criteria (units of measure)

- Information which was insufficient, inexact and outdated

Corresponding to the problems identified, the following objectives were identified:

- Increase sales through a reduction in out-of-stocks

- Cost reduction along the supply chain through, among other things, inventory optimization including promotions left-overs

- Learn, test and develop further

Within the cooperative agreement, the focus was placed on the following individual elements (The work process was supported through a work flow tool):

- Planning the promotion

- Forecast the promotion volume

- Control of outlet orders and inventory

- Monitoring the promotion sales

- Evaluation of the promotion after its conclusion

No results have been made public yet. The teams on both sides have expressed some commonly held beliefs about their work:

- We do promotion management with our partner, Internet supported with common systems, data and processes

- Through cooperation with our partner we are able to achieve more

- We have an improved promotions process

- We are convinced we can increase sales and reduce inventory

- It is doable

- CPFR begins with small steps. Start small and simple, be patient and expand

10.4.2 CPFR Internally

It is the responsibility of our CBD teams to hand-off the business plans they developed jointly with retailers to the demand planning group, so that the customer specific forecast is incorporated into a total forecast. In Germany in particular, information on planned promotions plays an essential role because enormous pikes in the forecast, production and delivery to the retailers and on to its outlets are daily business. The following image will serve to clarify.

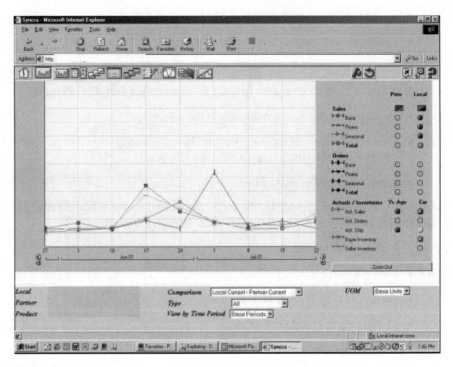

Legend:

I   Line: Sales of a retail chain(sale at POS according to scanner data)

—   Line: P&G deliveries to the distribution center of a retailer

■   Line: Delivery forecast for deliveries from P&G to the distribution center

X   Line: Average weekly inventory in the distribution center of the retailer

Source: Syncra/Procter & Gamble

Figure 10.6:   Forecast-Management of Procter & Gamble

The chart in Figure 10.6 shows the course of the delivery forecast, the P&G deliveries and the sales in the outlets at the weekly level. The sales peak in July is clear, along with the accompanying peak in deliveries, which was accurately anticipated eight weeks before shipment along with the development of inventory in the preceding two weeks. In the week of the promotion, sales with an index of 500 points over the normal volume were recorded. In order to ensure availability along the entire supply chain with such severe changes in demand, very good planning and communication are necessary on the part of all involved.

In order to support the CBD teams with planning and to improve P&G's internal communication, we began a pilot project in the first half of 2001 and began to test a tool named Syncra. Syncra was developed by Syncra Systems of Cambridge, MA. The system is designed to support CPFR. It is based on e-commerce standards and supports the communication between cooperating partners. Procter & Gamble chose Syncra as its CPFR software and Transora as its e-marketplace. In principle, the customer supervisors' have a large amount of data available to them, which they can use for forecasting. Depending on availability, this information is composed of items like delivery amounts from P&G to its customers, POS scanner data from its customers, details of the customer's warehouse activity and inventories, access to the customer's extranet, or historical information on sales targets during promotions. This data comes from different sources at P&G and the retail partner and is accessible through different systems.

The amount of effort required on the part of the CBD to use all of this information, for example, to estimate the promotional volume with the expected accuracy, is a substantial task. We have defined the following general requirements in order to support the process of volume planning; we want one tool for planning, plan supervision, and communication:

- Volume planning   →   Forecast

- Volume tracking   →   Delivery vs. Forecast

- Communication   →   Demand planning

The tool should make the data which comes out of the information systems at P&G and its customers transparent.

- Begins at the lowest level (week, EAN)

- With a compression of customer structure and product hierarchy

- Planned promotional business

- Planned base business

- Customer's POS data

- Customer's inventory

- P&G delivery amount

Syncra is a tool which meets these criteria, presenting the various pieces of information transparently in a tabular or graphic format. It is a user friendly system with a short learning curve. Access to Syncra is via a web browser after inputting a user name and password.

With the exception of the planned promotion, we load the above-mentioned information into the system. For the calculation of forecasts for base business, we prefer to use data on our customers' drafts from inventory or our weekly deliveries to their central depot. The structuring of product hierarchies is done in consultation with the CBD teams. It is the customer supervisor's job to create the forecasts in the system and to keep them current. That can take place online directly or through a tool based on Excel that automatically transfers planning data into Syncra. The planning time frame shown is three months and is displayed on a weekly level.

The test with selected CBD teams in Germany, Austria and Switzerland and the chosen product categories was successful. On the technical side, the flow of information met with our expectations. More importantly, the forecast accuracy of our CBD teams markedly improved. Currently we assume that six weeks before delivery, 80% of the delivery amount on EAN and at the weekly level can be estimated within a plus or minus 25% range. Similarly, the tools have proven themselves with respect to communication between CBD teams and demand planning. Both parties used the same system and worked with the same data. In addition, there was the potential to open the system to trade partners in order to support CPFR from the retail side. As appropriate to the success, the decision was made to proceed with a system wide implementation, so that by the beginning of 2002, all CBD teams and all product categories in Germany, Austria and Switzerland will be able to participate.

10.4.3 CPFR with Suppliers

The collaboration with factories and their suppliers is comparable to that between CBD teams and their customers. Of course the information exchange doesn't have to do with the finished product but rather with raw materials and packaging. After the production planning stands the production, storage and delivery to the suppliers is collaboratively determined. CPFR between all partners in the supply chain assures that information on the expected sale at the outlet flows through the entire chain and is translated into meaningful data at every stage. On a weekly (t) timeline, such a process appears as follows.

Activity	Week	Information basis
Execution of a promotion in outlets	t	EAN consumption units
Delivery to outlets	t−1	EAN shipment units

Delivery to retail central depot	t–2	EAN shipment units
Delivery to manufacturers central depot	t–3	EAN shipment units
Production	t–4	IAN internal article number
Delivery of raw material to plant	t–5	EAN, IAN
Production of raw materials	t–6	EAN, IAN

On the one hand, this example does not naturally apply to all manufacturers in all industries. On the other, it demonstrates that forecasting, forecasting accuracy and above all communication between all parties are the keys to success. Success is in creating product availability at the right time and at the right spot in the supply chain.

Procter & Gamble has begun several projects which, with the help of Syncra Systems, are testing CPFR between factories and suppliers. Here we use Syncra to support vendor managed inventory (VMI) as well. This means that based on the information in Syncra, our suppliers take over the responsibility for inventory control in our plants.

10.4.4 Experiences at Procter & Gamble with Pilot Projects

The use of CPFR across the entire supply chain is realizable even though there remain shortcomings in the system. Work is being done to rectify them. Interfaces between the systems are being developed. This has resulted in a unique opportunity to create global standards for data exchange. The desire for collaboration between business partners must be present on both sides and documented in a contract between them. CPFR must be brought to life by team leaders on both sides. The joint business plan is the basis for collaborative work in forecasting. To begin, the collaboration must set priorities. One should not begin with all nine steps of the CPFR model at once. Focus allows a quick start, which also allows both sides to learn quickly. One priority for CPFR between manufacturing and retail could be that one begins with sales forecasts for promotions. Inventory build up during new product introductions or with the more complex task of product redeployment (inventory reduction with the old EAN, inventory build up with the new EAN) are likewise appropriate for collaboration. To start with, various partners should analyze the same process so that they can not only learn from one another but also jointly recognize inefficiencies in the current process. The technology is important, but at the beginning it need not be perfect. What is essential is that the necessary information flow is not broken. Thinking long-term, we need to move towards automated forecast creation and exchange. Otherwise, the expansion of pilot projects is not scalable.

10.5 Epilogue

The CPFR concept was developed in 1997-1998 by a number of manufacturers and retailers in the US. In 2000-2002, CPFR is being discussed around the world and is getting accepted and supported as being a progressive concept. Its potential has been validated. The coming e-markets will support CPFR with their service. The necessary standards for the required data exchange are under development. It is up to us, the participants in the supply chain, whether supplier, manufacturer or retailer, to support the concept and to work towards the realization of its potential. No link in the chain can do it alone. It only works when we work together.

CHAPTER 11:

How to Scale Your CPFR-Pilot

Georg Engler
Accenture, Sulzbach, Germany

11.1 The Consequences of Cooperation for the Supply Chain

Retailers and manufacturers are currently undergoing major changes within their supply chains. Increasing competition, complex distribution channels, shortening Product-Life-Cycles and changing consumer patterns are challenging the FMCG (Fast Moving Consumer Goods) industry. Therefore companies must ensure that they are both flexible and agile enough to adjust to changing conditions.

Increasing supply chain efficiency requires that companies eliminate inefficiencies such as high inventory, out-of-stocks, poor service, limited information sharing and replenishment strategies that are not demand-focused.

Designing a synchronized and flexible 'breathing' Supply Chain is the basic requirement for gaining sustainable improvements and achieving competitive advantage.

The focus of Collaborative Planning, Forecasting and Replenishment (CPFR) must be on cooperation amongst the individual value adding steps within the supply chain and on the synchronization of the supply chain processes. Following are some examples of synchronized and value added CPFR activity along the supply chain:

- Collaborative promotion and event-management

- Collaborative sales and order forecasting

- Collaborative replenishment

In various countries, pilot projects and first implementation projects have proven that CPFR can deliver benefits and added value. To take advantage of the potential benefits, the realization of CPFR has to be proactively addressed by both trading partners involved in the collaboration.

Pilot Projects are demonstrating the following benefits[1]:

---

[1] Results of various European Pilot Projects.

Improved Management of Consumer Demand

The customers and their needs are the focus of the planning process. Customers' needs can be forecasted more accurately. Through better use of POS data, a simultaneous response can be generated along the entire supply chain.

Increased Forecast Accuracy Through the Development of a Single Forecast between the Trading Partners

The exchange of forecasting data between the collaboration partners and the development of a joint forecast by adjusting the planning process for the trading partners leads to increased forecast accuracy.

Sustainable Improvements in the Collaboration Relationship

Open communication between trading partners creates mutual trust and understanding.

Increased Sales

Reducing Out-of-Stock situations at the point of sale will lead to an increase in sales.

Inventory Reduction

By increasing the forecast accuracy and avoiding rush-orders, the planning horizon for both manufacturer and retailer is extended and therefore leads to decreased "buffers" for demand variations.

Reduction of Supply Chain Costs

Increased planning reliability leads to a better utilization of production capacity. Reduction of rush-orders decreases the need for manual intervention in the production process and therefore significantly decreases set-up and production times.

Better Use of Production and Supply Chain Resources

Reliable planning data allow the development of a long-term plan for the use of available production and logistics resources.

Increase Promotion Effectiveness

Increased transparency and coordination leads towards an increase in return on investment.

To gain long-term benefits from CPFR, a successful pilot project needs to be scaled and integrated within the internal business processes of the trading partners. Within CPFR pilots, data exchange is often handled on a manual basis (spreadsheet, fax etc. may be sufficient for a pilot) instead of using a collaborative software tool. Using manual processes means that the quality of the data will be limited and if put into the companies planning or production system, can lead to erroneous conclusions. For simulating the underlying business processes, manual data exchange is sufficient, nevertheless it is not an option for scaling CPFR throughout the company. The failed integration of business processes and collaboration software can doom a promising CPFR pilot to failure. Starting from the euphoric pilot results, gaps in system support will lead to employee frustration and thus resistance towards the initiative.

Parallel to a CPFR pilot, management must consider in advance how they are going to implement the CPFR initiative within their IT strategy and the overall company strategy.

Accenture and ECR Europe developed the "Guide to CPFR Implementation"[2], which describes in depth the different steps trading partners need to conduct to move from internal collaboration to pilot implementation and full-scale implementation of CPFR.

11.2 Supply Chain Collaboration – Are You Ready?

Retailers and Manufacturers are currently successfully piloting CPFR but full-scale CPFR implementations are not yet on the agenda. One explanation for the situation is that during CPFR pilot projects, companies get their first real impression of the complexity of full CPFR implementation into internal processes, organization and technology. Looking more closely, the complexity can be differentiated as IT-complexity and organizational complexity. To scale up the collaboration process company wide and with all major trading partners, company specific IT-solutions are required.

Organizational and cultural adjustments are more challenging to implement than the IT solutions. The organizational adjustments include structural adjustments, training of the changed functions and cultural adaptations to support the CPFR goals. Realization of cooperative benefits within the supply chain started in the early 1990s with the development of Efficient Consumer Response (ECR). All ECR methods are based on collaborative elements. The collaboration partners who have already implemented ECR methods (VMI, CRP, Category Management etc.) are already familiar with collaboration and thus have an additional advantage.

---

[2] ECR Europe "A Guide to CPFR Implementation", 2001

Those experiences can be used as a starting point to spread CPFR-Collaboration through the whole supply chain.

So far, supply chain optimization or collaboration has been based on peer-to-peer relationships within the supply chain, but the upstream or downstream aspects have been neglected. The transformation of the supply chain structure – from having a company focus to having a supply chain focus – requires adaptation of processes, organization (structure, culture and qualification) and the IT System within the company. Within these areas, paradigms and company values, which traditionally grow between and within the companies, will be replaced by collaboration. Rethinking and re-learning is required for employees in order to adjust to the rapid changes.

Collaboration Levels

Distinct levels of collaboration can be differentiated by several criteria:

Information and Data Exchange

The first level of collaboration is defined by the exchange of information and data without defining specific processes or following specific rules based on the idea that the exchange of information alone will have positive effects for the participants. The insights gained from information sharing can be used internally to adapt high-level processes to the requirements of the trading partner, thereby simplifying day-to-day work.

Bilateral Communication

In bilateral communication, the data and information exchange is focused on specific subjects that are of interest to the trading partners. The aim is to define common goals within the trading relationship and set up a communication plan to reach those goals. For the exchange of the data, industry standards or pre-defined standards can be used if necessary. Bilateral communication fulfills the aims of aligning the business of the trading partners and of enhancing the cooperation between companies.

Integration of Business Processes

The trading partner is involved in the strategic, tactical and operational planning and expects sustainable benefits from the partnership. Based on the exchange of information, the partners design collaborative business processes and agree on confidentiality. The benefit for the partners is the early exchange of information and therefore early involvement in significant trading relationship changes. Furthermore, the information can be used to internally align processes and procedures towards the requirements of the cooperation. The developed processes need to be integrated into day-to-day business.

Prerequisites for a Collaborative Agreement

A collaborative agreement is created by strategically establishing partnerships across company borders. For the trading partners, collaborative organization requires open communication, process transparency and identification with collaborative ideas. One of the advantages for partners is the cultivation of flexibility within an environment of constant change.

The following are the main characteristics of a collaborative agreement:

- It fosters knowledge exchange between partners

- It strengthens the collaborative culture

- It creates a proactive climate for problem resolution

- It establishes a collaborative incentive system

- It measures collaborative success

- It builds partnerships and win-win solutions

Knowledge Exchange between Partners

Collaborative organizations are defined by the exchange of knowledge. An understanding of behavior patterns or the knowledge of internal processes in partner organizations allows for better prediction and evaluation of events. The partners have to agree in advance on what kind of knowledge they want to exchange, the way the knowledge is exchanged and when the knowledge exchange will occur.

Knowledge Exchange is based on:

Data Exchange

Collaborating companies agree on the scope, format and type of data that is necessary to achieve the goals of collaboration. Within a CPFR project, items like weekly sales inventory data from the regional distribution center or the planned demand of a promotional item are of interest to partners.

Employee Support

Conducting collaborative projects requires support from several business and organizational units. The units contribute to the project team either as subject experts or by dedicating full time project support. The project team consists of team members from both companies.

Resource Sharing

When implementing IT solutions, the exchange of specialists across company borders can support project efforts significantly. Especially, smaller companies often do not have the required resources available. Very often, they are deployed in day-to-day business and cannot support the needed processes.

Strengthening of the Culture

Close and intensive contact between companies during collaboration will result in companies' own cultures being influenced by the culture of their partners. The exchange of small ideas and suggestions in the long-term results in large scale changes to the culture. Traditionally, major cultural differences exist between retailers and manufacturers. Influenced by the culture of the collaborative partner, in-house culture is critically reviewed and if appropriate, the necessary adjustments are made. The employees within a partner's organization should initiate adjustments within their own organization if possible, and proclaim the advantages of a collaborative culture through their actions. The collaborative spirit will influence even employees who are not directly involved in the collaboration.

Problem Recognition and Solution

Every innovation meets with difficulties and reservations on its inception. Compared to other initiatives, CPFR requires not only that such reservations be overcome within an organization but also within its trading partners.

Employee Hesitation

The hesitation and concerns of employees in planning an implementation of CPFR must be addressed. First of all, the employees tend to want to keep business as usual instead of taking the risks that they perceive to be associated with collaboration. To overcome this hesitation, it is necessary to establish open communications with all employees and to discuss the opportunities of CPFR for the whole organization. Employees have to live with the proposed collaboration in their day-to-day activities and therefore it is important that they understand and support the related concepts. Within a pilot project or inter-company collaboration, involved employees can get a feeling and understanding of the sort of collaboration being planned and profit from their experiences later on in a full scale CPFR implementation.

Know-How

Knowledge is required to set up the project's collaborative processes and to identify how IT can support collaboration. Management needs to prepare for the collaborative challenge by gaining the necessary competencies and knowledge.

Senior Management Support

The involvement and support from senior management is required to secure necessary resources and to coordinate the collaboration with the overall business strategy.

Resources

A collaborative project requires adequate resources in terms of project budget and team members. Senior management is responsible for ensuring that sufficient resources are available in terms of quality and quantity from the start.

Collaboration Partner Selection

The overall success of collaboration depends on the selection of an appropriate partner. The following questions should be considered while trying to qualify a partner:

- Can the relationship with the potential trading partner be characterized as open and trusting?

- Does the trading partner have strengths and weaknesses complementary to one's own organization?

- Does the trading partner have appropriate resources (personnel, IT, etc.) to make CPFR successful?

- Is the trading partner conducting other collaborative initiatives with one's company or with other organizations?

The complete questionnaire for a capability assessment of a potential collaboration partner can be found in the ECR Europe Publication "A Guide to CPFR Implementation"[3], which was jointly developed by ECR Europe and Accenture.

Establishing a Collaborative Incentive System

Through their joint responsibility for the supply chain, partners have to consider installing incentive systems that are linked to the achievement of their collaborative goals. Traditionally, incentive systems such as the annual bonus have been linked to squeezing the highest possible benefit out of trading partners, neglecting the efficiency of the supply chain. Within retailer-manufacturer relationships, the goal of the retailer is to obtain products at the lowest possible price, whereas the manufacturer is targeting high sales volume. As a result, high inventory levels occur due to forward buying behavior.

---

[3] Ibid.

Incentives should be oriented towards improvements in efficiency, such as inventory reduction, lead-time reduction or increased on-shelf-availability.

Measuring Collaborative Success

Continuous measurement of collaborative success based on agreed Key Performance Indicators (KPI) is required to ensure that:

- The actual developments and future plans are generating value for the collaboration partners

- The supporters of the collaboration, including senior management, receive relevant feedback and overcome any lingering skepticism. The generated information should be used to critically review the collaboration and to identify improvement areas

When installing a system to measure collaborative success, it is important to involve the controlling department to analyze its consequences for future planning. A recalculation of prices, including savings realized by the collaboration, leads towards a repositioning in the competitive landscape. Selling the same product at lower prices offers the possibility of significantly improving total sales.

A Partnership Win-Win Solution

The collaborative partners' expect higher sales and increased profits. The idea of win-win means a fair distribution of the efforts of the collaboration and the results. For the companies, a win-win is the incentive to intensify the collaboration. Within the collaborative arrangement, the partners must agree on how to distribute the benefits of collaboration. On the other hand, they must also provision for the risks of collaboration in the arrangement.

There are several different types of collaboration. For the purpose of simplification, we focus on downstream collaboration between retailers and manufacturers.

11.3   Guidelines for CPFR Implementation – From CPFR Pilot to Full-scale Implementation

11.3.1 What Is Important When Implementing CPFR?

CPFR implementation is based on long-term and all-encompassing planning between collaborative partners. Implementations vary in scope and intensity, depending on the underlying technical solution and the organizational and cultural integration of the partners.

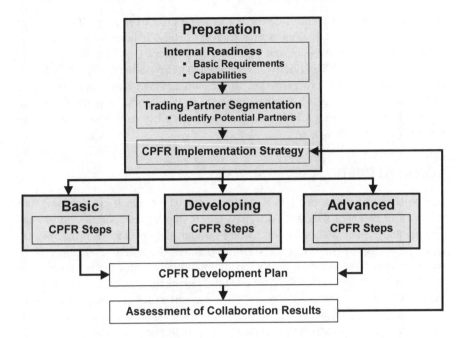

Source: ECR Europe

Figure 11.1: CPFR Implementation

Basic CPFR

The objective of Basic CPFR is to enhance collaboration within an organization. Basic CPFR doesn't provide an implementation framework for trading partners who are unwilling or prepared to collaborate, nor those for whom collaboration with partners would offer limited potential, but rather, provides a framework for those for whom collaboration within their own company may generate benefits. In some cases, it may be used to prepare the company for future CPFR implementation with trading partners. It aims to foster collaboration between departments within one company. For example, Basic CPFR brings together the Sales, Demand Planning, Marketing, Production, Purchasing, Logistics and Customer Support departments. Basic CPFR can focus on a few or all areas for collaborative processes. The potential benefits are significant, but limited, since no trading partners are involved.

Developing CPFR

The objective of Developing CPFR is to prove the CPFR concept and assist companies with an easily implemented CPFR initiative that will reap benefits. It also enables companies wishing to focus on supply chain integration to prepare the organization for an Advanced CPFR implementation. Developing CPFR implies generally limited collaboration with a trading partner. It is often restricted to a collaborative promotion plan and sales or order forecast collaboration, or to a reduced number of SKUs. It may also be used as 'easy-to-implement' CPFR that embraces all the CPFR processes and all the company SKUs and delivery points. There are however, limited potential benefits, as it does not integrate the whole supply chain. Developing CPFR can also be seen as a key entry level with trading partners (e.g. pilot phase).

Advanced CPFR

The objective of Advanced CPFR is to roll-out CPFR, reach critical mass and achieve full potential benefits. Advanced CPFR implies collaborating in promotion planning, sales and order forecasting through the development and maintenance of a close relationship with trading partners. Complete integration of all processes may be effected gradually, beginning initially with a limited scope. The collaboration process is usually automated through an advanced IT solution that is integrated with the company's back-office systems (ERP, Production Planning etc). Advanced CPFR includes the use of orders, POS and inventory data. Advanced CPFR may also include collaboration through one or many exchanges.

From Pilot to CPFR Implementation

In the preparation phase, trading partners have to assess their own capacities for implementing CPFR and selecting a corresponding collaboration partner. The steps from Developing CPFR towards Advanced CPFR are mainly determined by higher IT requirements and by the deployment of adequate resources for implementation. The benefits collaboration partners can realize from pilot implementation mainly include a significant reduction in variable costs, depending on the scope of the pilot and the SKUs involved. Those cost savings are based on inventory reductions along the supply chain, reduction in rush orders and administrative savings. Collaboration leads to a better balance of supply and demand and therefore gives an indication about savings that could be realized through full-scale implementation.

In most cases, a successful CPFR pilot is the baseline for rolling out CPFR and a full-scale implementation. Through pilot projects, companies can learn and gather experiences, which they are able to apply later for quick implementation.

After the pilot stage of CPFR, companies have either grown aware of the requirements for IT-collaboration tools or if a specific tool was used during the pilot, they have been able to assess its value directly. An additional advantage is that intra-company processes between departments have already been established. Good preparation during the pilot stage delivers advantages in terms of shortening set-up times when implementing CPFR.

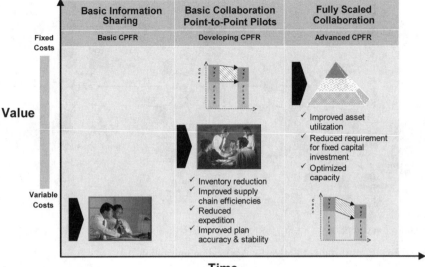

Source: Accenture

Figure 11.2:   Migration of CPFR Implementation

11.3.2 Complexity of CPFR Implementations

The complexity of implementing CPFR is based on two major components.

1. **Integration of Collaborative Processes between the Collaboration Partners**
    All processes between collaborating companies need to be identified, regardless of whether they are partially or fully automated. Depending on the collaboration goals, whether they are sales promotions, special events, regular sales or standard assortment processes, they all require detailed analysis. Detailed analysis allows one to optimize the processes in accordance with the collaborating partner's company. For all semi-automated processes, this means re-assessing the interface requirements.

2. **Collaborative Process Links to Internal Infrastructure**
    A detailed analysis of the existing IT-Infrastructure is required before implementing CPFR. Due to an increasing number of available systems, the system landscape in most companies is rather heterogeneous. Implementing a CPFR solution requires that an interface to link the systems peer-to-peer be identified.

    - Enterprise Application Integration (EAI) is a technology for the structured integration of different IT-solutions into the existing IT-landscape.

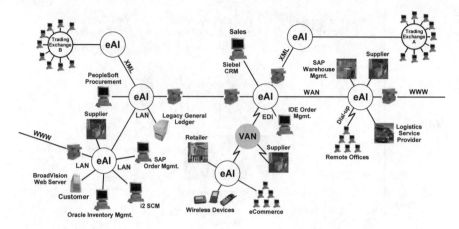

Source: Accenture

Figure 11.3:   Structure of Enterprise Application Integration

EAI ensures that the company is able to react quickly and precisely when adding additional applications to the existing IT-infrastructure by:

- Analyzing the existing business processes and workflows

- Defining and managing interfaces of the various applications

- Transforming and formatting of data and information and simultaneously synchronizing the information on the different systems and within various data sources

- Serving the data flow architecture between linked systems

All major B2B exchanges offer CPFR functionality. The Global Commerce Initiative is currently working on defining CPFR standards to ensure global applicability.

Technological Requirements for CPFR

A Successful CPFR implementation requires technical support. Many retailers and manufacturers are comfortable with the CPFR concept and have realized the benefits; however, few companies have implemented a fully scaled CPFR and realized sustainable benefits.

Why?

The answer is very simple. Internal processes, organizational status and the current IT structure are not prepared adequately for the challenge of collaboration. In a first step, the internal requirements need to be aligned to start a full-scaled CPFR imple-

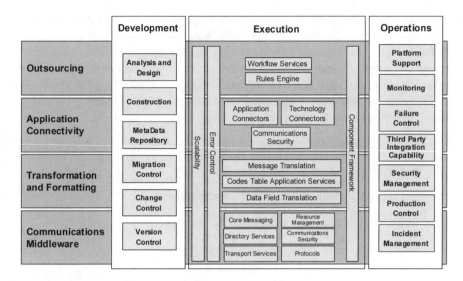

Source: Accenture

Figure 11.4: Major Components of Enterprise Application Integration

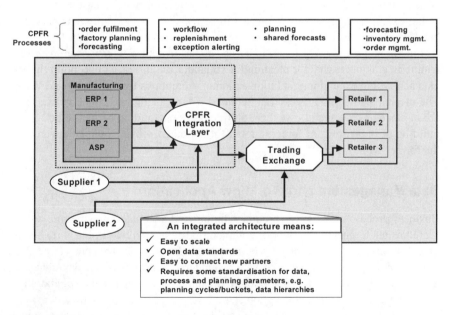

Source: Accenture

Figure 11.5: CPFR and Trading Exchanges

mentation. However, this investment cannot fully provide for the CPFR initiative. Companies must always change some of their processes and systems to solve specific business issues; for example, a company may need to develop on what would otherwise be an insufficient demand planning engine. Implementing a solution will often bring benefits, some of which may not be directly attributable to CPFR.

There are several areas which need to be addressed before starting collaboration. The critical areas for success are:

- The collaborative forecast challenge

- Data management and workflow application

- Forecast adjustment and exception management

- Trusting relationships among trading partners

- Difficulty of intensified data exchange

The Collaborative Forecast Challenge

Adjusting forecast detail for one or two trading partners is manageable, but for broader applications, this can be a time-consuming process and an opportunity for error or misinterpretation to arise. Manufacturers and retailers must address this issue and decide how willing they are to modify their current forecast formats.

For example, compressing a forecast from a weekly to a monthly time period or breaking down a national or category-level forecast to a SKU/location-level forecast might be the only way to get to a true "apples to apples" comparison. A proper comparison is necessary for meaningful collaboration in setting exception thresholds and taking exception-resolution action on exceptions that will truly add value. The mechanics of this process can be aided if forecasting and collaborative tools are in place or outsourced. Another solution is for one trading partner to perform a build-up or breakdown of forecast detail for the other, provided the latter can trust the former with this task.

Data Management and Workflow Application

Business process definitions, resources, timing and adequate infrastructure are all prerequisites to ensure the flow of collaboration-relevant data. In the early stages of CPFR implementation, a long-term strategy for the management of the data must be defined. The question of which standards will be used for data management requires an early decision. Without deciding on a standard, the collaboration cannot enter the next implementation step.

The automatic Data Retrieval Process, such as an e-mail system that provides forecasting updates within the internal planning systems can further spread and accelerate the usage of CPFR processes. There is an opportunity to use available, technically mature data management tools, or a range of external service providers who also offer services.

Forecast Adjustment and Exception Management

Resolving exceptions based on agreed upon exception criteria should have top-priority for partners. It seems simple, but priorities are not necessarily the same for retailers and manufacturers. Within a collaborative arrangement, it must be clearly defined what exceptions are and how the trading partners will resolve them. The collaboration process requires that the partners agree on a specific format for data exchange.

A major part of the collaboration cycle involves the "window of action" concept. The "window of action" is a period when the partners can address the final result within a pre-defined scope. Forecast changes can therefore be addressed within the "window of action" by each collaboration partner without the direct involvement of their counterparts. The idea is that the partners do not have to activate the collaboration process for small changes in the forecast.

Trusting Relationships with Trading Partners

Changing behaviors amongst trading partners is a major challenge that needs to be overcome in implementing CPFR on a scaled basis. In implementing CPFR on a full scale basis, one is confronted with a different mentality on the part of the trading partners than for a short-term pilot project. Additionally, the timeline for a pilot differs from a long-term strategic CPFR implementation. As the duration of the pilot project is limited, both sides can easily cancel the pilot if the results are not as expected.

Due to the shorter duration of a pilot, the cooperation of those involved is easier to assure than a full-scale implementation. In the short term, people can change their attitude because they might already have the end of the project in mind. A full-scale implementation becomes an ongoing collaboration and with no end in sight. Therefore it is more difficult for people to adjust to the new rules, since it demands lasting change. Trust in the accuracy of collaboratively developed forecasts is especially limited because companies tend to use incompatible methods for forecasting. Depending on company structure, different departments are involved in the forecasting process. Some may not be directly involved in the collaborative process and may not be able to assess the consequences of their actions.

If all the forecast information is not shared amongst partners, it can impair transparency along the supply chain. To avoid this situation, trading partners must adjust the roles and areas of responsibility for their decision makers and stakeholders in the changed environment. This is an especially difficult step for the retailer – manufacturer relationship because in such a collaborative relationship, both are focusing on the customer and trying to act accordingly. Historically this has not been the case because customer focus has been limited.

A joint business plan emphasizes the goal of customer centricity due to a common understanding of the partner's business processes and working patterns. The development of a joint business plan is only possible if each organization allows and supports those kinds of changes.

Difficulty of Intensified Data Exchange

So far the term data exchange has been used in a negative way, even though it is a part of our daily business. In speaking about collaboration, data exchange is seen from a different perspective.

Collaboration does not mean that there is free and uncontrolled data flow between companies. Instead, collaboration regulates the data exchange and uses data in the best possible way to support management decisions. Therefore the collaborative partners have to decide on rules for the exchange of data, including who is to provide which data and of what quality.

Experience has shown that within collaborative relationships, the strongest trading partners try to force their ideas on partnering companies. In the supply chain, a possible effect might be that a retailer provides POS data to all following members in the supply chain.

Intensive data exchange should be established between all supply chain members, independent of their current position. At first sight, it might seem ridiculous to send POS data to one packaging supplier, but if the supplier has the knowledge and infrastructure to use the data, there is no reason to exclude him or her. Each collaborator must individually agree to the extent he is willing to share data and to what extent it makes sense to exchange data along the supply chain. It is necessary that partners are open to share data and overcome traditional boundaries for data exchange.

11.4   Collaboration – the Outlook

Supply chain collaboration is a logical step in optimizing the supply chain. Through collaboration, the trading partners will be able to fulfill customer needs such as flexible delivery, shorter lead-times and On-Shelf-Availability. Furthermore, collaboration will include transportation planning.

Cultural changes and the necessary process adjustments between the trading partners will be the main challenge for the implementation of a collaborative scenario.

New technologies will allow faster collaboration between companies by providing sophisticated tools to cover the interaction between the companies and by improving data quality. The transactional business-to-business approach quickly leads to decreased costs. For large-scale supply chain optimization, companies must develop individual collaborative models which best represent their own collaborative strategy.

PART 5:

What's Next? – The Future of Collaborative Customer Relationship Management

Part 5 deals with the future development of CCRM. Chapter 12 describes how as category management gets more and more day-to-day business, new and sophisticated solutions to attract the consumer may evolve. Alexander H. Kracklauer, D. Quinn Mills and Dirk Seifert teamed up with two authors from one of the most renowned companies for category management – Procter & Gamble. Together with Michael Leyk and Steffen Rübke they describe new directions in category management, making it clear that category management in the 21st century must be integrated with the overall retail strategy. From a long-term category management perspective, it is of particular significance that the entire strategy and situation of the company is analyzed together. So far, the individual optimization of categories has not been coordinated with the overall retail strategy and has therefore been relegated to an operational level that, in the best cases, has coincided with the corporate strategy by chance.

Chapter 13 addresses collaborative category management in the inter-connected world of the Internet. Markus Großweischede, Head of the Competence Center for Multi-Channel Management at the University of Essen, Germany, shows how category management can work for online shops. The goals of category management in the virtual market place need to be guided by a philosophy that is based on evolving an orientation towards the target customers. Conventional retailing methods must be accommodated to this new situation. The technological opportunities that the internet delivers have allowed categories to be directed more strongly at target groups than in bricks-and-mortar outlets. Großweischede explains the nine phase process to achieve this goal.

CHAPTER 12

New Ways of Category Management

Alexander H. Kracklauer
BayTech IBS, UAS Neu-Ulm, Germany / Harvard Business School, MA, USA

D. Quinn Mills
Harvard Business School, MA, USA

Dirk Seifert
Harvard Business School, MA, USA

Michael Leyk
Procter & Gamble, Schwalbach, Germany

Steffen Rübke
Procter & Gamble, Schwalbach, Germany

12.1 Introduction

The retail sector is currently one of intense competition, great opportunity and great risk. For example, stagnating productivity per unit of retail space, excess total retail space and hyper competition from Wal-Mart and Target have driven firms like K-Mart into bankruptcy. A retailer that tries to differentiate itself from competition primarily through offering aggressive prices often faces catastrophic results.

How can this situation be rectified? How can retailers create value without squeezing prices frequently and risking further decreases in profitability?

A promising possibility for improved differentiation from competitors and for improved value creation comes from efficient consumer response. Optimized supply chain management and category management in cooperative arrangements between manufacturers and retailers can create useful potential. While on the logistics side of the equation, projects on cost reduction in the supply chain have proven successful, there remains considerable potential in collaborative category management. Since opportunities for cost reduction are becoming exhausted in retailing (resulting in a service wasteland), differentiation from the competition via improvements in assortment management is the next logical step.

This chapter describes a new approach to strategic assortment planning and control. The processes discussed here have already been tested in pilot projects and show the practicality and superiority of the method. Assortment, shelf presentation and promotions can be strategically guided and be used for gaining profile in the marketplace. Sales and earnings increases on the order of 15 to 20%, depending on the category, are the rule, not the exception.

12.2   The Retail Strategy Determines the Assortment

Category management the way it is most often practiced today is not a new approach. Companies that have used these methods for specific categories have reported increased customer loyalty and cost savings. Because of the complexity of the complete process, even large retail and manufacturing companies have thus far been able to initiate only a few projects of limited scope.

A seldom discussed weakness of CM projects is the fact that the individual optimization of categories is often not coordinated with the overall retail strategy, and is therefore, relegated to an operational level that in the best cases coincides by chance with the corporate strategy. For long term category management, it is of particular significance that the entire strategy and situation of the company is analyzed together. It is necessary to understand the goals and strategies of the organization and to gain knowledge about their strengths and weaknesses. This information must be kept in mind in all subsequent decisions.

The first step in category management is the development of a retail strategy. In the second step, category plans are derived. The third step concerns itself with the implementation of plans and their realization in retail outlets. In the fourth and final step, category performance is evaluated and corresponding adjustments made in the preceding steps.

In the context of building a retailer strategy, an overview of all essential categories is created and their significance towards meeting the objectives of the company as a whole is identified. This analysis forms the basis for the selection of categories, which will be closely examined in subsequent phases and in doing so efficiently distributes limited resources such as time, money and personnel to individual categories. At the same time, strategic partners can be chosen for individual categories. The following checklist identifies the questions that need to be addressed in the development of a retail strategy:

1. Who are the target customers of the retailers? Are they being reached?

2. Why are target customers valuable?

3. With whom are the retailers competing against for their target customers?

4. What are the opportunities retailers have for improving their position vis-à-vis their competition?

5. Which categories are strategically important for the target customers?

6. On which categories should the retail organizations concentrate to achieve maximum penetration with their target customers?

12.3   Defining Categories from the Customer's Perspective

The product mix seen in the market today is, as a rule, a product of history; the placement in the market is oriented more towards internal necessities and logistical requirements than on customer needs. Customers often go astray in their attempts to find products quickly and easily. This phenomenon has its roots in insufficiently defined categories that are not customer oriented.

Categories should be closely aligned to the needs of the customer and should map the buying decision process of the consumer. As an example, a spatial separation of the categories associated with baby care would be impractical; the products serve the satisfaction of specific consumer demands. Coordinated placement and marketing of products is expected by consumers; in addition, the extent to which the consumer would expect other categories and segments like baby lotion or shampoo appropriate for consolidation is also worth considering. Understanding the consumer and investigating his or her buying behavior through joint projects is of critical importance to retailers and manufacturers. A category should be defined so as to include all articles that serve the same function for the consumer and thereby logically constitute a single entity.

The process of category definition according to the model of Tochtermann and Lange is presented below:

After category definitions are fixed, product segments and sub-segments must be identified. The deciding factor lies in the accurate characterization of the target consumer's buying decision process in each of the categories. Information on consumer behavior often comes to the retailer in the form of buying decision trees. The following illustration is of an analysis by Glendinning consultants and illustrates the effects of different approaches. Figure 12.1 shows the traditional category structure as it developed over time in the retailing of food products.

In contrast, Figure 12.2 shows the way in which the consumer views the category. Sweets are primarily purchased for a particular occasion, which has nothing to do with conventional segmentation. Important criteria for the buyer's decision are parameters like "share with family" or "for me now". This of course has consequences for category management. It is, for example, conceivable that children's sweets have their own department with concomitant marketing support (such as in-store sampling or children's parties or sweets sold as gifts in a special packaging).

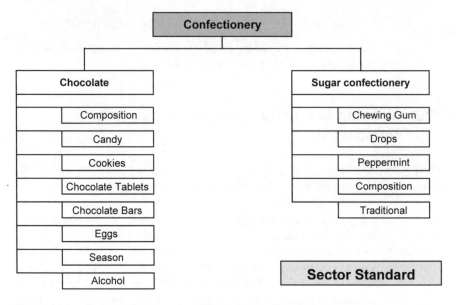

Figure 12.1: Category Structure According to Sector Standard

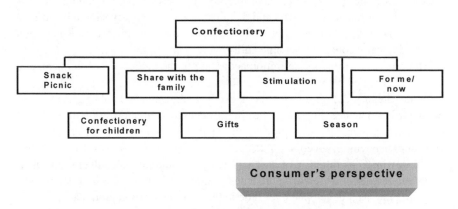

Figure 12.2: Category Structure from the Consumer's Perspective

The structure and segmentation of categories reflects typical buying decisions within the category. Restructuring of a category, therefore, can lead to new perspectives and approaches for winning customers.

The process of category definition and segmentation are preconditions for the fixing of a category role. This step is often discussed in industry publications as the core of category management while the overreaching corporate and marketing goals (such as building a particular image for a product line or creating a distinction for a particular store) present themselves at the category level. For retailers who define families as target groups, the above mentioned segmentation of sweets could be the starting point for developing further contact with this target group. The determination of individual category roles offers the best approach in distinguishing oneself from one's competitors.

12.4 Category Roles: How to Attract Target Groups

The analysis of category roles should serve to answer the following questions: Which categories are strategic in the market? Which categories are meaningful for the target group? And on which categories should the retailer concentrate to achieve optimal penetration among its target customers?

The categories are distinguished by four typical roles: destination, preferred/routine, occasional/seasonal and convenience.

1. Destination: The retailers position themselves as the preferred merchant of a category and present themselves as being so to target customers. Such categories enjoy above-average demand and add measurably to the top line. As a rule, 5 to 7% of all categories fit this role.

2. Preferred/routine: The retailers are preferred merchants in a category and can improve their image with target customers. These categories represent 55 to 60% of all categories, and have a very high consumer value and generate earnings.

3. Occasional/seasonal: The retailers position themselves as a primary seller of this category in order to strengthen their image in general. This group is responsible for high consumer value and comprises of 15 to 20% of all categories.

4. Convenience: The remaining 15 to 20% complete the category mix; their role is primarily to generate earnings.

To classify their roles, categories are investigated according to their indices: 1. Market data such as sales or growth rates, 2. Consumer data such as market penetration or degree of loyalty, and 3. Financial indices of the company like return on investment. For completeness, data on the corporate image or on the overlap between the demographics of category purchasers with the actual target group can be examined too.

The following table presents a classification model whereby quantitative data is organized based on the aspects being considered.

Table 12.1:   Classification Model for Quantitative Category Data

Outlet	Class	Turn-over (Rank)	Penetra-tion (%)	Spend-ings per Year ($)	Purchas-ing Fre-quency	Spending per Purchase ($)	Share of Basket (%)	Growth vs. Year Ago (%)
Super-Market	High	1-10	>40	>30	>7	>10	>50	>5
	Medium	11-90	6-40	8-30	2-7	2-10	30-50	0-5
	Low	>90	0-6	0-8	0-2	0-2	0-30	<0
Con-sumer Market	High	1-10	>20	>30	>7	>10	>75	>10
	Medium	11-90	3-20	8-30	2-7	2,5-10	50-75	0-10
	Low	>90	0-3	0-8	0-2	0-2,5	0-50	<0
Hyper-Market	High	1-10	>35	>50	>8	>10	>100	>10
	Medium	11-90	10-35	10-50	2-8	3-10	60-100	0-10
	Low	>90	0-10	0-10	0-2	0-3	0-60	<0
Drug Market	High	1-10	>25	>20	>8	>10	>20	>10
	Medium	11-90	5-25	8-20	2-8	3-10	15-20	0-10
	Low	>90	0-25	0-8	0-2	0-3	0-15	<0
Dis-counter	High	1-10	>60	>35	>8	>8	>50	>20
	Medium	11-90	10-60	6-35	2-8	2-8	35-50	0-20
	Low	>90	0-10	0-6	0-2	0-2	0-35	<0

After the data is classified, roles can be ascertained. On this basis, existing resources are allocated to the categories.

Table 12.2:   Significance of the Indices for Individual Categories

Indices		DESTINATION-CATEGORY	PREFERRED-CATEGORY	OCCASIONAL-SEASONAL-CATEGORY	CONVENIENCE-CATEGORY
Market	How high is the category's national turnover?	High	High/Medium	Medium	Medium/Low
	What is the estimated future development? (Consumption trend)	High	Medium	Medium	Medium
Shoppers	How many households are reached with the category? (Consumer Household Penetration)	High	High/Medium	Medium	Medium/Low
	How often do consumers shop in the category? (Purchase Frequency)	High	High/Medium	Medium	Medium/Low
	How high is the average ticket excl. category?	High/Medium	Medium	Medium	Medium/Low

Table 12.2 (continued)

Indices		DESTINATION-CATEGORY	PREFERRED-CATEGORY	OCCASIONAL-SEASONAL-CATEGORY	CONVENIENCE-CATEGORY
Financial Indices	How high is category Turnover at retailer?	High	High/Medium	Medium	Medium
	How high is the retailer's margin in the category?	Low	Medium	Medium	High
	How high is the category share compared to overall market share of the retailer?	High	Medium	Medium	Medium

12.5 What Is Not Measured Will Also Not Be Attained: Category Evaluation and Performance Analysis

The successful management of a category requires that its status be determined. Category evaluation entails the analysis of relevant data on the category in view of the market and the customer. The goal is to have a clear understanding of the current capacity of the group (strengths and weaknesses) as well as be able to identify the corresponding potentials of the group. The category evaluation cannot, however, rest on a pure technical analysis alone. H.E. Butt, a leading North American retailer in category management, has moved to let qualitative evaluations play a role in target group marketing. There are, for example, supply chain partnerships with manufacturers of Mexican products that bring relatively little earnings for the retailers, but which are important for Hispanic customers. In the German market, it is well known that a failure to provide regional specialties can lead customers to do their business elsewhere.

The evaluation of categories can also lead to a reformulation of their roles. If it becomes clear that customers who buy a specific category spend, on an average, 80% more money in one shopping trip on daily necessities, a study of this target group is merited.

The category performance analysis establishes the essential goals and measurement criteria for groups under analysis. In practice, however, this is often limited to a results based criteria. Though it is important to have widespread management through data on net earnings and stock on-hand, it is internally focused and therefore requires customer data to be completed. The measurement of data like customer penetration, customer loyalty, average purchase volume and image of the retail brand draws management's attention away from the most important component of category management: the customer.

The measurement criteria for a category must be reflective of the category's role. The goal of a destination category is, first of all, to increase sales and market share, with an occasional group contributing to the earning power. This must be observed in the setting of goals, and above all, should be reflected in the assessment system of both the category manager and the buyer.

As a rule, retail and manufacturing develop performance criteria on a yearly basis with the opportunity of modifying and adjusting business plans in a quarter yearly cycle. The corresponding review can be done with the help of CM scorecards.

Table 12.3:   Customer and Results Referenced Measurement Criteria for Category Performance

Customer Focused Measurements	Result Oriented Measurements
• Household Penetration • Purchase Frequency • Loyalty • Spending Intensity • Basket Size • Image of Store	• Net Profit • Operating Cost • Average Retail Days On-Hand Operating Cost • Return on Investment • Category Share

12.6   Category Strategies and Tactics: How Do I Differentiate Myself from the Competition?

Many campaigns in retail marketing suffer from a certain degree of arbitrariness and interchangeability. The ever-present struggle to define price as the main instrument of building customer relationships shows minimal flexibility and creativity in strategy. The fixing of category roles just described can help find different marketing parameters for each group. To that end, the construction of a category strategy follows from the previously determined category roles. The destination category can be aggressively positioned with value offers vis-à-vis competitors through innovative strategies like "speed-to-market" marketing and conspicuous placement for 'genuine' product introductions. Occasional and seasonal categories like fireworks support a strategy of raising customer frequency. And finally, the convenience category offers a method for improving image in that a broad assortment of goods makes for simpler and more comprehensive one-stop shopping. Category strategies should always be in harmony with the super ordinate corporate and the corresponding marketing objectives must be set towards the desired target group. The strategies thus generated create a framework for retail marketing.

The best strategies fail when they are not fully realized in the field. Category tactics formulate the specific steps for the best possible implementation of the category strategies just described. The core areas for the development of tactics are product mix policy (which products the retailer should carry long term), in-store presentation, pricing policy and promotions. The following figure shows the connection between category roles and tactics.

Table 12.4: The Connection between Category Roles and Tactics

Category-Role	Tactics			
	Assortment	**Shelf presentation**	**Pricing**	**Promotion**
Destination	**Broad and deep Assortment** • Best variety in the market • Premium products	**Very Good In-store Location** • High customer touch • High customer frequency • Big areas	**High-Low-Pricing Strategy** • Price aggressive promotions	**High Level of Activity** • High frequency • Different media
Preferred/ Routine	**Broad Assortment** • Important brands • Private label program	**Average Location** • Multiple placing	**Competitive Pricing** • Consistent • Fair and transparent	**Average Level of Activity** • Flyer as main advertising tool • According to flyer appearance, medium frequency
Seasonal/ Occasional	**Seasonal Assortment** • Changing suppliers • Different topics	**Good Location** • Locations with strong awareness • High customer frequency	**Competitive / Seasonal** • Premium priced with exclusive products	**Seasonal Activities** • Different media • In-store Promotion • frequency: saisonal
Convenience	**Reduced Assortment** • Other brands with significant turnover and earnings	**Available Location In-store** • Small areas Near to main general assortment	**Accepted pricing level** • Within a 15% range compared to competition	**Few / No Advertising** • Selected media

In the product mix policy for a destination category like baby care, it is critical to have a broad and deep assortment available. Diapers, for example, should be made available in different package sizes. Several price classes in different brands should be in store as well. Essential to in-store presentation is that 'baby care' is given an appropriate layout in a high traffic area of the retail outlet. In pricing policy, high-frequency products like diapers are targeted to get the customer into

- Did you align merchandising with overall strategy and is it focused on target customers?
- Do you fulfill the customers' expectations?
- Is the category definition reflected?
- Is the assortment structured?
- Does the in-store presentation support buying habits?
- Is the consumer's purchase decision tree reflected?
- Are you going to use cross-selling and up-selling opportunities?
- Is the location according to category role?
- Is meaningful advertising in store possible?
- Does the consumer easily find the category ?

Figure 12.3: Checklists for In-store Presentation

the outlet with aggressive pricing. Appropriate measures can then be used to force the shopper into larger purchases. This can be achieved either through the placement of high revenue segments in the vicinity of typically low profit destination categories or by simply advertising using flyers. The retailer's special sales events should be advertised throughout the media with billboards and posters or through local radio stations. This would attract the desired target group into outlets. What may appear at first to be a simple process is in fact very complex. The number of criteria for success is listed in the following 'checklist' for the placement of categories.

12.7   Without a Scorecard, It's All for Nothing: Measurement of Category Performance

The measurement of category performance is a continual process – one that cannot simply be done sporadically or only once. The resources invested are profitable only when the monitoring of category results fuels learning in the CM organization. One cannot assume that ambitious objectives can be achieved without any changes to the initial plan. Professional category management relies on quick correction for achieving even better results. Therefore, continuous reviewing of the implementation, along with measuring of plan fulfillment and adjustment statistics, becomes a foreground activity.

Table 12.5:   Example of a Scorecard

Measurements	Category			Trade Execution	Industry Execution	Data Source
	Current Figures	Plan Objectives	Revised Objectives			
Total Market Development of Category						Household Panel
Total Market Development of Category at Channel						
Total Category Dollar Sales at Channel						
Promotion Share of Category at Channel						
Average Price of Category at Channel						
Development of Category at Retailer						Retailers Data
Total Market Share Retailer FMCG						
Category Market Share of Retailer						
Promotion Share of Category at Retailer						
Average Price of Category at Retailer						
Gross Margin Dollars/Sq Feet Selling Area						
Dollar Sales						
Units or Equivalent Volume						
Category Penetration						Household Panel
Avg. Market Basket						
Propensity						
Loyalty						
Market Share Retailer						
No. of sku's vs. competition						Industry
Pricing Index vs. Competition						
No. of promotions vs. Competition						

In developing a scorecard, two things must be considered. First, the parameters for success must be agreed upon by retailer and manufacturer in a way that they feel committed; the principle of reciprocity is maintained and neither party exercises an excess of power. Second, the parameters must be clearly defined so that no one gets lost in the details.

12.8 Perspective

The category management process described here, when used in a retailer's overall strategy, offers an alternative to price wars with competitors and provides an opportunity for differentiation from the competition. Through focused, target group-appropriate assortments, the consumer can again be made enthusiastic about a company, consciously choosing the company on the basis of a clear profile of the firm as the best retail outlet for her or his shopping. This result is a win-win for both retailer and customer.

CHAPTER 13:

Collaborative Category Management on the Internet – Basics to Create and Manage Consumer-Focused Assortments in Online-Shops

Markus Großweischede
Competence Center Multi-Channel-Management, Universität Essen, Germany

13.1 What's Going on in Online Business?

Retailers and manufacturers are eager to tap the new sales and profit source offered by the introduction of the Internet as a trade channel and the prospects are looking good. Through additional virtual sales outlets, the spending per capita, loyalty of existing customers, and recruitment of new customers will be increased. Through direct marketing and the commitment to profitable consumers within the framework of Customer Relationship Management, one assures oneself of an above-average contribution to overall profit.

The reality of the situation however is not so glorious: online shoppers get lost in large product offerings, or search in vain for articles and product descriptions.[1] If the virtual shopping cart is actually filled, many customers leave the web site before actually making a purchase. Studies in the US estimate these "silent losses" on initiated but unfulfilled transactions at 28 to 43%.[2] The reasons include not only a lack of trust in the payment process, high shipping costs and technical problems with the web site, but also problems in guiding the user through the web site and in the accessibility of desired products. All this serves to diminish the comfort level of many potential customers on the Internet's two dimensional marketplace.[3]

The creation of a customer-oriented assortment and shopping experience presents an essential challenge. This applies to purely virtual competitors like Peapod in the US and LeShop in Switzerland, and also to established multi-channel retailers like Tesco in England or Safeway and Wal-Mart in the US. How can sales and

---

[1] Bauer et al. 1999, Fittkau & Maaß 2001, Haupt/Ansorge 2001

[2] Compare Rehman 2000, p.19, and Boston Consulting Group 2000, p. 21

[3] Boston Consulting Group 2000, p.21

profit potential be realized when the requirements of customer-oriented assortment determination and control have not yet been met?

The key to the answer lies with the customer himself, i.e., in his or her online shopping behavior. If it is assumed that "e-shopping is a fully new enterprise with its own demands"[4], one can conclude that customers and business conventions in the virtual world are essentially no different from those in the real world. On the Internet, the retailer and his suppliers face old challenges. Customer guidance systems and product placement must accommodate the demands of buying behavior. The product assortment must be oriented to the customer in its breadth and depth. Promotions must be coordinated between sales partners and tuned to particular target groups. To reach these goals, it is necessary for retailers and manufacturers to collaborate on their assortment control systematically. The knowledge about the customer that each partner has must be synergized. It is for these purposes that customer-oriented assortment planning and control, also known as category management, is being developed and used in traditional retailing outlets.

The term 'Category Management' (CM) refers to a market-oriented process of managing categories as strategic business units in retail.[5] Thereby, specially chosen suppliers can be named category captains or category consultants to consult retail on categories defined from the perspective of the consumer in contrast to product groups traditionally defined by the products themselves. The manufacturer's

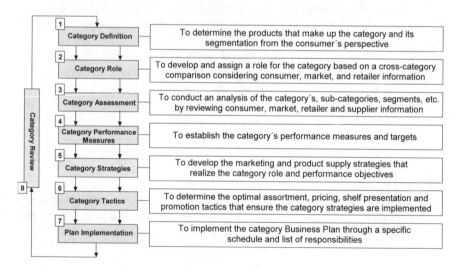

Figure 13.1: The Classic Category Management Process[6]

---

[4] OC&C 1999, p.6

[5] Müller-Hagedorn/Zielke 2000

[6] ECR Europe 1997, p.21

knowledge is used by the retailers to optimize their product line and thereby to distinguish themselves from the competition. This practice is being used primarily by grocers, but also by others in the consumer goods business. Individual cases have documented significant revenue and return on investment increases, although not without high demands, especially in the area of cooperative information management, which was often neglected in the past.[7]

Figure 13.1 depicts a classic category management process. Can it be adapted to the virtual world? For online shops, the following features of category management should be considered against the backdrop of the situation in electronic trade channels.

13.2 Category Management for Online Shops

In June 2001, a research group called "Category Management for Online Shops" was founded under the auspices of ECR Germany, Austria and Switzerland. The goal of this group of dedicated retailers and manufacturers was to successfully apply the classic category management model to e-commerce. By deriving conceptual formulations and work content and integrating it all into a workable business solution, the objective is to generate a general framework for systematic collaboration in the electronic trade channel that emphasizes on faster decision-making and execution and focuses on adequate control mechanisms in the e-marketplace. The process to be introduced in this article is the first conceptual work to come out of the research group.

Category management, in large part because of improved access to consumer data, has opened a larger window of opportunity in e-retailing. Product mix can be more strongly directed at target groups through online retailing rather than through comparable efforts at bricks-and-mortar outlets. This fact is reflected in a comparison (in Figure 13.2) between the classic definitions[8] and the modified definitions[9] of Category Management when the latter is applied to online stores.

13.3 Requirements for and Demands on the Process

A number of partially interdependent factors must be considered in the modeling of category management for online stores. Besides generic factors like organization, cooperation, technology and resources, some factors are of particular interest and are listed below.

---

[7] Schröder et al. 2000

[8] ECR Europe 1997, S. 8

[9] Compare figure 2.

„Conventional" Category Management	Category Management for Online Stores ...
is a continuous retailer/supplier process	
– of managing categories as strategic business units	– of managing *target group specific* categories – allowing the usage of *one-to-one* marketing activities,
... producing enhanced business results by focusing on delivering costumer value.	

A Category ...

– is a distinct, manageable group of products/services	– is a *target group specific*, manageable group of products/services
... that consumers perceive to be interrelated and/or suitable in meeting a consumer need.	

Source: ECR Europe 1997, p. 8; ECR D-A-CH 2001

Figure 13.2:   Deriving the Definition of "Category Management for Online Stores"

13.3.1 Consumer Behavior in Multiplexed Systems

The starting point for product-mix policy measures in category management is the attitude of the buyer. In the case of category management for e-commerce, an approach could be developed, which *prima facie* considers only the behavior of the customer online. The customer however moves in a network of different trade channels. Empirical studies on the alternating influence of trade channels for the US,[10] Europe[11] and Germany[12] show that individual transactions are increasingly conducted in several trade channels. As an example, the customer could inform himself or herself in detail on the Internet about a product seen in a catalogue, examine it at a conventional outlet, order it online with a credit card, pick the goods up in person to save on postage and finally exchange them there because there were defective after obtaining yet more information online and in person. See Figure 13.3.

---

[10] National Retail Federation et al. 2000, p.4 f. and the examination by Shop.org et al. 2001, p.6

[11] Boston Consulting Group 2001, p.15 ff

[12] Silberberger 2001

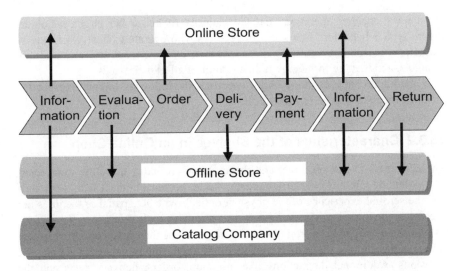

Figure 13.3:   Use of Several Channels During a Single Transaction

Customer needs must be met via multiple channels and the buyer's decision-making process must be seamlessly supported. The future of e-retailing will, for this reason belong, to the integrated multiplexed retailers – the so-called 'click and mortar' companies.[13] The question then is to what extent is the category management process proposed for online shops valid? Is it only valid for pure plays or valid also for multi channel companies? To answer this question, consumer behavior in the multiplexed system should be considered. Three types of behavior have been identified.

- Type 1 uses one channel exclusively, e.g. only shops in a conventional outlet. (consistent behavior)

- Type 2 uses different channels for different products, some store bought, others online. (hybrid behavior)

- Type 3 uses several channels based on the individual situation, and within the context of individual purchases. (multi-option behavior)

When a multi-channel retailer's market research shows that customers are exhibiting type 3 behavior, product mix determination and control should be coordinated across channels. From the retailer's perspective, CM would then have to develop into a multi-channel approach in response to the growing revenues accountable to the new channels. This conclusion is only compelling when the retailer in question

---

[13] Calkins et al. 2000: p.144 ff.; Vishwanath/Mulvin 2001, p.26 f.

has a multi-channel operation, and the majority of his or her target customers Figure type 3 behavior. This goes for retailers who operate exclusively in the e-marketplace also. They must consider that their customers are active in multiple channels, and that the former are unlikely to meet all of their needs.

In the interest of illustrating online specifics, the following Internet perspective on CM processes will be brought forth.

13.3.2 Characteristics of the Shelves in an Online Shop

The customers in a retail outlet and those online are likely to be the same ones. The points of sale however differ greatly.[14] The personal contact with sales staff and the sensual experience of the physical outlet – whether spatial or tactile is not present in the digital world, or if it is present, only in limited measure. The cognitive maps customers have from those experiences lose their value online or inhibit the learning of a new mode of acquiring information, finding products and making decisions. Additional distractions like minimum orders, delivery costs and the coordination of delivery times lead, on the whole, to a significant change in the purchase decision process relative to the habits formed in conventional outlets.[15]

For the retailer, the Internet offers significantly fewer restrictions than a conventional outlet. This applies especially to the collection of data on the customer and his buying behavior, the range and time-referenced flexibility of assortments, as well as the systematic possibility for interaction with identifiable customers and the reaction options to their actions. I f the navigation and transaction data generated at the retailer's website is supplemented with information from external partners, good demographics and segmentation information on customers can be readily obtained. Cross-selling and up-selling are then assortment specific and comprehensive too.[16] The virtual outlet allows the use of multiple placement, a fundamental of assortments directed at target customers.[17] It is noteworthy that the customers' ability to process the information with which they confronted, as well as the size of their computer screens ultimately limits the 'shelf space' available. For this reason alone, a target customer oriented assortment, possibly with only limited offers can be advantageous. The limited 'shelf space' can be and must be used in a very efficient way The goal is to support customers in their decision-making process, not to overtax their already strained concentration with a boundless range of goods.

Carrying the principle of orientation to the customer and correspondingly his or her target group a step further, categories for specific target groups can be defined.

---

[14] Ahlert 1996: p.140

[15] Schröder 2001: p.2 ff

[16] Wiedmann et al. 2001: p.38

[17] Großweischede 2001: p. 318 ff

Not only the digital components of the offering, but also the product groups can be broken down into subcategories or articles and assembled into bundles according to customer profiles. In principle, any desired comprehensive or special arrangement of the product mix is thereby possible all the way up to being a "Shop of one assortment".[18] The conditions to change conventional CM are thereby characterized by objectively defined product groups and create a comprehensive customer oriented approach. This is, however, not to be seen as a revolutionary restructuring of the retail offering. In applying all measures of CM, online or in an outlet, the central requirement must be met: the presentation of product must correspond to the natural purchasing process of the target customer.

13.3.3 The Impetus of Customer Relationship Management

A study in the US investigated how each customer group influenced the success of an online grocer (see Figure 13.4). The profitability of different groups was simulated using data on the market, firms in the market and the target groups, including infor-

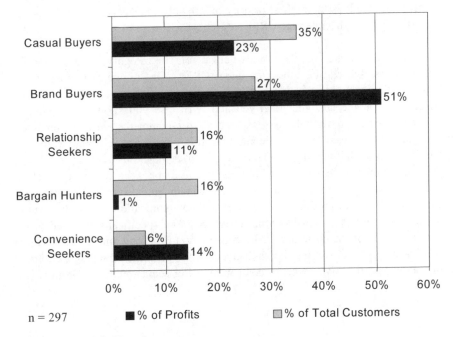

n = 297   ■ % of Profits   ▨ % of Total Customers

Source: Chu et al. 2000, p. 8

Figure 13.4: Customer Segment Profitability Analysis

---

[18] Albers/Peters 1997: p. 73

mation on their purchasing behavior. So called brand-name buyers appreciate convenience and are not very sensitive to pricing. They are responsible for 51% of profits although they represented only 27% of the regular customers. In contrast, bargain hunters, representing 16% of the market contributed 1% to total earnings.[19]

That it is economically sensible to orient a product line toward profitable customer groups and to develop their loyalty is a lesson learned long before the advent of e-commerce. Indeed, in the wake of declining customer loyalty in the consumer goods market and through the expansion of cost intensive electronic retailing, the attraction and retention of profitable market share is more central than ever. Therefore, the term 'customer relationship management' (CRM) suggests that via complete and comprehensive customer management, customers and their needs should become the focus of corporate strategy. CRM includes all customer-oriented measures which contribute to raising customer profitability and customer lifetime value.[20]

Through the compilation of all customer information, a unified corporate-wide or cooperation-wide customer profile is created in order to better understand the needs of the customer and to better fulfill them across all channels. The orientation to customer needs is the highest priority of category management. Kracklauer & Seifert, for example, interpret CRM as a consistent extension of category management.[21]

One-to-one marketing plays a particular role in category management for online shops, and can be subsumed under CRM. "One-to-one marketing means being willing and able to change your behavior toward an individual customer based on what the customer tells you and what else you know about the customer."[22] The customer, who is registered at an e-commerce website, communicates his or her needs through, among other things, an order. Through every further interaction: additional orders, product inquiries, reactions to direct marketing, the activity on the website, the retailer learns more about the customer. Purchase history and other information on consumer behavior rounds up the customer profile. The offering of products and services and communication can, in the form of implied or explicit personalization, always be more specifically trimmed to the specific needs of the customer.[23] The construction of a long and stable customer relationship gives the online shop a distinct advantage in the future competition of the buying profile. Even when a comparable offer seems only a click away, the

---

[19] Chu et al. 2000: p. 7 f

[20] Emmert/Buchta 2000: p. 27

[21] 2001: p.52

[22] Peppers et al. 1999: p.151

[23] Riemer/Klein 2001: p.149

competitor still does not know anything about the preference structure of the customer and cannot offer him a comparable solution.[24]

The more precisely the preferences of the customer, but not only in the way of product categories or brand names, are known, the more precisely the individual cluster of needs can be filled through personalized service. In the framework of assortment composition, this can lead to offering customers, who have been identified as dog owners, products consistent with those of dog owners (implied personalization). Consumers without pets would probably not show this category of goods although there is the danger that they feel patronized. Better indications are for a demand-tailored product-mix composition delivered by the customer himself (explicit personalization).

In the use of personalization tools, it should be recognized that customers prefer changes they have initiated to those controlled by the retailer. In particular, product suggestions based on the knowledge of other customers' purchases can meet with resistance.[25] Customer orientation should also not be interpreted in a way that limits the personalized palette of goods and services so as to countermand the firm's objectives. Furthermore, one must be careful in the use of implied personalization, not to permanently change web presence and category structures so as to irritate the customer instead of encouraging additional purchases.[26] Not everything that can be achieved technically makes sense economically. This is especially true for e-retailing.

13.3.4 Cooperation between Retailers and Manufacturers

Category management is commonly considered to be the same as the cooperation on product mix between retailers and selected suppliers. Just as a manufacturer can design his product line according to the tenets of category management alone, a retailer can try to optimize his product mix without the help of a category captain.[27] The real benefit of category management is achieved, however, when customer data is compiled and the resources of both retailer and manufacturer used cooperatively.

Retailers can use suppliers' product group-specific knowledge in order to better orient their product mix to the customer and thereby to distinguish themselves from competitors. Category captains usually have an informational advantage on competition. They strengthen the trust between trade partners and have the opportunity to influence the product mix in order to support 'their' product groups and brand-driven objectives. However, the opportunities described are countered by

---

[24] Peppers et al. 1999: p.152

[25] Burke 2000: p.17

[26] Schröder 2001a

[27] Großweischede 2000: p.4 f.; Holzkämper 1999: p.49 ff

attendant risks. Cooperating retailers and manufacturers risk a drain on their know-how. One could imagine that partners regard the relationship opportunistically and contrary to their agreement give sensitive information to their partner's competition. Category captains must under certain circumstances make recommendations at the cost of their own product and portfolio in categories where a competitor profits excessively from their consulting. Additionally, in conventional retailing, small businesses suffer from the extensive consulting work required in the CM process. That is why some manufacturers are very reluctant to take over the role of a category captain.

On the Internet, the revenues and expected gains in cooperation relative to conventional retailing are marginal. So under which conditions can a retailer expect the support of his or her suppliers in the development and implementation of a category management system? The answer seems simple. The partners must receive a net benefit from the cooperative agreement.[28] An initially disappointing cost-benefit ratio is acceptable when long-term advantages are expected.[29] For the retail organization looking to amortize its considerable investment in the electronic infrastructure, there are several reasons for calling for online collaboration in the framework of category management:

- Support in the determination of comprehensive and channel specific assortments

- Improvement of the understanding of purchase behavior – online and in a multiplexed system through quantitative and qualitative market research

- Use of the manufacturer's brand name appeal to overcome buyers' inhibitions about buying online

- Secured access to profitable market share in the e-commerce arena

- Access to the manufacturer's existing Internet knowledge-base including the technical aspects of online marketing

- Creation and expansion of relationships to include leading manufacturers (applies to representatives of retailers who are either only or primarily Internet based)

On the side of suppliers, the economic incentive to enter cooperative agreements is lesser than ever before. In the online grocery business – a relatively unsuccessful sector of e-commerce up until now, even top-name products may have less than € 50,000 in yearly revenues per retailer. As a rule, it is brand-name manufac-

---

[28] Meffert 1981: p.102

[29] Anderson/Weitz 1992: p.19

turers, who desire a presence for their target groups in all relevant trade channels. In supporting e-retailing, they can expect the following benefits:

- Information about online consumer behavior and in the case of click-and-mortar retailers, about the multiplexed purchase decision process

- Improvement of the management of integrated trade channels particularly in the manufacturer's own organization

- Secured and strengthened brand identity through direct control

- Access to profitable customer groups in the realm of e-commerce

- Use of direct customer feedback on the new and further development of products

- Access to virtual test markets for market research

- Hindrance of competitors in accessing the e-marketplace

- Distinction in the eyes of the consumer of having a multi-channel presence

- Distinction in the eyes of the trade partner as being a comprehensive leader in category management with potentially positive effects for conventional retail outlets

In addition to the economic objectives of increasing revenue and profit, CM can also be used for a mutual improvement of data collection and customer contact a concept that is also referred to as Collaborative Customer Relationship Management.[30] Activities directed at target groups, including information exchange and a coordinated customer approach, place extensive requirements on the database, especially in the implied personalization of bundling.

13.4 Category Management for Online Shops

The control of the product mix on the Internet represents a significant yet unexplored topic in both theory and practice. The first attempts at electronic CM are found in *Pramataris/Doukidis* [31]. *Großweischede* derived a set of recommendations for target group oriented phases from there. In the following described proc-

---

[30] Kracklauer/Seifert 2001: p.54 f.
[31] 2000

ess (based on the research of the CCG[32]), the insights of the firms gained in conventional retailing are included. Additionally, the experiences of retailers and suppliers in e-commerce are considered. To test their viability, the proposed measures were first operated as pilot projects.

13.4.1 Overview

In cooperatively organized category management, two cases can be identified. There is first the cooperation of a retailer, be it a multiplexed organization, e.g. Wal-Mart, or a retailer which can only be found online, e.g. LeShop, with a manufacturer on the one hand and a *subsequent cooperative agreement* of both partners on the other hand. At the beginning of a cooperative agreement, there are three phases to be covered which serve strategic direction and coordination. These phases do not, as a rule, need to be recreated by repeat agreements, although their results are regularly reviewed and if necessary amended. For this reason, the model is organized in two parts: strategic direction and coordination. The operational configuration is shown in Figure 13.5.

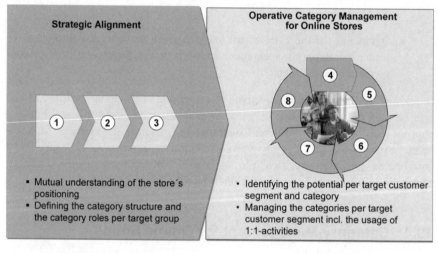

Source: Roland Berger Strategy Consultants, ECR D-A-CH

Figure 13.5:   The Bipartite Category Business Planning Process for Online Stores

---

[32] Maasen/Locher 2001, Großweischede et al. 2002

13.4.2 The Phases of Strategic Direction and Coordination

Phase 1: Positioning

To begin, the scope of positioning must be coordinated and approved. This means that the cooperation partners must discuss the target groups, how the partnership will differentiate itself from the competition and what the essence of the tender will be. A common understanding of the target group, its needs structure and differentiation strategy, is essential for the success of the partnership.

In many cases, while identifying the most attractive target group, the consumer typology derived through studies of conventional retailing and often e-commerce can be checked for its suitability. The temptation to only use data from Internet sources (demographic and purchasing behavior) to define target groups should be resisted. For one, consumers are active in a multi-channel marketplace, and for another, offline segmentation criteria should be considered.

This is how the Swiss grocer LeShop.ch, based on qualitative and quantitative data about consumer behavior and customer profitability, determined that young families with children and a working mother should be its target group. Only following an analysis of current and future competition can the so-called value proposition be derived, showing that the store is committed to providing benefits to the consumers (e.g. Le Shop.ch's motto is: "Our vision is convenient buying").

Phase 2: Target Group Specific Category Definition

For the definition of categories, which can vary from retailer to retailer according to target group, the search and buying habits of the consumers must be fathomed. As known in conventional CM, but not always executed,[33] a combination of qualitative and quantitative market research, such as focus groups, the evaluation of click stream data from buyers and non-buyers, invoice analysis etc. is necessary.

In the structuring of categories according to consumer behavior, product use and solution-oriented measures can be combined. The resulting structures are not free of duplication; rather they overlap one another in a fashion analogous to the preference structures of the individual customers. Individual articles are assigned to multiple categories where appropriate. Peapod, for example, combines classic product-oriented categories such as frozen foods and beverages with solution-oriented categories like baby's place or meals made easy (see Figure 13.6). Tesco offers direct delivery of fourteen so-called warehouses additional to the local grocery assortment from the outlet. Warehouses comprise categories like baby and toddler ("you and your child"), books and music, electrical and home living, fashion and flowers.

---

[33] Schröder 2001 b

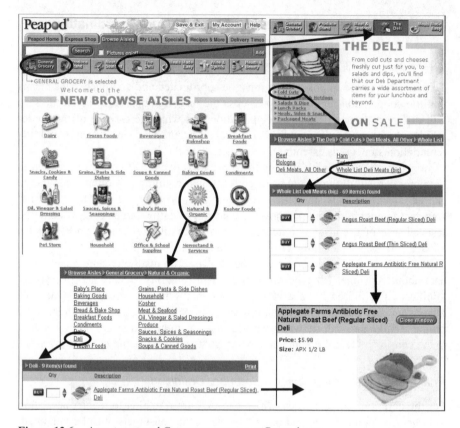

Figure 13.6:   Assortment and Category-structure at Peapod.com

The availability of a technical solution for personalizing categories, implicitly or explicitly, has hardly been used. A study of German Internet retailers by *Kotzab/Madlberger* came to the conclusion that none of these companies used virtual shop design or bundled products and services.

Phase 3: Target Group Specific Category Roles

In this phase, categories are assigned roles. In principle, they are no different than classic CM. Here, the question that must be answered is: Which categories are relevant for the target customers? Resource allocation accompanies the definition of category roles according to category and target group. The mistake made in CM with conventional retailing – that of assigning isolated roles to categories, instead of coordinating between them, should not be repeated.

To develop different categories for different target groups, the significance of specific categories for specific market segments must be understood, both in the real and virtual retail environments. For this purpose, uni-variate statistical research and variation analysis according to sales, frequency, penetration affinity index etc. and clickstream research according to loiter time, page views etc. can be done. In the end, the objective is to determine the significance of the categories relative to the competition. The comparison between what is bought in conventional outlets vs. online can reveal that certain categories can be better distinguished on the web.

Based on the consumer behavior of its target group of working mothers, LeShop.ch defined the profile-based categories 'Babies', 'Bio' and 'Pets'. For young mothers, baby products have special significance. Qualitative market research showed that young families in particular place a high priority on nutrition and that this target group is also likely to have a pet.

Steps in Operational Category Management

When the segment and category-spanning phase of strategic determination and coordination is complete, the operational planning of the categories can begin. Ideally, the project is not a one-time affair, as is often the case in conventional retailing, but a continually evolving process between online retailers and manufacturers. (See Figure 13.7)

Phase 4: Target Group Specific Category Evaluation

The basis for operational CM groups is the sales and earnings potential attributed to each target segment. The goal is to understand the reason why identified potentials have not been exploited. To that end, pockets of opportunity must be sought

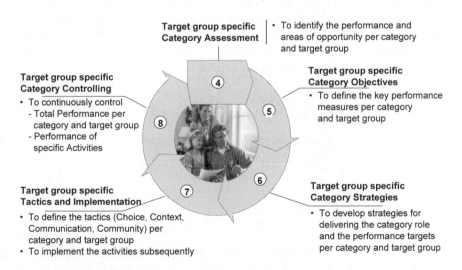

Source: Roland Berger Strategy Consultants, ECR D-A-CH

Figure 13.7: The Five Operative Category Management Steps

based on consumer profiles through the comparison of external and internal benchmarks.

External benchmarks to the extent that they can be determined are indices like customer acquisition rates, customer conversion rates, the level of customer loyalty enjoyed by online competitors in the same market, and best practices retailers from other markets. When opportunities are identified, the details can be researched. "How do customer approach and marketing mix differentiate themselves?" or " Which differences exist in the applicability of the tender for e-retailing?" are examples of exploratory questions. Another is the comparison of the consumer behavior of the target group and category online vs. that in retail outlets according to demand fulfillment, frequency etc.

In the framework of internal benchmarking, the comparison of categories with similar characteristics in the e-marketplace is important. From this perspective, differences in frequency and repeat sales can be investigated with inquiries about the inter-category overlap with the customer profile of the dominant group or specific marketing mixes. It can be possible that similar inter-category differences exist for competitors as well, in which case data collection can pose a larger problem. In the second step, the differences between online consumer behavior in general and the target groups are analyzed. Can this be, for example, explained by a softening in demand or by the fact that customers are now fulfilling their demand through competitive e-retailers or through other channels?

Many of the questions demand an analysis of an online shop's existing database. With the help of a data mining application, consumer behavior can be investigated. In the case of LeShop.ch, one can examine sales down to the level of a single purchase by an individual consumer. This Swiss e-retailer guarantees its manufacturing partners access to this data mining application in the framework of it cooperative category management agreement. Legal restrictions of cause are strictly observed. With the help of these tools, the database can be analyzed according to different dimensions and at various levels of aggregation. (see Figure 13.8) For example:

- Customer type (Total, target customer, regular target customer etc.)

- Age, gender, location, or language of the consumer

- Category and article

- Time of sale

- Manufacturer and distributor of the article(s)

Also, in this phase, it is necessary to support database analysis through qualitative, ideally comprehensive market research studies. Manufacturers offer category-specific support through panel investigations or ad hoc studies.

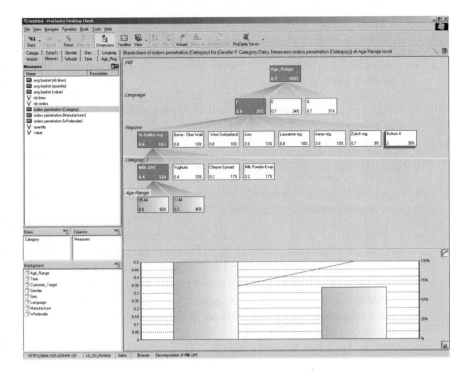

Source: ECR D-A-CH 2001

Figure 13.8:   Data-Mining-Tool of LeShop.ch

Phase 5:   *The Results of the Evaluation Phase Form the Basis for the Determination of Performance Objectives*

These are determined for each target group and category. First, the overall goal, like earnings, market share, frequency, transaction value etc. has to be determined. To operationalize this, a list of success factors for each target group and category is derived. In the last step, target values of the indices are established based on category valuations. These values hold good for each category and target group, whereby in a consolidated overview, the effects on e-retailing are analyzed in total. As with classic CM, online category management also uses a scorecard. In contrast to conventional retailing though, every index of consumer behavior (frequency, transaction value, satisfaction) can be more rigorously monitored.

Phase 6: Target Group Specific Category Strategies

After the role is fixed, the category valuated and the performance objectives derived, the marketing strategies of each target group and category are to be defined. They serve as an orientation framework for the determining target-group specific activities in Phase 7. Four strategies are available which can be combined and are only roughly distinguishable from one another.

- Quality and additional value: large selection, supplemental product information and service

- Value: meet basic shopper needs and offer competitive prices; quick and easy shopping

- Service and problem solutions: Comprehensive information and consultation, superior, personalized customer service.

- Experience: Large selection, comprehensive information and consultation, personalized customer service

- The appropriate strategy or combination of strategies is chosen with respect to the target customer's needs and the chosen category must harmonize with the category role. For example, the multiplexed English grocer Tesco pursued a decisive strategy with its 'You and your child' category. (www.tesco.com/youandyourchild/) Nearly everything was presented – from detailed information on children in the form of brief articles, chats and roundtables through a customer club ('baby club', 'toddler club') to a connection to a live external community (iVillage.uk).

Phase 7: Target-Group Specific Tactics and Implementation

From the strategies, specific target-group tactics are derived for each category and implemented. Their use must be evaluated in view of their contribution to performance objectives. The individual tactics group themselves into the four areas shown in figure 13.9.

- Choice: tender and price

- Context: presentation

- Communication

- Community: interaction and virtual communities

Under the four "C"'s, the traditional measures of marketing mix can be subsumed: the 4 "P"'s. In any case, this reflects the increasingly useful aspects of the Internet unique to it in e-commerce. The tactics covered here differentiate themselves from those used in conventional retailing.

While all of the activities mentioned here cannot be explained in detail[34], their use can be described through a case example. Imagine an Internet retailer who has

---

[34] More at Großweischede 2001

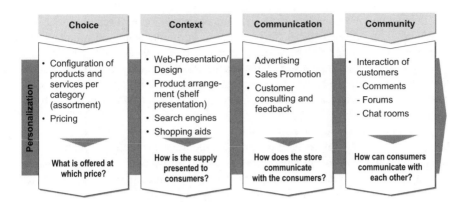

Source: Roland Berger Strategy Consultants, ECR D-A-CH

Figure 13.9:   Target Group Specific Activities

defined the category 'everything for children'. This category has been assigned a destination role. The target group of the e-retailer is young mothers, who are always busy. Their needs can be filled through a combination of strategies, 'experience', 'service' and 'solutions'. Based on available data and the capabilities of the retailer's software application, the retailer is able to tender a personalized offer. He can offer potential customers an individualized, current and demand-sensitive product mix and present it in a way especially attractive to them.[35] Mothers are presented products based on their buying history and the age of their children. In this way, the category 'everything for children' changes over time in step with the age of the child. Beyond the products of their suppliers, the retailer links other merchants who offer products and services of interest to their target group. The service of a childcare provider and a tutor are integrated in their partner program.

The corresponding category partner of the e-retailer, a leading producer of baby products, has learned through intensive interviews that for many who belong to the target group but have not purchased online, Internet shopping is too unfamiliar. The majority of these potential customers miss the orientation and logic of the in-store experience. The retailer knows that the customer should be granted the navigation bar and search systematics of her choice.[36] It can be concluded that the shopping environment made available should be most amenable to the customer's existing cognitive structures. The best case would be a three-dimensional space reminiscent of a conventional retail outlet. Therefore, with the help of a category captain, the retailer creates 3D shelves for the category 'everything for children' from which customers can place their items in a virtual shopping cart with each mouse click.

---

[35] Tomczak et al. 1999: p.116 f.

[36] Morganosky/Cude 2000: p.24

The creation of a complete virtual 3D store is possible, but because of the limited bandwidth on the Internet, this has yet to be implemented on a large scale. The effect of 3D shopping on consumer behavior therefore cannot be conclusively evaluated.[37] Current empirical research results from *Diehl/Weinberg* (2002) show however that virtual shelves have similar effects on consumers as real ones. Thereby, the experience of shelf design from traditional CM can be used in the creation of 3D shelves in a virtual store.

In addition to tactics from the fields 'Choice' and 'Context', the example above identifies several areas of potential cooperation for retailers and manufacturers. This can lead to the integration of a shop into shopping solutions. In the tactical area of 'Communication', brand name manufacturers of perfume are making web modules available that are integrated into a web site. In this way brand equities of highly charged products should be secured on the Internet. Manufacturers and retailers can test the efficiency of advertising and promotions on a neatly defined market segment through their web presence. The same goes for calculation of reaction to pricing policy in promotions as well as everyday prices. For instance, one day in March 2001, the multiplexed retailer Schlecker offered a far broader selection of Nivea products in its virtual stores than in its conventional locations. These products were priced 17 to 35% lower. In similar tests, five other brand name manufacturers participated and received access to all the data thereby collected.[38] Through the direct interaction with the customer, marketing efforts can be tested together and in combination with one another online. Implications can be derived from the results that are relevant for the marketing mix of both conventional and online retailing.

In this way, an online presence has something to offer to CM in conventional retailing, in underdeveloped efforts in cooperative development, and in introduction of new products.[39] In the area of new product introduction, a virtual presence offers an inexpensive test market. Participants in product tests can be selected from narrowly defined target groups. Market tests are likewise precise with respect to the target group and not immediately visible to the competition. In an environment where the customer and the contents of his shopping cart are known, not only can products be ideally tested, but ideas about new products and the further development of existing ones under nearly laboratory conditions. A project run by the Swiss franchise of Henkel and LeShop.ch signifies the potential of such cooperation. The laundry detergent MiniRisk, produced without allergic ingredients, is offered exclusively to customers of LeShop and supported with targeted online and offline promotions. Under such conditions, the effectiveness of a marketing campaign can be observed precisely.[40]

---

[37] Burke 2000: p.19

[38] Wolfskeil 2001

[39] Borchert 2001: p.50; Großweischede 2000: p.186

[40] Hofstetter/Locher 2001

Phase 8: Target Group Specific Category Control

At the end of the first iteration of the rolling business process, a check on effectiveness and variance is introduced. It should be ascertained whether or not agreed upon objectives were achieved in the manner expected and if not, shortfalls should be identified in a timely fashion and their root causes uncovered. For this purpose, selected indices of success at the category level of each target group must be reviewed. In the area of quantitative measurements the process can be automated. Instruments for the measurement of qualitative indices like customer satisfaction must also be institutionalized. In the case of a shortfall relative to the ideal value, an attempt has to be made to identify the measures that contributed to the shortfall. By the same token, exceptional success needs to be documented. Identifying shortfalls and successes can lead through feedback loops in CM to improved tactics.

Summary

The use of category management in e-retailing provides a marketing framework for the realization of cooperative, customer-oriented product mix policies. It does not distinguish itself fundamentally from the classic model of category management, even though the specific methods available for use on the Internet are unavailable in conventional retailing. Moreover, the opportunities for electronic interaction with the customer are used to sharpen the focus on target groups in the management of categories. Target potential customers can be precisely identified and their behavior analyzed in detail instead of having to resort to the often too-highly aggregative, level of national sales figures.

If the customer is known and his or her behavior online is systematically documented, one-to-one marketing activities down to the level of individual assortment control can be employed. The limits are not necessarily technical ones; rather they are set by consumer behavior online and offline which serves as the starting point for assortment management. It is important to consider in particular the role of the thought processes in the online buyer's decision making. For the same reason, CM business processes must reflect the fact that different trade channels influence one another. For online retailers who belong to a multiplexed system it is not sufficient to optimize the virtual store and the product offered in isolation.

For conventional retail, there are new opportunities to learn from online CM. Instead of simply using existing product groups without further thought, as is often observed, the success of need based categories can be examined. Furthermore, an e-presence allows the testing of marketing schemes on target groups and the introduction of new products under ideal conditions. Considering the incentives and the increased availability of customer data, it can be expected that comprehensive, multiplexed cooperation between retailers and manufacturers in e-retailing has more leverage than when only applied to conventional retailing.

Ready access to data must not lead to blind faith in data, and must not end in electronic controls that steer product mix automatically. The contributions of qualitative market research to differentiation from the competition are easily as important in the virtual environment as the physical one.

Finally, CM for e-retailing will lead to increasing integration of the inter- and intra-category marketing mix. The boundary blurs appreciably between the assortment-oriented uses of CM and those that primarily serve to strengthen customer contact, like CRM. The development of multiplexed retailing will increase this tendency.

References

Albers, S. and Peters, K. (1997): Die Wertschöpfungskette des Handels im Zeitalter des Electronic Commerce, in: Marketing ZFP, Heft 2, pp. 69-80.

Anderson, E. and Weitz, B. A. (1992): The Use of Pledges to Build and Sustain Commitment in Distribution Channels, in: Journal of Marketing Research, Nr. 1, pp. 18-34.

Bauer, H. H., Fischer, M. and Sauer, N. E. (1999): Wahrnehmung und Akzeptanz des Internet als Einkaufsstätte – Theorie und empirische Befunde, Wissenschaftliches Arbeitspapier Nr. 26, Institut für Marktorientierte Unternehmensführung Universität Mannheim, Mannheim.

Borchert, S. (2001): Führung von Distributionsnetzwerken – Eine Konzeption der Systemführung von Unternehmungsnetzwerken zur erfolgreichen Realisation von Efficient Consumer Response-Kooperationen, Wiesbaden.

Boston Consulting Group (2001): The Multichannel Consumer – The Need to Integrate Online and Offline Channels in Europe, o.O.

Boston Consulting Group (2000): Winning the Online-Consumer – Insights into Online Consumer Behavior, o.O.

Burke, R. R. (2000):Creating the Ideal Shopping Experience – What Consumers Want in the Physical and Virtual Store, hrsg. von KPMG LLP/Indiana University, USA, o.O.

Calkins, J. D., Farello, M. J. and Smith Shi, C. (2000). From retailing to e-tailing, in: The McKinsey Quarterly, Nr. 1,pp. 140-147.

Chu, J., Sun, M., Rastogi, S. and Berzins, A. (2000): The Year 2000 Online Retailing Agenda, Bain & Company/Mainspring eStrategy Brief, Boston, Cambridge.

Diehl, S. and Weinberg, P. (2002): Vergleich der Wirkungen von realer und virtueller Ladengestaltung aus verhaltenswissenschaftlicher Perspektive, in: Ahlert,

D./Olbrich, R./Schröder, H. (Edit.): Jahrbuch Handelsmanagement 2002, Frankfurt am Main.

ECR Europe (1997): Category Management Best Practices Report, London.

ECR D-A-CH (2001): Category Management für Online-Shops – Dokumentation des Soll-Prozesses, Dokumentation der Ergebnisse der ECR D-A-CH Arbeitsgruppe „Category Management für Online-Shops", Köln/Bonn.

Großweischede, M. (2001): Category Management im eRetailing – Konzeptionelle Grundlagen und Umsetzungsansätze am Beispiel der Lebensmittelbranche, in: Ahlert, D./Olbrich, R./Schröder, H. (Edit.): Jahrbuch Handelsmanagement 2001 – Vertikales Marketing und Markenführung im Zeichen von Category Management, Frankfurt am Main, pp. 293-337.

Großweischede, M. (2000): Category Management aus Sicht der Lieferanten des Lebensmitteleinzelhandels – Grundlagen und ausgewählte Ergebnisse einer empirischen Studie, in: Ahlert, D./Borchert, S. (Edit.): Prozessmanagement im vertikalen Marketing – Efficient Consumer Response (ECR) in Konsumgüternetzen, Berlin u.a., pp. 159-192.

Haupt, U. and Ansorge, P. (2001): Internetshopping-GAU – vom Design-Störfall zur Umsatzkatastrophe, in: Klietmann, M. (Edit.): Kunden im E-Commerce – Verbraucherprofile, Vertriebstechniken, Vertrauensmanagement, Düsseldorf, pp. 53-71.

Hofstetter, W. T. and Locher, D. P. (2001): MiniRisk@LeShop.ch, Präsentation für den CCG/ECR D-A-CH-Arbeitskreis „Category Management für Online-Shops" auf dem 2. ECR-Tag, Track „eDemand Side Forum", Bonn, 6. September 2001.

Holzkämper, O. (1999): Category Management – Strategische Positionierung des Handels, Göttingen.

Homburg, C. and Sieben, F. G. (2000): Customer Relationship Management (CRM) – Strategische Ausrichtung statt IT-getriebenem Aktivismus, in: Bruhn, M./Homburg, C. (Edit.): Handbuch Kundenbindungsmangement – Grundlagen, Konzepte, Erfahrungen, 3. Aufl., Wiesbaden, pp. 473-501.

Kotzab, H. and Madlberger, M. (2002): Internet-basierte Distribution im stationären Handel – Empirische Erfahrungen aus Dänemark, Deutschland und Österreich, in: Ahlert, D./Olbrich, R./Schröder, H. (Edit.): Jahrbuch Handelsmanagement 2002, Frankfurt am Main.

Kracklauer, A. and Seifert, D. (2001): Category Management – Stellen Sie die richtigen Fragen, in: Absatzwirtschaft, Nr. 6, pp. 52-55.

Maasen, S. and Locher, D. P. (2001): eCategory Management: Category Management für Online-Shops – Konzeption eines Soll-Prozesses, Präsentation für den CCG/ECR D-A-CH-Arbeitskreis „Category Management für Online-Shops" auf dem 2. ECR-Tag, Track „eDemand Side Forum", Bonn, 6. September 2001.

Meffert, H. (1981): Verhaltenswissenschaftliche Aspekte vertraglicher Vertriebssysteme zwischen Industrie und Handel, in: Ahlert, D. (Edit.): Vertragliche Vertriebssysteme zwischen Industrie und Handel – Grundzüge einer betriebswirtschaftlichen, rechtlichen und volkswirtschaftlichen Betrachtung, Wiesbaden, pp. 99-123.

Morganosky, M. A. and Cude, B. J. (2000): Consumer response to online grocery shopping, in: International Journal of Retail & Distribution Management, Nr. 1, pp. 17-26.

Müller-Hagedorn, L. and Zielke, S. (2000): Category Management, in: Albers, S./Herrmann, A. (Edit.): Handbuch Produktmanagement, Wiesbaden, pp. 859-882.

National Retail Federation, Biz.rate.com and J.C. Williams Group (2000): Channel-Surfing – Measuring Multi-Channel Shopping, o.O.

OC&C (1999): Strategische Einsichten – Electronic Shopping News 3/99, Düsseldorf.

Peppers, D., Rogers, M. and Dorf, B. (1999): Is Your Company Ready for One-To-One Marketing?, in: Harvard Business Review, Nr. 1, pp. 151-160.

Pramataris, K. C. and Doukidis, G. I. (2000): The Category Management Process in the Virtual Retail Environment, in: Corsten, D. and Jones, D. T. (Edit.): ECR in the Third Millenium, Brüssel, pp. 46-51.

Riemer, K. and Klein, S. (2001): Personalisierung von Online-Shops – und aus Distanz wird Nähe, in: Klietmann, M. (Edit.): Report Online-Handel, Düsseldorf, pp. 141-163.

Schmickler, M. (2001): Management strategischer Kooperationen zwischen Hersteller und Handel – Konzeption und Realisierung von Efficient Consumer Response-Projekten, Wiesbaden 2001.

Schneider, U. (2000): Rauer Wind im Handel? Neue Chancen durch Wissensmanagement, in: Foscht, T./Jungwirth, G./Schnedlitz, P. (Edit.), Zukunftsperspektiven für das Handelsmanagement, Frankfurt a. M., pp. 125-137.

Schröder, H. (2001a): Intransparenz und Kaufrisiken beim Electronic Shopping – Was E-Retailer über die Kunden im B2C-Bereich wissen sollten, Arbeitspapier Nr. 9 des Lehrstuhls für Marketing & Handel an der Universität Essen, Essen.

Schröder, H. (2001b): Wer hat bei Category Management an Efficient Shelf Presentation gedacht? – Informationen für kundenorientierte Flächenzuteilung und Warenpräsentationen im Lebensmittel-Einzelhandel, in: Ahlert, D./Olbrich,

R./Schröder, H. (Edit.): Jahrbuch Handelsmanagement 2001 – Vertikales Marketing und Markenführung im Zeichen von Category Management, Frankfurt a. M., pp. 261-291.

Schröder, H., Feller, M. and Großweischede, M. (2000): Zum Status quo von Category Management und Supply Chain Management – Ergebnisse einer empirischen Studie, Arbeitspapier Nr. 6 des Lehrstuhls für Marketing & Handel an der Universität Essen, Essen.

Seifert, D. (2001): Efficient Consumer Response – ECR-Erfolgsfaktorenstudie Deutschland – Supply Chain Management, Category Management und Collaborative Planning Forecasting and Replenishment als neue Strategieansätze, 2. ed., München.

Shop.org, J.C. Williams Group, BizRate.com (2001): The Multi-Channel Retail Report, Executive Summary, o.O.

Silberberger, H. (2001): Der Multi-Channel-Kunde: Eine multidimensionale Herausforderung, Vortrag im Rahmen der 2. Handelsblatt-Jahrestagung Marketing-Management im E-Commerce „Multi-Channel-Strategie im Marketing", Mainz, 19.-20. November 2001.

Tomczak, T., Schögel, M. and Birkhofer, B. (1999): Online Distribution als innovativer Absatzkanal, in: Bliemel, F./Fassott, G./Theobald, A. (Edit.): Electronic Commerce – Herausforderungen, Anwendungen, Perspektiven, Wiesbaden, pp. 105-122.

Vishwanath, V. and Mulvin, G. (2001): Multi-Channels: The Real Winners in the B2C Internet Wars, in: Business Strategy Review, Nr. 1, pp. 25-33.

Wiedmann, K.-P., Buxel, H. and Buckler, F. (2001): Hybrid-Commerce: Zukunftsoption für Anbietersysteme der „New- und Old-Economy", in: der markt, Nr. 1, pp. 31-39.

Wolfskeil, J. (2001): Online im Verbund – Schlecker und Markenartikler, Test von Internet-Aktionen, in: Lebensmittel Zeitung, Internet-Edition www.lz-net.de, Funddatum: 23.03.2001.

PART 6:

Conclusions and Key Takeaways

Alexander H. Kracklauer
BayTech IBS, UAS Neu-Ulm, Germany / Harvard Business School, MA, USA

D. Quinn Mills
Harvard Business School, MA, USA

Dirk Seifert
Harvard Business School, MA, USA

The last chapters showed how fast the consumer goods industry develops. ECR as a concept has not yet come to an end. ECR is a tool to satisfy consumer needs, but it needs vertical cooperation, innovation and technological advancements.

One of the most important requirements is that ECR continues to be successful in the development of new concepts on the demand and supply side. Collaborative Customer Relationship Management is the leading concept for the demand chain.

The last few chapters showed how rapidly the consumer goods industry is developing. Customer Relationship Management as a concept is still valuable; it is a tool for satisfying consumer needs, but requires innovation, vertical cooperation and technological advancements. Many companies have failed to understand that a technological rollout of CRM specific software is not sufficient to succeed in the market. Capital expenditures for attracting the customer continue to be unavoidable. Old methods of marketing – direct mailings or banner ads are no longer sufficient to attract and retain customers. It has also become clear that many companies are disappointed by the CRM implementation achieved so far. Large expectations remain unfulfilled. It is critical for CRM initiatives – collaborative or not – to first determine business goals and strategies. Software and state-of-the-art technology achieve cannot achieve any outstanding results by themselves. First, companies must develop a customer value growth strategy and recognize key business leverage points before they discuss the role of technology. Second, they must focus on key customers and channels, their points of contact, and the generation of relevant data in order to develop outstanding CRM initiatives. Third, they need to develop customer-centric metrics, which enable the whole organization to be focused on customer acquisition, retention and development. The enterprise, in the end, should be understood as a learning organization; one in which appropriate test-and-learn approaches are encouraged and often lead to its advancement.

In the second section, after having presented the principles of successful CRM and explained that CRM is not merely a technological development, we elaborated on the new concept of Collaborative Customer Relationship Management. CCRM is a new strategic approach in the consumer goods sector and represents a significant advancement in the joint effort between supplier and retailer to meet and exceed customer expectations. Like CRM, CCRM also focuses on the customer, but uses capabilities along the value chain to maximize customer lifetime value. Different participants in the value chain possess different kinds of knowledge about the consumer. The unification of the different views leads to a global picture of the customer. Often enterprises pursue similar targets because suppliers and retailers are interested in increasing the loyalty of their customers. While the retailer forces this for his own stores, the manufacturer is interested in brand loyalty. A cooperative strategy among dealers and manufacturers can contribute to both parties achieving their objectives by using the strengths of their partners. Value – adding partnerships are based on the use of differentiation in marketing as well as on the elimination of non-value adding costs in the supply chain. Higher consumer satisfaction and increased brand and store loyalty are results of successful cooperation between industry and trade.

By observing the core process of CRM and the points of contact between consumers and retailers, countless mutual opportunities that result in added value can be uncovered.

Since consumer information is mainly contributed by the supplier, the possibility of realizing additional value-chain opportunities in sales will increase dramatically through cooperative partnerships. Quantitative and qualitative market research by the supplier will facilitate up-selling or cross-selling. In combination with trade's analytic options (e.g. docket analysis), there will be numerous possibilities for business development (e.g. specific merchandising programs).

In marketing and logistics, most existing partnerships between industry and trade already have successful cooperative business models. Jointly prepared in-store and on-line promotions and direct mailings are good models of the capabilities resulting from a mutual marketing program. The Internet provides new areas of cooperation. There is also tremendous potential in the field of customer service and customer loyalty programs. Consumer databases of large trading companies can be used to run loyalty programs right down to the level of individual outlets. Further, there is also the possibility of identifying profitable customer segments jointly and tying them to the specific outlet or brand.

With the concept of cooperative customer relationship management, the whole process chain is realized. Apart from the technologies, which are necessary for the implementation of this chain, the mutual confidence between trade and manufacturer is a necessary condition for cooperation. Both exchange internal and external data as well as strategic considerations about their target and jointly decide on their future business potential. Multi-functional teams and harmonized information technologies along the value chain are important prerequisites for effective customer management.

Logistical functions must also serve customer relationship management processes. Out-of-stock scenarios, products of poor quality and huge non-value adding costs that result in increased retail prices are but a few examples of mismanaged logistics, which annoy the customer. It is therefore obvious that marketing and logistics must be integrated; for example, to integrate CPFR processes into the Customer Relationship Management, IT infrastructure plays an important role. CPFR uses cooperative planning tools like Syncra, and other developments like Advanced Planning and Scheduling tools. The Internet is opening new dimensions in the use of technology through developments like extranets and web-EDI. Besides suitable IT infrastructures, the integration of logistics in the framework of Customer Relationship Management requires having appropriate organizational prerequisites. Multi-functional teams are an important organizational prerequisite: they facilitate synergies in, for example, the design of joint promotions or in the supply chain. They also simplify the search for customer specific solutions and provide knowledge and flexibility vis-a-vis the changing demands of both business partner and consumer.

The advantages of cooperation between value chain partners are significant and can lead to several value improvements. Reduced out-of-stocks, lower inventory costs, and better data to mass customize products are some of the advantages for the supplier and the retailer.

A global study by Deloitte Consulting shows the advantages of CCRM and integrated value chains. Based on its research, Deloitte Consulting concludes that consumer businesses with clear customer focus and linked customer management and supply chain operations are twice as profitable as other companies. Digital loyalty networks are far ahead of their competitors in key measures like sales growth, market share, customer service, return on assets and other goals, and are more likely to meet their goals in generating shareholder returns. They are digital in that their demand generating and supply chain operations are linked through information technology, loyal in that high customer loyalty and profitability is their objective, and networked in that their supply and demand related functions are linked to those of suppliers, customers and other business partners to form a virtual network.

Marketing Cooperation: Differentiation of Value Chains to Beat Competition with Collaborative CRM and CM

It is clear that the marketing tools of CCRM can boost customer retention and satisfaction. Joint initiatives between manufacturers and retailers in the context of CRM can enliven customer management.

In Customer Relationship Management, the marketing expenditures are measured against the degree of loyalty of the consumers in an attempt to achieve the maximization of customer lifetime value. The focus is on the customers, less so on category roles. It is possible to examine a complete lifecycle based customer analysis. Based on this information, an appropriate adjustment can be made on the desired target groups. In the next step, appropriate category roles are assigned in order to acquire, retain and develop the target customer. If, for example, one finds that families with children in the age of 0-6 years are big spenders in his or her channel, it might make sense to assign destination categories like baby food, diapers etc.

Not only can the assignment of category roles help customer relationships thrive, Category Management as a process itself can help to retain customers. Considerable customer information is generated in the process of CM and can be used to strengthen and expand customer loyalty. Market research companies are able to facilitate data gathering and can offer sophisticated market research methods. This is true for every single step in the Category Management process in the strategic part (role of the category, strategy of the category) as well as the tactical part (category tactics and review of the category).

In their article, Dr. Tweraser and Dr. Barrenstein of McKinsey&Co. illustrate how category management helps maximize customer value. Category management helps companies design product offerings for the target customer. It is based on a deep understanding of the attitudes, expectations, motivations and behaviour patterns of existing and potential customers. Broader reach, stronger brand and retailer loyalty, growing market share and greater customer satisfaction – category management that is well done offers retailers and producers great advantages. With category management, companies design creative product offerings for defined target groups like gardening fans, breakfast lovers or families with small children. CRM tools help refine product offerings: customer cards, surveys and panels provide valuable information for category management. Combining data, breaking rules, understanding target groups, and mobilizing employees – all are essential for successful category management. Increased sales, higher market share and growing profits – successful category management has so much to offer. What better reason to overcome the barriers and launch a joint pilot project!

Cooperative Logistics: Cost Reductions and Basis for Customer Retention

The optimization of the supply chain through logistics will, without doubt, continue to be an important factor for success. Consistent orientation of logistics to the demands of the customer will be required. CPFR (presented earlier in this book) places collaboration in the foreground. All participants in the supply chain work together to define the most precise forecast possible. The exchange of information serves to control the flow of goods. Information is usually already available in most cases. Most of it, however, is separate, confined to specific firms and unusable by others in the chain. Thereby the potential for optimization lies in the bilateral exchange of all relevant data for all participants. According to Schröder, Director of Customer Logistics Management for Procter & Gamble, Europe, the replenishment period i.e., the time from the purchase of the product by the consumer to its reorder process and its production, typically takes at least ten to fifteen days. The goal of CPFR is to reduce this time to three days. From an average of 103 steps in the replenishment process, 40 should be eliminated through CPFR. Thereby, cash flow could improve and cost savings through reduced inventory could be around 25% to 60%. Other objectives like the reduction of out-of-stocks through an availability of at least 98% and responsiveness to changing market conditions and consumer demands will be directly perceived by the customer and rewarded with customer satisfaction. Customers only profit from cost savings when they are passed on to them.

What's Next – The Future of Collaborative Customer Relationship Management

The next step in the consumer goods industry will be the integration of logistical and market driven processes along the value chain. A clear orientation to target group customers together with the use of new technological possibilities will define the future of the firm.

New challenges bring with them new opportunities. In Category Management, new possibilities exist through the integration of retail strategies in the control of product mix and through reduced overall complexity. Assortments must be seen through the eyes of the customer and categories understood as the means of differentiation, to be realized through corresponding category management strategies and tactics. This is the way to achieve long-term benefits in the area of product mix.

The Internet offers retailers the opportunity of an additional trade channel to increase sales. The Internet however requires a different approach to assortment design. While the needs of the customer remain principally the same as in traditional retail, the Internet offers the opportunity of mass customization and personalization. One-to-one marketing, vision and goal-setting in traditional retail is thereby possible. At the same time, better customer data can be collected than ever before, and purposefully used. This leads consequently to an interweaving of Category Management and Customer Relationship Management. The development of multiple channels can only strengthen this trend.

The trend of CCRM's dynamic development in recent years has become clear. The exchange of core data via paper and diskettes has disappeared. New developments like Data Warehousing, Web-EDI, e-Markets and Extranets are not merely technological advances. They have added new dimensions to collaboration. Strategic and operative competencies paired with comprehensive and technically advanced IT will contribute not only to cooperation, but to comprehensive networks.

After having focused on improving internal processes and systems as well as external processes, companies must subsequently build strategic alliances. This includes a collaborative hub with different key capabilities in logistics, transportation and marketing. The last step comprises the realization of the network economy, where companies focus strictly on core competencies and competitive advantages and work closely with all kinds of business partners based on global standards and open, intelligent technologies, thereby creating real value for their customers.

This book shows that CCRM can be an excellent tool for consistently exploiting potential synergies in supply chain partnerships. In the face of massive consolidation in the international retail landscape and among suppliers, individual companies will no longer compete with one another. On the contrary, whole supply chains will vie for higher efficiency and revenue growth. CCRM is a definitive concept for actively and successfully orchestrating this paradigm shift.

Editors

Prof. Dr. Alexander H. Kracklauer

Prof. Dr. Kracklauer is the director and founder of the BayTech Institute of Brand and Sales Management (BayTech IBS) at the University of Applied Sciences (UAS) Neu-Ulm. Further, he teaches Marketing and Sales Management at the University of Applied Sciences Neu-Ulm and advises major corporations and consulting companies. In 2002, he was the head of a CRM research group and visiting scholar at the Harvard Business School. Before joining the Harvard Business School, Prof. Dr. Kracklauer worked as a Head of Sales with Procter & Gamble, Germany. He has also held senior positions in the Key Account and Customer Marketing Management of Procter & Gamble. Prof. Dr. Kracklauer's research focus is Customer Relationship Management, Strategic Sales Management and Strategic Marketing. He has published articles in renowned journals like "Harvard Business Manager", "International Journal of Retail and Distribution Management" etc. and is a much sought-after management speaker.
Contact: akracklauer@hbs.edu

Prof. D. Quinn Mills

Prof. Mills teaches Leadership, Strategy, Organizations and Human Resources at the Harvard Business School. Before he arrived at Harvard he had taught at MIT's Sloan School of Management. He also advises major corporations and consulting companies. Prof. Mills is the author of many books including "Wheel, Deal and Steal: Deceptive Accounting, Deceitful CEOs, and Ineffective Reforms," and "Buy, lie and sell high – how investors lost out on Enron and the internet bubble", "The Empowerment Imperative" etc. and articles including The New York Times, Wall Street Journal, Chicago Tribune, Los Angeles Times, Business Week and others. Prof. Mills' research focus is Leadership, CRM, Strategy, Human Resources and e-Learning. He is a Fellow of The National Academy of Human Resources.
Contact: dmills@hbs.edu

Prof. Dr. Dirk Seifert

Prof. Dr. Seifert is head of a CPFR research group and visiting scholar at the Harvard Business School. Beside that he teaches Management and Marketing at the University of Massachusetts. Together with Prof. Mills he is developing new corporate e-learning formats. Before joining the Harvard Business School, Prof. Dr. Seifert worked as a Director with Bertelsmann. He has also held senior positions in the Category Management of Procter & Gamble and with the International Marketing Department of Bayer. Prof. Dr. Seifert's research focus is CPFR, Efficient Consumer Response, Customer Relationship Management, Strategic Marketing. *Contact: seifert-d@gmx.de*

Contributing Authors

Eric Almquist

Eric Almquist is a Vice President and member of the Board of Directors of Mercer Management Consulting. He specializes in customer-focused business strategies. His work has focused on corporate brand strategy development, development of branded value propositions, marketing experimentation, and data-driven marketing. He is a Trustee of the Marketing Science Institute.

Dr. Peter Barrenstein

Dr. Peter Barrenstein is a Director in the Munich Office of McKinsey & Company. He is one of the core members of the international Strategy and Organization Interest Group and for some years chaired the German Marketing and Consumer Goods Industry Group. During his work with McKinsey, Dr. Barrenstein has focused on addressing strategic and organizational issues as well as designing and implementing operative improvement programs for German and European companies of various industries – primarily in service, retail and packaged goods companies. Before joining McKinsey in 1980, Dr. Barrenstein was a lecturer and assistant professor in marketing and retailing at the University of Erlangen-Nuremberg, Germany. He holds a degree in economics from the University of Cologne and a PhD from the University of Nuremberg, Germany. He also worked for a large department store and spent some time in a purchasing office of a retailer in Hong Kong.

Dr. Michael Barz

Dr. Michael Barz is a freelance business consultant. He has conducted extensive work on customer-centric strategies and business concepts. Apart from strategic and organizational issues, he has also been involved in projects designing and implementing (e)CRM concepts for German financial services companies. Before acting as a freelance consultant, Dr. Barz worked as an internal consultant for the German subsidiary of one of the Big-5 European insurance companies and as an analyst and consultant in management consulting and corporate venture capital. Before, he was lecturing and giving seminars at the University of Sussex, U.K. and worked as an advisor to the Russian government. He holds a degree in business economics from the University of Hanover, Germany and a PhD in economics from the University of Sussex, U.K.

David Bovet

David Bovet leads the European supply chain practice at Mercer Management Consulting, where he is a Vice President. He focuses on customer-driven supply chain design and implementation. He is the co-author of *Value Nets: Breaking the Supply Chain to Unlock Hidden Profits* (Wiley & Sons, 2000), introducing powerful digital business designs that deliver on the customer promise.

Jim Duffy

Jim Duffy is a Partner in Deloitte Consulting Global Consumer Business Practice with a focus on driving ROI by implementing Digital Strategies. Prior to joining Deloitte Consulting, Jim was CEO of Benchmarking Partners, where he led the development of best practices for collaboration, such as CPFR, between retailers and manufacturers. Jim holds a Master's degree from Columbia University, New York, USA.

Georg Engler

Georg Engler is a Manager with Accenture. He is based in the Frankfurt Office, Germany and specialized in Supply Chain Management and the development of CPFR® solutions.

Matthias Groß

Matthias Groß is a Senior Consultant Category Management at AC Nielsen. He studied business administration at the University of Hamburg, Germany and started his career at Melitta Haushaltsprodukte GmbH & Co. KG. There he worked in the Trade Marketing, Product Management and Category Management Department. Then he changed to Tchibo Frisch-Röst Kaffee GmbH in Hamburg taking over the responsibility as a Head of Sales Management, 2001 he changed again to AC Nielsen.

Markus Großweischede

Markus Großweischede graduated from the University of Essen, Germany, in 1996. He spent four years as research fellow at the Chair of Marketing & Retailing, headed by Prof. Dr. Hendrik Schröder. After having founded a start-up business supported by the German retailer Karstadt´s incubator KQ-Lab, he developed the concept of a public-private research partnership in multi-channel-management – the Competence Center Multi-Channel-Management, a joint initiative by the University of Essen and the University of Münster, Germany. His focus areas are Multi-Channel-Retailing, e-Commerce and Category Management.

Peter Hambuch

Peter Hambuch has been with Procter & Gamble since 1980 where he held several management positions in the Customer Business Development. In recent years his main focus has been on the implementation of innovative concepts like Category Management and Efficient Consumer Response. His department is supporting multifunctional customer teams of Procter & Gamble Germany, Austria and Switzerland. He studied Mathematics at the University of Saarbrücken, Germany.

Carla J. Heaton

Carla Heaton is responsible for promoting collaborative efforts across the operating company subsidiaries of MMC (Marsh Inc., Mercer Consulting Group, and Putnam Investments). Prior to this, she spent 16 years as a Vice President in the Financial Services Industry Group of Mercer Management Consulting, specializing in growth-oriented strategy development, customer value management, business process redesign, and organization transformation. Her CRM clients included retail banks, credit card companies, investment management firms, and insurers.

Scott Hines

Promoted to Senior Vice President in 1999. Responsible for the development of JDA's In-Store Systems as well as setting the technology direction for JDA's suite of products and advancing new technology ventures. Served as Vice President of Store Systems from 1997 to 1999 with responsibility for the development of JDA's In-Store Systems. Joined JDA in 1993 as Associate Director of Store Systems product development and promoted to Director in 1996. Prior to JDA, spent two years as Director of MIS for US Hosiery Corporation and four years as President of DataWorks, Inc. Education: BS Molecular Biology, Carnegie Mellon University, Pittsburgh, USA.

Peter Koudal

Peter Koudal is a Director at Deloitte Research. In his research capacity, Peter regularly works with leading global companies, e-business technology providers, academic institutions, and other think tanks. His research has been covered in leading business media around the world, including Business Week, The Economist, Financial Times, Fortune, Handelsblatt, The New York Times, Nihon Keizai Shimbun, and the Wall Street Journal. He holds a Cand. Oecon degree from Aarhus University, Aarhus C, Denmark.

Michael Leyk

Michael Leyk is trade marketing manager for laundry products in Austria/Switzerland at Procter & Gamble. After his studies of business administration at the University of Mannheim, Germany he joined P&G as national key account and marketing manager. There he was responsible for the cooperative marketing and category management with leading trade customers.

Jens Ohlig

Jens Ohlig is the Head of Customer Business Development in the Frankfurt office of AC Nielsen. He graduated from the University of Siegen, Germany and started his career with a trainee program at AC Nielsen. Then he worked as an Account Manager, Account Executive and Key Account Manager, calling on customers like Unilever, Kraft and Beiersdorf. In 1998 he changed to Reckitt & Colman, Germany as Sales Development Manager and established the Category Management Department. Since 2000 he is again working with AC Nielsen.

Dr. Frank T. Piller

Dr. Frank T. Piller is a lecturer and research fellow at the Department of General and Industrial Management at the Technical University Munich (TUM), Germany and Director of the Research Center Mass Customization and Customer Interaction at the same institution. His research areas are strategic technology & innovation management, customer integration & customization, and strategic management. Frequently quoted in The Economist, Financial Times, Business Week, among others, he is seen as one of Europe's leading experts in the field of mass customization and personalization. Frank T. Piller is a managing partner of *Think Consult*, a Munich based management consultancy firm specializing in customer interaction, service innovation and mass customization.

Stephen Pratt

Stephen Pratt is the global leader of Deloitte Consulting's Customer Relationship Management (CRM) practice. Stephen has helped clients throughout North America, Europe and Asia develop and implement CRM strategies to increase shareholder value. His clients include Microsoft, General Motors, Hewlett Packard, Telstra, and Barclays. He has a Bachelor's degree in Electrical Engineering from Northwestern University, Illinois, USA and a Masters degree from the George Washington University in St. Louis, USA.

Prof. Dr. Dr. h.c. Ralf Reichwald

Prof. Dr. Dr. h.c. Ralf Reichwald is head of the Department of General and Industrial Management at the Technical University Munich (TUM), one of Germany's leading universities. His research interests lie in the empirical research of organizational structures, the application of IT in organizations (collaboration, distributed work and cooperation forms), as well as innovations in the service sector and leadership excellence. He serves as a lead advisor of the German Ministry of Research & Development and is member of several scientific associations. Prof. Reichwald was a guest professor at the University of Texas at Austin, USA and Syracuse University in New York, USA and holds a permanent guest professorship at the University El Manar in Tunisia.

Steffen Rübke

Steffen Rübke is trade marketing manager for paper products in Germany/Austria/Switzerland at Procter & Gamble. After his studies of law, history and political science at the Universities of Saarbrücken, Germany and Bergamo, Italy he joined P&G as national key account manager. There he was responsible for cooperative marketing with leading trade customers. Since May 2002 he is visiting lecturer for strategic key account management at the University of Applied Sciences in Neu-Ulm, Germany.

Dipl. -Inform. Christian Schaller

Christian Schaller is a research scholar at the Department of General and Industrial Business Management at the Technical University Munich (TUM), Germany (Head: Prof. Dr. Dr. h.c. Ralf Reichwald) and partner of the consultancy firm *Think Consult*. The focus of his research lies in the areas of customer relationship management, service management and knowledge management. He is currently leading several research projects within these fields, and gives lectures and seminars for students. Prior to joining the department he studied computer science and business management, and then worked for several years in consultancy (Accenture (former Andersen Consulting), Droege & Company). Here, his main interest lay in processes and strategies, in particular in the fields of e-business, finance and the transport industry.

Dr. Stefan Tweraser

Dr. Stefan Tweraser is an Associate Principal in the Vienna Office of McKinsey & Company. During his work with McKinsey, Dr. Tweraser has focused on addressing strategic marketing and organizational issues as well as designing and implementing operative improvement programs for retail and retail banking companies.

Niko Warmbrunn

Niko Warmbrunn is a national key account manager at Procter & Gamble Germany. He studied business administration with emphasis on European Management at the University of Applied Sciences FHDW Hannover, Germany.

Index

* Processes. Marketing. Management.

J. Becker, M. Kugeler, M. Rosemann
(Eds.)

Process Management

A Guide for the Design of
Business Processes

2002. Approx. 370 pp. Hardcover
€ 49,95; £ 35,-; sFr 86,-
ISBN 3-540-43499-2

Process Management is a
compendium for modern de-
sign of process-oriented companies. The included recommendations are summarized
in a series of checklists for
each stage of the project. The
book integrates insights of
modern organization man-
agement and current ap-
proaches to information systems.

S. Hougaard, M. Bjerre

Strategic Relationship Marketing
2002. 371 pp. Hardcover
€ 44,95; £ 31,50; sFr 77,-
ISBN 3-540-43161-6

This book encompasses
strategical as well as operational points of view and
gives a complete overview of
strategic relationship marketing and the theoretical ratio-
nals and paradigms. The authors introduce the concept
of relationship networks and
discuss how to deal with the
influence of relationship. Relationship marketing is dealt
with as a real marketing disci-
pline integrating economics,
institutional factors, behavioral
aspects and strategy.

R. Maier

Knowledge Management Systems
Information and Communication
Technologies for Knowledge Man-
agement

2002. XII, 574 pp. 70 figs., 111 tabs.
Hardcover **€ 74,95**; £ 52,50;
sFr 124,50 ISBN 3-540-43406-2

Information and communication technology (ICT) is often
regarded as the enabler for
the effective and especially
the efficient implementation
of knowledge management.
The book presents an almost
encyclopedic treatise of the
many important facets, concepts and theories that have
influenced knowledge man-
agement and integrates them
into a general knowledge
management framework con-
sisting of strategy, organization, systems and economics.

Please order at your bookstore!
More Information: www.springer.de/economics

Springer

All Euro and GBP prices are net-prices subject to local VAT, e.g. in Germany 7% VAT for books.
Prices and other details are subject to change without notice. d&p · BA 00490-4/1

Druck: Strauss Offsetdruck, Mörlenbach
Verarbeitung: Schäffer, Grünstadt